# YA WANNA GO?

PAUL STEWART

Foreword by Terry O'Reilly

Printed in the United States of America

Layout by Judi Fennell



Digital ISBN: 978-1-7328772-0-7
Paperback ISBN: 978-1-7328772-1-4
Hardback ISBN: 978-1-7328772-2-1

# Table of Contents

# Dedication

So much is owed to so many by so few. Thank you is not enough. Without those listed below, and their helping hands, I would not be here to write a book and share with you the life I have lived.

My mother, Helen Stewart: The poster picture of an Irish mother. I had clean clothes, enough to eat, went to good schools, and was bestowed with enough Irish guilt to last a lifetime. Whenever I was in it up to my neck, she was there to support and then clean me up after my fights.

My dad, Bill Stewart: father to me, friend to many. He was the epitome of what a father, teacher, and a coach should be.

My wife, Lori Stewart: She paid attention to Katie Couric's message on television and made me go and get checked for colon cancer. She has been a great mother to our two sons. I give kudos to this Minnesotan woman who has had to live with a man who only has black and white crayons in his crayon box. It isn't easy living with a guy who's always right.

My sons, McCauley and Maxwell: I am proud of you both and want nothing but the best for you, no matter where life takes you. Anything I do or say, I do from love.

My sister, Pat McDonald: More than a sister; can I say enough about a person who walked me through my darkest days and helped me be about my father's business?

Katie Couric: In the days following the death of her husband, Jay, from colon cancer, Katie thought more of her fellow man than her sadness. Without her message about colon cancer, I would never have known I was sick.

The doctors who saved my life: Drs. Gary Kearney, Sue Kelley, Jacob Lokich, Steve Camer, Gerald Sweeney, Gerwin Neuman, Ian Dunn, and Diane English. Without them, I would have made it to Harvard… as a cadaver.

All of my coaches, mentors, teachers, and my lifetime of friends: Without you, there would not be a Paul Stewart, nor this book.

—P.S.

# Acknowledgments

Just as with officiating or playing hockey, writing a book is a team effort even on an autobiographical project. This book would not have been possible without the assistance of these people I would like to mention.

Chris Smith: Chris sat up many nights, with me in Russia and him in Boston. Chris tirelessly worked as a writer with me on my dream to have a book we could be proud of. Chris and his family have been friends for years. Chris Smith, without whose assistance and professional ability, my book would still be a dream and likely stuck somewhere in Siberia.

Bill Meltzer: My editor, my spit-and-polish man, confidant, and friend. Bill and I have worked together on my blogs for *Hockey Buzz* and *The Huffington Post* for several years. Bill has done all that an editor could and should do with any manuscript: a fresh set of eyes on a labor of love.

Liza Sherman, Esq.: Liza has utilized her passion for the law by accepting my book challenges with great passion which helped fuel the final efforts to get my book to print. Writing a book isn't just about using letters to form words. One must follow up by crossing all of the Ts and dotting all of the Is. Liza has made certain that we are in line and able to go forward with this book, maintaining class and dignity, and being able to pass the white glove test for the legal side of publishing.

David Hughes: In the search for photos to support this book, David has been a mighty miracle man.

Kevin Harrington: Friend, neighbor, and brother. Kevin and his family are the epitome of class. Everyone should have a friend like Kevin.

Jim McDonough: My longtime friend, a huge supporter of and for special needs children. He is also a friend and vital supporter of my life's work.

John Harwood: Speaker of The Rhode Island House Emeritus

and a brilliant lawyer from Pawtucket. My center at Penn and my lifetime friend: The "Rocket."

Cathy Harrop: Is there a woman who does more for hockey than this First Lady of Rodman Rink? I think not. Wednesdays are my Chinese Buffet tradition with Cathy. Ding Hao!

George Hailer, Esq.: If you have to go to war, you want George in the foxhole with you.

Steve Hagwell: Commissioner of ECAC Division 1 hockey. We have been a team for thirteen years. Steve's confidence and support has been pivotal for my life in hockey.

Marina Riva: My great friend. Whenever there was a glitch, Marina, former captain of the URI Women's Hockey team used her brilliant mind to unravel my problems.

Bryan Hicks: I don't have just two sons, I have three. Bryan has been a person who, despite age differences, can be older and wiser than I can be.

Dmitry Antipin: My fourth son who landed years ago in America to play hockey and go to school. Dima has become exactly what a great American could and should be.

Terry Johnson: You left us too early. He was "Uncle Buck" to my boys and my brother from another mother. We shared many delightful rides across Canada together.

Brian and Wendy Collier: Thank you for your unwavering support and friendship. I regret that I live here and you in Toronto. I miss our times together.

David Langford: My other brother from another mother, my running buddy; you were there for me in my darkest hour.

Peggy and Betty Waffle, along with Fay and Hank Bolster and their daughter Bonnie and son-in-law Joe: You kept a good eye out to make certain Ken Holland didn't starve, and you were like a second family to me when I was a rookie living in a motel in Binghamton, always with a hot meal, a warm home, and good friendship. Ken and I were always well looked after, so thank you.

David Matheson, Esq. and Philip Healey, Esq.: My two "Great" Canadian friends. These men truly represent what one would call the "BEST" in people. The best fighters in close quarters, they are the epitome of winning with class.

Scotty MacPherson and Elena: The two best roommates and

friends one can have in Moscow (or just about anywhere). You are like family to me.

John McCauley, Frank Udvari, Dutch van Deelan, John Ashley, Lou Maschio, Jack Butterfield, Gordie Anziano, Bud Poile: All are present in spirit. Without these men and their patience in teaching me to referee, I might still be the night manager of a Laundromat.

Scotty Morrison, Bryan O'Neil, Jim Gregory, John Zeigler, Bill Wirtz, Harry Sinden, Dale Hamilton Powers, Brian Burke, Bill Daly, Gary Bettman, Rene Fasel, Alexander Medvedev, and Dmitri Efimov: The patient but anxious parents waiting up to see if I could navigate home safely. Without their unwavering confidence and unending support, my career might have ended before it started out behind the rhododendrons at the Wirtz family farm.

My brother officials at all levels of hockey: Too numerous to mention, especially the linesmen who steered me with great advice to referee with courage and passion. You all helped me last twenty years on the ice.

The trainers and equipment managers across hockey: When everyone else was mad at me, you always showed class in your support and friendship.

The ladies and gentlemen of the NHL offices in Montreal, Toronto, and New York: the friends who are still my friends and who work behind the scenes. I prize your caring loyalty and the way you've stood by me. I know who you are, and I love you for that.

The players, coaches, and teams for whom I skated as a player and as a referee: It was not just a pleasure, it was my dream to be out there with you.

Thank you, Terry O'Reilly, for writing the foreword to this book and for giving me a chance to prove myself in my NHL playing debut nearly forty years ago.

Bryan Lewis, Andy van Hellemond, and Colin Campbell, for whom I labored as an official and, later, a supervisor in the NHL after John McCauley passed: I have used all that I learned from you as I administer, coach, teach, supervise, and lead officials both in North America and while I was in Russia. From watching and applying your lessons, I know that the boss must be even-handed and must treat his people firmly, fairly, and honestly. As the boss, I must have one can of paint, one brush, and one stroke. That it's a business, never personal. For all you have done by example, I am a better boss.

Paul Stewart

FINALLY, TO THE FANS OF HOCKEY ACROSS THE WORLD: OH, TO BE YOUNG AGAIN! I MISS YOU ALL MORE THAN YOU KNOW!!!!!!!

# Foreword

Recently, I received a call from Paul Stewart, telling me about his soon-to-be-released book, *Ya Wanna Go?* I had to smile, because that phrase triggered a host of memories. That question had been put to me many times in my playing career, and I might have asked it a few times myself.

In fact, Stewy asked me that on the evening of his first NHL game in the Boston Garden on Nov. 22, 1979. After our scrap, he challenged and fought Stan Jonathan and then Al Secord before he was sent to the locker room. The NHL Rule Book mandated "three fights and you're out."

I am quite sure that if it were not for that rule, Stewy had enough courage, stamina, and enthusiasm to go through our whole lineup that night.

Stewy had great passion for the game of hockey, and when he recognized that his playing career was coming to an end, he took a hard and smart look at becoming a referee. And the rest is history. His twenty-year career as a referee is a remarkable achievement. He's earned enshrinement in the United States Hockey Hall of Fame for his contributions to the game, and it was a well-earned achievement.

Because of his experience as a player, Stewy was more patient with a belligerent player who would question his call, and he would often diffuse the tension with a smile or humorous quip. He had a reputation as an official who would "let the players play." He has a wonderful story to tell from the perspective of a man who both played and refereed in the NHL. He's the only American to do both.

Stewy has been a good soldier in the New England community, as former director of the Boston Bruins Foundation and various other charities, and I wish him all the best in his new venture. I look forward to reading his book—if he gives me a free copy.

—TERRY O'REILLY

# Preface

When I was a boy, my father, Bill Stewart Jr., often invited me to accompany him to special events, such as the Beanpot or to Cornell University for the weekend to watch him referee a hockey game.

In his straightforward manner, he'd ask, "You wanna go?" The answer was inevitably yes. I always wanted to go. By my father's side was where I always wanted to be as a young boy. It was where I learned the virtue of tireless work, digging deeper than you ever knew you could, and commitment to myself and to others. Some people call it grit, some call it dedication, and some call it perseverance. One thing is certain, though: I got it from my father.

My older sister, Pat, is fond of telling a story about the day I was born that shows my grit came early. My mother overheard a nurse in the hallway saying the Stewart baby was in very rough shape. I had stopped breathing; the nurses rushed me out of the nursery and up to the NICU. Apparently, I was up there "as blue as can be." I had two hernias and one of my lungs had collapsed. The doctors had to operate on me before my parents could take me home from the hospital. But the only place I was ready to "go" at that point was home with my family. Pat says I've been a fighter since the day I was born.

The phrase "You wanna go?" took on a much different meaning later in my life. It's something hockey players have said to opponents for years, locking eyes as one player issues a challenge to fight. A split second later, the combatants cast aside their gloves and sticks and away they go.

In the second period of my debut as a player in the National Hockey League—November 22, 1979, in the Boston Garden to be precise—Boston Bruins tough guy Terry O'Reilly stared at me and uttered, "Ya wanna go?" Or maybe I said it first. Either way, we were both quite willing to go.

That night, I also fought Stan Jonathan and Al Secord. A born-and-raised Bostonian, I earned the Dorchester Hat Trick in my NHL debut.

What's a Dorchester Hat Trick, you ask?

Well, I'm sure you've heard of the Gordie Howe Hat Trick: one goal, one assist, and one fight in a game. A Dorchester Hat Trick, named in honor of the traditionally rough-and-tumble area of Boston where I spent part of my formative years, is three fights and an automatic game misconduct. This night was a harbinger of many more nights and many more fights to come. My career in professional hockey was largely defined by my willingness to "go." I racked up 1,242 penalty minutes in 285 professional games.

Much of my life has felt like a series of battles. Very little has come easily to me professionally or personally. Say what you will, but nothing was ever just handed to me. I had to fight, either literally or metaphorically, every step of the way.

Friction is a part of hockey and certainly has been a part of my life. But I take a lot of pride in the fact that one thing that even my harshest critic could say about me was that I never backed down from a challenge. My background and upbringing made backing down from a challenge something I feared more than just the challenge itself.

That grit served me well later in my career when I made it back to the NHL for a second time. When I became a referee, I soon realized that I would have to learn on the job. Like the other challenges I'd faced, it didn't come easily or quickly. I received a lot of calls from the league office in Toronto about certain decisions and actions that I made. As my career progressed, I had to deal with bosses who openly wanted to drive me out of the business because they didn't like my style, my nationality or my strong-willed personality. Yet I worked tirelessly at my craft.

Of course, not every fight was in the interest of winning a game or standing on principle. Some have been an actual matter of life and death. That do-or-die attitude has gotten me through all of my life's battles. But all of that grit and determination were simply preparation for what would prove to be the battle of my lifetime—my fight against cancer.

American historical legend tells of how naval commander John Paul Jones responded to a taunt from his British counterpart urging surrender of his ship by saying, "I have not yet begun to fight!" Jones ultimately captured the British ship, the HMS Serapis, in a famous 1779 battle in the North Sea.

I can relate.

On February 23, 1998, not even twelve hours after my wife, Lori, gave birth to our first child, McCauley, I was informed that I had stage IV colon cancer. A large, malignant tumor was in my colon. Then they discovered a secondary tumor at my liver after they opened me up. The doctor told me that, had I waited even another few weeks to get checked, my chances of survival would have been virtually zero. I faced surgery and chemotherapy, with a significant possibility that I would not make it five years, if that.

Dying was a non-option to me, though. I was definitely *not* ready to "go." I had to be alive for my family. That's why I had the will to fight and beat cancer. If not for Lori, McCauley, and my younger son, Maxwell, I would not be here today. They are the reason I made it. I fought for them. I fought because I knew of no other way.

I've defeated the odds so many times in my life, not by luck, but by sheer will and hard work. I've never allowed other people's perceptions of me to color my own ambitions. My life story is filled with several remarkable events, twists, and turns. I've been called an overachiever more than once. I gladly accept that description. I am an ordinary man willing to fight for his dreams at any cost.

It is my aim to inspire those who feel that their dreams may be impossible to achieve. With hard work, dedication, and an unwillingness to fail, anything is possible, no matter what. Never believe anyone who tells you otherwise.

You can realize your dreams—no matter what they are—so long as you are willing to fight for them and pay the price it takes to achieve them. How much are you willing to fight? How much sacrifice is too much for you? These are things that determine your success.

Like my Dad would ask, "You wanna go?" Let's start the journey.

—PAUL STEWART

# CHAPTER 1: The Miracle Man

If my sister, Pat, thinks I came into this world fighting my way to survival, I come by it honestly. My father and grandfather may not have been pugilists, but they were models of the value of hard work and tireless determination. It is what people call "grit." They were the greatest role models I ever had in my professional and personal lives. Let's put it this way: If I am half the man that Bill Stewart, Sr. and Bill Stewart, Jr. were, I've still done pretty well for myself. Often, I have been asked if I am as tough as they were. I think I may be half as tough and that still makes me tougher than most.

It all started with my grandfather, Bill Stewart, Sr. He had a remarkable career in two different professional sports: hockey and baseball. Born in Fitchburg, Massachusetts in 1894, my grandfather was raised in working-class Boston. He grew to stand only about 5'6," but he was rawhide tough and a fine natural athlete. In high school, he was a standout in baseball, hockey, track, and freestyle wrestling. To this day, I have a vintage newspaper clipping which states how my granddad beat Jim Thorpe in the 100-yard dash in a 1912 track meet in East Boston after Thorpe returned home from the Summer Olympics in Stockholm, Sweden.

Baseball was perhaps Bill, Sr.'s best competitive sport. A fine pitcher with good control, in 1913 he signed a contract to play for Worcester in the New England League. He worked his way up in the minor leagues to pitch for the Louisville Colonels of the American Association (13-10 record with a 2.71 earned run average in 216 innings pitched), as well as playing for Montreal in the International League. During his minor league playing days, my grandfather roomed with baseball legend and Hall of Fame manager Joe McCarthy, who served as skipper of Louisville before McCarthy spent twenty-four years as a major league manager for the Chicago Cubs, New York Yankees, and Boston Red Sox.

As much as he loved sports, my grandfather was even prouder to be an American. He believed strongly that freedom comes at a price and that everyone has a responsibility to help preserve that freedom. Bill, Sr. became the first professional baseball player to enlist for service in World War I. He served in the Navy for the duration of the war. After World War I, he signed a Major League contract with the American League's Chicago White Sox. Unfortunately, my grandfather suffered a major setback that cost him his chance to pitch in the big leagues. While working as a census taker in Boston in 1919, he fell down an icy flight of steps, injuring his pitching arm and shoulder. He never had the same velocity or control again.

Despite his misfortune, moping wasn't in my grandfather's character. He simply found other ways to stay involved in sports. He became a minor league manager, occasionally inserting himself in games as a relief pitcher. As a manager, my grandfather coached the 1921 Boston University baseball team and converted then-BU ballplayer Mickey Cochrane into a catcher. Cochrane eventually played thirteen Major League seasons, winning the American League MVP twice. The Baseball Writers' Association of America inducted Cochrane into the National Baseball Hall of Fame in 1947.

Late that decade, my grandfather also started working as an umpire and proved to be a natural for the demands of the job. Focusing exclusively on the officiating side of baseball by 1930, Bill, Sr. was hired by the National League in 1933 and began his lengthy umpiring career at the top level. Bill, Sr. was a Major League baseball umpire from 1933 to 1954, working four World Series (1937, 1943, 1948, 1953) and four All-Star games (1936,1940, 1948, 1954). Later, he was a scout for the Cleveland Indians and Washington Senators.

Among Bill, Sr.'s umpiring career highlights are working home plate in the second no-hitter of Cincinnati Reds pitcher Johnny Vander Meer's record two consecutive no-hit games. Later, he was the first Major League umpire to eject Jackie Robinson from a game. In 1951, Bill Stewart was the crew chief of the umpiring crew that worked the famous three-game playoff between the New York Giants and Brooklyn Dodgers.

Even with his feet firmly entrenched in the big leagues of baseball, my grandfather found himself drawn to the world of hockey, as well. During 1910s and 1920s, my grandfather would come home from wherever baseball had taken him to work for Walter Brown, who ran the Boston Arena. While there, and among his other duties, he coached hockey for various teams in Massachusetts, as well as working as a hockey referee during the baseball off-seasons. In 1928, eleven years after its inception, the National Hockey League hired Bill Stewart as its first American-born and -trained referee. He officiated in the NHL for a period spanning three decades. To date, my grandfather is still one of just four U.S.-born referees to work in the Stanley Cup Finals in the long history of the NHL. The others are Hall of Fame member Bill Chadwick, as well as Dennis LaRue and Chris Rooney. I reffed for seventeen years in the NHL. It was never my assignment to work in a game where they hoisted the Cup, a bitter pill that I had to swallow.

In the summer of 1937, my grandfather received an offer from Chicago Black Hawks owner, Maj. Frederic McLaughlin, to serve as coach and general manager of the NHL team. A native Chicagoan and a Harvard University graduate, McLaughlin served in the U.S. Army during World War I, rising to the rank of major. Even after returning to civilian life, McLaughlin insisted on being addressed as "The Major" for the remainder of his life.

Maj. McLaughlin, heir to his family's lucrative coffee business, first became interested in sports team ownership prior to the start of the Great Depression. In 1926, he purchased a controlling interest in Chicago's fledgling NHL hockey team. The owner nicknamed the team the Black Hawks (later shortened to one word), in honor of his former Army infantry battalion, which was nicknamed the "Black Hawks." The Major's wife, Irene Castle, designed the team's now-famous Indian head logo. McLaughlin was fiercely patriotic. That is part of the reason why he was drawn initially to my grandfather, a fellow World War I veteran who wore his American citizenship with great pride.

Apart from being a proud patriot, McLaughlin was a nutcase. He was one of the worst bosses to work for in the entire history of the NHL. In eighteen years of owning the Black Hawks, he hired and fired eighteen different coaches.

My grandfather and the Major made for a volatile mix. Bill, Sr. wasn't about to be pushed around by his boss, and McLaughlin hated to employ anyone with a strong personality as much as he hated to employ anyone with a weak personality. They co-existed for one reason: they shared the goal of seeing Americans succeed in hockey.

Steering a team featuring eight Americans on the roster at a time when the NHL otherwise almost entirely comprised Canadians, my grandfather coached the Chicago Black Hawks to the 1937-38 Stanley Cup. In the Finals, the Hawks downed the favored Toronto Maple Leafs in four games in a best-of-five series.

Prior to Game One of the Finals in Toronto, the team learned that starting goaltender, Mike Karakas, would be unable to play. He had broken his big toe in the clinching game of the semifinals, and backup Paul Goodman was also out of commission. The Hawks requested that the NHL let the team use New York Rangers goaltender Davey Kerr to fill in, but the Maple Leafs balked at the idea and the league refused the request.

At the suggestion of Black Hawks' captain Johnny Gottselig, my grandfather reluctantly decided to offer former New York Americans backup goaltender Alfie Moore the opportunity to become Chicago's goaltender to start the finals. Moore lived in Toronto and had once been a solid NHL goaltender, despite playing as the backup to Hall of Famer Roy Worters.

The problem? Alfie drank himself out of the NHL and had spent the past season in the American Hockey League. With the season over, he could devote himself fully to nightly bar-hopping. He was finally tracked down at one of his favorite local watering holes—it took the Hawks several tries to find the right one at the right time. Moore had about a dozen drinks in him by the time he was finally brought to the Black Hawks hotel. He slurred his words and hadn't changed clothes in at least two days. My grandfather was not amused.

"Get him out of my sight," he said to Gottselig. "There is no way that guy is going to start in goal for us."

"We have no other choice, Bill," Gottselig said. "Someone has to be in goal. I can't do it. No one else is going to volunteer. Alfie is a good goaltender. He will be fine in the game." My grandfather sighed. "Okay, it's your playoff prize money and the Cup at stake. If you really think he's our best option at this point, I will trust you."

Speaking to Moore, my grandfather told him he'd be in goal against Conn Smythe's Maple Leafs in the Stanley Cup Finals. The goaltender beamed. "That Connie Smythe is a son of a bitch," Moore roared drunkenly. "That bastard is going to regret the day he picked [Turk] Broda over me! I'll show that Connie Smythe!"

"Save it for the game," my grandfather said.

Although my grandfather didn't really trust Moore, he did trust Gottselig. The Black Hawks players basically babysat Moore until game time, using the old-fashioned remedies of cold showers and endless cups of coffee. As fate would have it, the emergency goaltender outplayed Broda, and Chicago won the series opener, 3-1.

Goodman was ready to go for Game Two. As a result, NHL President Frank Calder disqualified Moore from playing in the rest of the series. The Maple Leafs won the next game, but the Black Hawks rebounded to win each of the next two games, winning the Stanley Cup. The Major was ecstatic. He told everyone who would listen that Bill Stewart was the most brilliant hockey coach ever born. A miser by nature, McLaughlin even gave Alfie Moore a gold watch and three hundred dollars cash at the insistence of his coach. In the meantime, the newspapers took to calling my grandfather "the Miracle Man" for what he accomplished.

My grandfather was the first U.S.-born coach of a Stanley Cup champion. It would be another fifty-three years until the second one emerged when Hall of Fame coach "Badger" Bob Johnson guided the 1990-1991 Pittsburgh Penguins to the Stanley Cup. Despite my grandfather's unprecedented accomplishment, McLaughlin's happiness lasted only until his team failed to roar out of the gates the next season. Just twenty-one games into the 1938-39 season, with the Hawks sporting a record of 8-10-3, he fired the "Miracle Man." The Major told the media that my grandfather had lost his effectiveness as a coach. After his tumultuous tenure as the Black Hawks' coach, Bill, Sr. returned to refereeing for the duration of his NHL career.

In the mid-1950s, Bill, Sr. decided to return to coaching hockey when he had the opportunity to coach the U.S. National Team in 1957. Featuring a squad that largely comprised the roster that would win Olympic Gold in Squaw Valley three years later, my grandfather coached the U.S. Men's Ice Hockey team to a record of 23-3-1. Unfortunately, the U.S. State Department elected not to send a team to the IIHF World Championships in protest of the Soviet Union's invasion of Hungary, so that was that.

Brothers Eddie and Jack Kirrane played for that team. Jack, a U.S. Hockey Hall of Fame inductee, was then twenty-eight years old, but Eddie was just seventeen and the youngest player selected to represent the U.S.A. Eddie felt extremely excited to make the roster but also a little scared about playing for my grandfather.

"He was a well-built guy," Eddie said about Bill, Sr. "He had legs like hydrants and arms that were strong and muscular, and I was petrified. He would just look at you and stare at you at first. And I'm kind of thinking, 'What the hell kind of guy is this guy?' There was no smile or no nothing." But Eddie soon came to learn a different and kinder side to my grandfather.

"He treated me like a son," Eddie said. "He turned out to be one of the best friends I ever had in my life." My grandfather made Eddie, the youngest player on the squad, stay back with him while other veteran players went out at night. "He'd make sure I was in bed at a certain time and I was eating the proper foods," Eddie said. "He took me under his wing."

Ed described Bill Stewart, Sr. as being a very quiet coach behind the bench. "His pep talks, they weren't yelling or screaming," Eddie said. "He never swore. He raised his voice very, very little. It was just the look and the way he'd stare at you. You knew he meant business. He could say a thousand words with one look."

Despite the ultimate decision not to permit the team to compete in the IIHF World Championship, the team competed throughout Europe in other contests. The team landed in Scotland and played there, as well as in England, Germany, and Sweden. "Everywhere we went over there was by train or bus," Eddie said. "He always made sure he was sitting in front of me or behind me, but mostly beside me. He said, 'Eddie, come to the front of the bus and we'll talk.'"

Eddie recalled how much my granddad loved scally caps and had great national pride. "He bought scally caps for all of us and they were red, white, and blue, and we had to wear them everywhere," Eddie said. "We couldn't go without that hat. One day, during a train trip in Switzerland, for some reason I stuck my head out the window and the cap flew off. He said, 'Stop the train. Stop the train.' He pulled the cord. We had to stop the train and I had to run back about a quarter of a mile to get the cap. I'll never forget that."

Eddie listened to many of my grandfather's stories while they were together, away from Eddie's other teammates. Eddie said my granddad talked with him a lot about his controversial call in the bottom of the eighth inning of scoreless Game One of the 1948 World

Series between the Cleveland Indians and Boston Braves. "He'd always bring that story up to me and said, 'It was that angle of the camera—that camera that made the call look bad!'" Ed recalled. "He also loved Willie Mays," Eddie added about my granddad. He recalled a favorite Mays story my granddad had shared with him:

"He said (Mays) got in that batter's box one time and the pitcher was about to pitch the ball and the catcher said something to Willie and Willie turned back at him and said, 'Oh, yeah?' and the ball came in for strike one. And then it went on again the next time. The pitcher was about to pitch the ball and the catcher again spoke up and said something to Willie. And Willie turned around and looked at him (the catcher) again and pitch went by and Bill said, 'Strike two!' So Willie stepped out of the box, got the mud out of his cleats, and stepped back into the box and said, 'I'm not listening. I'm not talking. I'm looking to hitting the ball over the fence.' Sure to hell, he hit the ball, hit a home run. The way (Bill) told it, it was comical. Any stories he'd tell, they always had that little comical twist in there."

Ironically, Eddie ended up coaching me when I played Pee-Wee hockey in Brookline. Eddie said I share my granddad's sense of humor. When I was growing up, Bill Stewart, Sr. was always just "Grampy" to me. It wasn't until I was a little older that I realized just what a unique and important figure he was in both the NHL and the Major Leagues in his various job capacities.

Before officiating my first game in Montreal, I talked with the security guard, a friendly, chain-smoking guy who sat outside the referees' dressing room. The guy's name was Raymond. He had worked the same job ever since my grandfather had served as an NHL referee. He was a nice man who spoke English in an exceptionally thick Francophone accent. I asked him if he remembered my granddad.

"*Oh, sure but you are bigger den 'eem,*" he replied in his heavy accent. "*Ya know, 'e was not so big, but 'e was one tough guy.*" After the game, Raymond entered the dressing room with a fresh cigarette hanging from his lips.

"*Paul, de big guy, 'e is outside, and, em, 'e want to come in to see you,*" Raymond said.

"Sure. Who's the big guy?" I asked.

"*Paul, dis is Montreal,*" Raymond replied, incredulously. "*Dere's only one big guy in dis town.*"

"OK, well, send the Big Guy in," I said, still unaware of who he meant.

The door swung open. The two French Canadian linesmen who worked the game with me sat on the other side of the room and saw the "Big Guy" before me. I couldn't see him because the door was blocking my view. Both linesmen reacted like the Pope himself had entered. Seeing their reaction, I stood and looked toward the door. There he was: the legendary Maurice "Rocket" Richard.

The Hockey Hall of Famer holds the distinction of being the first NHL player to record 50 goals in 50 games, which he did during the 1944-45 season. He potted 544 goals and added 421 assists for 965 points during his 978 NHL game career. He lived much of his life in Montreal and played all 18 NHL seasons with the Canadiens. The Rocket was such a legend there that the then-Montreal Expos (now the Washington Nationals of Major League Baseball), wore a patch with Richard's number 9 on their home and away jerseys for the remainder of the 2000 season after Richard died on May 27 of that year.

I nodded my head as he looked at me and stuck my hand out for him to shake.

*"Are you Stewart?"* Richard asked, with a similar Francophone inflection as the man who had introduced him.

"Yes."

*"You can sit down,"* he said.

I did exactly as he instructed.

*"I seen you ref the game here tonight,"* Richard continued. *"I come in to ask you a question. Did you have a grandfather who reffed in this league?"*

"Yes."

*"I remember him,"* Richard said, taking a seat beside me. *"I don't like that guy."*

He was joking. We all laughed and Richard slapped my knee. Richard asked Raymond to get us drinks. Raymond returned, carrying a gin-and-grapefruit-juice for Richard.

The Rocket became a regular visitor whenever I was in town. He always drank the same concoction when I was around him. He visited the referees' dressing room nearly every game I worked in Montreal throughout my NHL officiating career until he began battling abdominal cancer and eventually died of respiratory failure.

We shared several laughs together. My father, Bill Stewart, Jr., and ex-referee Bill "The Big Whistle" Chadwick both told me on separate occasions that my grandfather once ejected "Rocket" from a game in Montreal because of something the right wing had said to him. The two got in each other's faces, then two crazed fans rushed down from the stands and onto the ice to attack my grandfather.

My granddad knocked down both fans, one with a forearm and the other using a left hook and also his metal whistle, striking the fan on the temple with it, "causing a gash and much blood," wrote sportswriter Tim Cohane in his book *Bypaths of Glory*. Cohane also mentioned another Montreal fan tried to reach out at my grandfather from the stands. My grandfather threw an uppercut and knocked the third fan over his seat.

Chadwick, a Hall of Fame NHL referee who later became the voice of the New York Rangers, officiated the game with my granddad. Chadwick told me he and my grandfather went into the Montreal dressing room after the game and my granddad pointed in Richard's face while standing on his toes so he could get closer to the much taller Richard.

My grandfather happened to be wearing long underwear. All anyone one could see was the sleeve of the long underwear going up and down while he kept making his point to the Rocket!

That night in Montreal, Bill Stewart, Sr. left the arena through the angry crowd, holding up his skates with the blades pointed at the fans for protection. It was him against all of Montreal, or so it must have seemed to him.

Throughout my playing and officiating careers, several hockey stars, such as Richard, sought me out because they wanted to meet the grandson of the legendary Bill Stewart, Sr. They all spoke glowingly of him. Hall of Famer Milt Schmidt said about my granddad, "He was a very strict official. Not the greatest skater in the world, but he managed. He was very strict and he was highly thought of. … He was not only a great referee who was deeply thought of, but he was also a great hockey coach."

Being the grandson of Bill Stewart, Sr. definitely had some advantages. For one, knowing greats like Schmidt through my grandfather's work certainly had its perks. In 1981, between my careers as a NHL player and referee, former Cincinnati Stingers teammate Tim Sheehy and I went to the Boston Garden without tickets on the night Marvin Hagler boxed for the world championship there. Unable to score tickets, Sheehy and I went to the Garden Club, managed by Schmidt.

"What have you been up to lately, Paul?" Schmidt asked.

"I'm doing some reserve police work in Yarmouth," I answered.

"Do you have tickets to tonight's fight?" Schmidt later asked during our conversation.

I told him that I did not.

"Ah, well, let me see that police badge of yours," Schmidt said.

I pulled it out, and Schmidt stared at it.

"The guy you're chasing just went through that door so go ahead and go get 'em," Schmidt said, referring to the door from the Garden Club into the Boston Garden. Sheehy and I walked into the Garden and watched the fight up in the press box with then-Boston Bruins Head of Public Relations, Nate Greenberg.

I often think about anecdotes like this one and how lucky I am to be able to share these relatively unknown stories about legends, allowing their personalities to shine through. I'm able to do this only because my grandfather introduced me to great men such as Schmidt at a young age and I remained close with them over the years.

Another legend who told me he respected my grandfather deeply was Hall of Fame defenseman, Eddie Shore. I met Shore during the 1977-1978 hockey season in Springfield, Massachusetts. At the time, I played for the AHL Binghamton Dusters. We traveled to Springfield to play the Springfield Indians. During the game, I fought Minnesota North Stars first-round draft pick, Bryan Maxwell.

Between periods, my coach, Larry Kish, entered the dressing room and summoned me to the hallway. I figured Kish wanted to scold me for something, maybe the fight with Maxwell. Instead, he stood out in the hallway with an older gentleman who wore a camelhair coat and top hat. I didn't know it immediately, but the gentleman was Shore.

"You're bigger than your grandfather," Shore told me, grabbing my hands. "You've got bigger hands than he did. But are you as tough as your grandfather?"

"People tell me I'm half as tough, which means I'm still pretty tough," I replied.

"He was a tough guy, but he was a good guy," Shore said before revealing his identity to me.

The way Shore, Richard, and others asked to meet me showed me the level of respect and credibility my grandfather and family had established. People respected my grandfather, and rightfully so, considering Bill Stewart, Sr. truly made his mark as a legendary sports figure in the first half of the twentieth century.

There were others, too. I met Hall of Fame defenseman Ching Johnson once when my Pee-Wee hockey team played in a tournament in Washington. Johnson, there at the rink, walked down to talk with me specifically because he knew my grandfather. Maple Leafs legend Red Horner and Chicago Blackhawks legend Mush March, who scored the first goal in Maple Leaf Gardens on Opening Night 1931, both came to see me in the dressing room during the final game before the Maple Leaf Gardens closed its doors. They, too, wanted to meet Bill Stewart's grandson. I also was extremely honored to meet them and King Clancy, another player-turned-ref, that night.

With so many people who knew my Grampy for his professional achievements, I feel exceptionally fortunate that I was one of the few who knew him as family. My grandfather greatly shaped my early life through his dynamic personality and love for sports, and by passing those things down to my father, Bill, Jr. Despite all they had in common, however, my grandfather and my dad weren't clones. My dad spent his life as a modest high school teacher and coach who lived within his own means. Dad always taught me and my siblings to recycle our bottles and cans for five cents apiece and my mother often cooked us minute steaks.

My grandfather, conversely, owned an orange juice squeezer, an ice-maker, overstuffed chairs, a player piano, oriental carpets, and a grandfather clock, all luxuries at the time. His sister worked as his housekeeper. Grampy's home consisted of three bedrooms, three bathrooms, and three telephones—one telephone on each floor. I hardly knew what to make of it all. I didn't know whether he was a millionaire. All I knew was that he and his lifestyle impressed me greatly.

Bill, Sr. owned a beautiful house in Jamaica Plain, a neighborhood in Boston. He built it himself and paid for it up front with $13,000 cash, his bonus money from Chicago winning the

Stanley Cup. The house resembled a mini-museum. World War I spiked German Army helmets, including one coal scuttle helmet, sat on display. (I'm unsure how he obtained them because I don't think he ever traveled overseas during his service in the Navy. He actually boxed in the Navy, too).

Bill, Sr.'s wife, my paternal grandmother, Gertrude, was a native of Nova Scotia. She died of breast cancer in December 1949, several years before my birth in 1953. In the latter stages, Grandmom's cancer spread to her lungs and brain, and she died in the master bedroom. The house—which I later lived in after my grandfather died—always seemed a little aery for that reason. I never felt alone there. The imprint of my grandmother's lipstick remained on a crucifix that was in the master bedroom. She had kissed the crucifix the night she died. My grandfather barely stepped foot in the master bedroom during the final fourteen years of his life. He slept in my dad's old bedroom and his diary tells of 1949 being the worst year of his life.

Sports memorabilia and autographs, including framed photos of Rocky Marciano, Knute Rockne, and "Shoeless" Joe Jackson, hung in the basement of the home.

One of my fondest childhood memories is of my sister, two brothers, and me sitting at the kitchen table together, listening as my granddad and father drank tea and talked about old-time athletes. My siblings and I sometimes traveled with my granddad when he scouted baseball players nearby. He always bought us ice cream at games. When he whipped out his wallet, he had more money than I'd ever seen. He carried twenty- and fifty-dollar bills with him, and he always taught me to put the larger bills in the inside, with an elastic band holding it all in a tight roll.

Grampy was a great storyteller. He had a lifetime of stories to tell because he had seen and done it all.

"'Shoeless' Joe Jackson was the best baseball player I've ever seen—better than Babe Ruth," he told me. "Babe Ruth was good, don't get me wrong. But he would've been better if he didn't drink so much." My grandfather told stories about other famous ballplayers he met or umpired, including Stan Musial and Lou Gehrig. One of the funnier anecdotes he ever told me was about Leo Durocher, the Hall of Fame manager. My grandfather described Durocher as "snippy and snide."

"Durocher kicked me once after I ejected him from a game," my grandfather told me. "I have a picture of it. I used to fold my arms when someone got in my face because I didn't want to reach out and punch him. I did it to hold myself back. But I told Durocher which hotel I was staying at and the room number. I said to him, 'When the game's over, I'll meet you there. Whoever leaves the room first, wins.'"

My granddad's most controversial call during his umpiring career came during the bottom of the eighth inning of scoreless Game 1 of the 1948 World Series between the Cleveland Indians and Boston Braves. It was the call he'd told Eddie Kirrane about. The Braves had a runner, Sibby Sisti, on first and a base runner, Phil Masi, at second. Bob Feller was on the mound for Cleveland and threw a pickoff to second base where shortstop Lou Boudreau covered and swiped down a tag on Masi. My grandfather called Masi safe. Masi scored the eventual winning run on a hit later that inning. Lots of people knew about the call from the newspapers; I was one of the lucky few who got a firsthand account. An Associated Press photo appears to show Boudreau tagging Masi, but my granddad always defended his call, remaining adamant that Boudreau missed the tag, even though certain angle views might have made it seem as though the tag had been made.

My grandfather was an extremely honest man. If he was wrong, he admitted it. If he wasn't sure, he said he wasn't sure. Even in the privacy of talking to his young grandson, he told me he'd made the right call on the tag play. "Photos can lie," he told me. "It can be unintentional or it can be intentional. Maybe the angle just isn't the best one. Maybe the photo was doctored to sell more newspapers. All I know is, I was five feet away and I saw what happened very clearly. No one else had my vantage point."

Since the Indians won the Series—their last championship to date—guys like Feller and Boudreau were able to smile about the play years later (even if they continued to insist that the umpire got it wrong). My grandfather and the Indians' two Hall of Fame members made some money together in later years talking about the Series on the banquet circuit, especially around Cleveland.

My grandfather was a wise man in many, many ways. I never forgot what he told me about that long-ago tag play in the Fall

Classic. When I later started my own refereeing career, I learned that he knew what he was talking about with cameras not always having the best perspective on a close play. Grampy was right, as usual.

When I was seven years old, he took my brothers and me to eat at the Ritz-Carlton in Boston, a place with fresh strawberries during the winter and real whipped cream, not the type from a can. I was impressed. I became more impressed when we then walked over to watch a Boston Red Sox game at Fenway Park and we went in through the back entrance. We always entered through the back or side door at stadiums. We sat upstairs in the press box where I met announcer Curt Gowdy. As my grandfather chatted with Red Sox owner Tom Yawkey, and as my brother and I watched the game, I felt a hand on my back. I turned and glanced upward. There stood the most beautiful woman I had ever seen. I fell in love instantly. She had dark hair, beautiful skin, and distinct red lips. She was rather tall, too.

"You're Bill's grandchildren?" she asked. She introduced herself as Mrs. Yawkey. I was thinking only one thing—"I am in love with you, Mrs. Yawkey." She took me to get a soda. Years later, in 1990, the Junior Baseball Park League in Boston was renamed the Yawkey League because it was funded by Jean Yawkey and her foundation. One of the league's conferences also had been named in memory of my father. I umpired the first game there and Jean Yawkey, at age eighty-one, threw out the first pitch.

"I hope you don't mind me saying so, but I met you years ago when I was a little boy," I told Mrs. Yawkey after she threw out the first pitch. "I came to Fenway with my grandfather, Bill Stewart, and I just wanted to tell you that you're just as beautiful today as you were that day. I fell in love with you all those years ago."

Whenever I matter-of-factly told the kids at school I met Mrs. Yawkey, Milt Schmidt or someone else famous, they would tell me I was a liar. It hurt my feelings and raised my ire. I never was one to brag about myself. I'd fight them for not believing me. At the time, I just thought all I was doing was telling the truth and they were being deliberately hurtful. Meeting those figures was just part of my life, and I was trying to let others share in it. It took many years for me to appreciate the rare, behind-the-scenes access my grandfather's notoriety afforded us.

My grandfather was a kindly man by nature. There was no doubt that he loved his family. However, he was definitely not demonstrative and showed little open affection. That is perhaps why I clearly remember him hugging and kissing me two months before he died of a stroke at age sixty-nine.

It was at Christmastime. I was ten-years old and he pulled me up onto his lap. I commented about how he had not decorated his house that year. He never purchased a Christmas tree but always had decorated the home, including putting fresh cut greens on his mantel over the fireplace.

"Next year, I'll come over and help you and we'll put up the lights together," I said.

"I'll count on that," he replied.

As I went to slip off his lap, he hugged me tightly and kissed me. His scruffy beard rubbed against my face. The unkempt appearance was unusual for him. He always had been so well-groomed. He had always presented himself as a very dapper man, often wearing a Palm Beach suit and straw hat. In hindsight, I think he knew he didn't have much longer left to live. Eight weeks later, on February 18, 1964, my grandfather died.

The call came that my grandfather died of a stroke on a Tuesday morning during February vacation. My dad and I were about to leave for a hockey practice at Bajko Rink in Hyde Park. I sat there with my family at the kitchen table eating a bowl of Kix. We only had one phone at our Dorchester house. It hung in the kitchen and had a long cord attached. My whole family cried together there. There would be no more chances for my dad to drive his dad to the airport for spring training. There would be no more stories about Gehrig, Jackson, and Ruth. There would be no decorating the house with him that next Christmas.

Walter A. Brown, the first owner of the Boston Celtics and also known for his contributions in ice hockey, attended the funeral as well as many Red Sox representatives. I had never been to a wake before. It felt very painful. I recall every moment, every smell, every scene, to this day.

Later in life, I sat in the dressing room in Chicago before officiating a game—the last that I would work in that building. The security man knocked on the door and told me Blackhawks principal owner Bill Wirtz wanted to see me.

Mr. Wirtz came in holding a book called, *Hockey Chicago Style: History of the Chicago Blackhawks*. He told me if anyone in the NHL hockey league deserved that book, I did. "You're as much a part of our family as anyone," Wirtz said, turning the book to page where there was a picture of my grandfather holding the Stanley Cup. Wirtz then told everyone in the room about how much he liked my grandfather and how Bill Stewart, Sr. had given him a job as a stick boy when he was a child.

The benefits of being Bill Stewart, Sr.'s grandson transcended event tickets, rubbing elbows with legendary athletes, and having exclusive access to exclusive places. I like to think I received some of my toughness and grit from my grandfather who—despite his short stature (which was the same as my dad)—was as tough as nails. He never missed any of his NHL reffing assignments until a cut he sustained one night resulted in a staph infection. In baseball, Grandpa also umpired 714 straight National League games until suffering from appendicitis. I similarly never missed any assigned games until being diagnosed with cancer.

Physical strength and endurance are apparently genetic; maybe grit is as well.

Life became tougher after my grandfather died. Everything suddenly changed. It was a tumultuous year in general. My granddad died and I found out Santa Claus was someone who disappeared from belief as you got older. My family moved into my grandparent's Jamaica Plain house. I changed schools. I left all my friends I had grown up with. Even President John F. Kennedy had been assassinated a few months earlier in November, 1963 and we watched as Lee Harvey Oswald got shot on live TV. Like the rest of America, I suddenly had to grow up and learn the complexities of this world. Most of all, I felt sad because I would never see or speak with my grandfather again. Death has hit me hard over the years. But the stories of my grandfather—and my father, as you'll read in the next chapter—continue to live on as I think about them frequently and sometimes chuckle when I am alone. I believe that my grandfather and father's spirits still live on inside me. I sometimes can hear them chiding me or encouraging me when I am in a tough spot.

The stories they told me had impact. The night before the NHL officials went on strike in 1993, longtime NHL center Craig MacTavish challenged me to a fight after a Los Angeles/Edmonton game as I left former player Billy Harris' bar/restaurant in Manhattan Beach, California. I uttered a familiar refrain that my grandfather had used when Durocher challenged him to a fight.

"I'm at the LAX Marriott in room #2527, by the hot tub and the pool. Meet me there," I told MacTavish. "Whoever leaves first wins."

## CHAPTER 2: Coaching To Teach

My dad, Bill Stewart, Jr., was, in many ways, the foil to my grandfather's larger-than-life persona. One way in which they were similar, though, is in that my dad was a fighter. Not only was he a fighter, but he taught me to fight and what was worth fighting for.

Born on October 11, 1919 to Bill, Sr. and Gertrude of Boston, my dad was the only child. My dad stood at only about 5'6", but he had big arms and it meant something when he fixed an eye on me.

Like my grandfather, my father wasn't the most demonstrative of the love he felt for his wife and kids. He wasn't one to kiss and hug us, but he showed us love by his deeds and actions. He led by example.

Dad taught physical education and health and also coached three sports (varsity football, hockey, and baseball) for thirty-seven years at Boston English High in Boston, Massachusetts, where his dedication went unmatched. He missed only ten days of work in all of those years. And those ten sick days came consecutively as he recovered after breaking his coccyx while refereeing a hockey game at Yale. He reffed both high school and college hockey, as well as football. He umpired baseball. He worked several NCAA Championships in Hockey. He reffed nineteen Beanpot Tournaments Games. He reffed many top college football games with the likes of Staubach and Gogalak playing in them. He umped in Omaha in the College World Series. He was a great sports official. He understood the game, the rules, and the players.

He was a graduate of Boston English, and excelled there in varsity football, hockey, and baseball. He's one of eight athletes from the Class of 1937 to be inducted into the English High Hall of Fame. After graduating, he attended Lawrence Academy, a preparatory school in Groton, Massachusetts, for two years and then he matriculated at the University of Notre Dame in South Bend, Indiana. His mother, Gertrude, lived at the Bismarck Hotel in Chicago, Illinois while her husband, Bill Stewart, Sr., coached the Chicago Black Hawks. She insisted her only son graduate from Notre Dame. She wanted my dad to receive a Catholic education and she also probably liked him living relatively close.

My father played Notre Dame freshman football but broke his leg, so his roommate Frank Murphy, who later joined the United States Marine Corps, pushed him to classes in a wheelbarrow. My dad remained on the football team but never played in a varsity game. In our cellar were all the autographed pictures from those teams. Dad also played Notre Dame baseball and helped launch a club hockey team on Saint Mary's Lake. He was teammates with 1943 Heisman Trophy winner, quarterback Angelo Bertelli, and the great Lou Rymkus who later played for the Washington Redskins and Cleveland Browns before becoming the first head coach of the Houston Oilers in 1960. Bertelli and Rymkus earned fame through football, but my dad told me they also showed talent in hockey as well. I am told my grandfather provided all of the young men with hockey equipment likely from the closets of the Chicago Black Hawks. Dad bled Blue and Gold. The Notre Dame Fight song was even the recessional at his funeral.

After graduating Notre Dame, my father spent three-and-a-half years serving in the United States Army Air Corps before returning to Massachusetts where he became a graduate assistant football and hockey coach at the University of Massachusetts at Fort Devens, a G.I.-Bill extension college. From there, he returned to Boston English where his influence and love for so many students were constant, although he never cared about gaining recognition. My father was exceptional in so many ways, and sports the vehicle through which he made his impact on others. But his strength of character transcended any of his achievements in sport. He was a true friend and a role model to his students.

Two days after my father died, one of his former students and athletes, legendary sports columnist Will McDonough, wrote in *The Boston Globe* that Bill Stewart, Jr. was like a second father to him. He wrote, "When I had last seen him three weeks ago, he was in pain and, at that time, knowing it might be the last time, I told him that he meant everything to me and that I loved him. I was speaking for me then, but I write now for the thousands like me who, over the past four decades, have shared the joys of the life of William J. Stewart, Jr., husband, father, coach, educator, role model."

My dad drove McDonough, then his star quarterback and pitcher, to school each morning and home from practice each night. He did it to make sure that the tough Southie kid who lived in the Old Colony Project in South Boston came to school each day because he saw McDonough's potential not only in football and baseball, but in the classroom and real world as well. He wanted McDonough to become a successful adult. My dad later brought McDonough to Northeastern University, helping him enroll there.

"What are you thinking about doing with your life?" my dad asked McDonough.

"Maybe being a writer," McDonough replied. Knowing several Boston sportswriters, Dad drove his former star quarterback to *The Boston Globe* for the very first time, where he got McDonough a position as a copy boy. McDonough eventually became a renowned and respected journalist. He worked at *The Boston Globe* until suffering a fatal heart attack in 2003.

Dad's good deeds earned him gratitude and devotion from so many. Every Thanksgiving, a turkey, a crate of oranges, or something got dropped off on our back steps because, somewhere along the way, my dad had done something for somebody. He had given someone a ball or baseball bat. He had given someone cleats or a ride to school. My dad never had to demand respect; he earned it. That's why we Stewart kids never got in trouble with underage drinking and other laws. I know I never wanted to disappoint Dad.

There were times, I remember, where, as a child, my dad's actions downright confused me. One of those instances was when he and I visited Tim McAuliffe's sporting goods store in Boston. At the time, Carl Yastrzemski played left field for the Boston Red Sox, and Yaz became one of the very first hitters in Major League Baseball to wear a batting helmet with a protective earflap. Yastrzemski began wearing it briefly after teammate Tony Conigliaro got beaned in the left eye batting against the Angels on August 18, 1967.

McAuliffe had a helmet with an earflap in stock and wanted to show my father. While we stood in the store, this street urchin of a boy walked in and wanted to buy a fitted Major League Baseball wool cap. The caps sold for probably ten dollars and the kid pulled all the money he had out of his pocket and ended up being two dollars short. McAuliffe told the boy he did not have enough money. The young boy left the store dejected. Moments later, McAuliffe walked away for a minute or two. My dad handed me two one-dollar bills and whispered to run after the boy and give him the money. I did and the boy returned to buy the hat. Later, when my dad and I drove home, I asked him why he had not just given the boy the two dollars immediately. "I didn't want to do it in front of McAuliffe because it would've been embarrassing for the boy," my father replied. "But he should've given that kid that hat for eight bucks. Two bucks—what's the difference?" Using that reasoning, my dad probably would not have succeeded in the business world, but he made a huge impact in the real world.

I remember my dad kissing me only once. Like my grandfather, Bill Stewart, Jr. did not demonstrate open affection, but made up for it through compassion. He had such a profound, positive effect on my life it's difficult to put it all into words. Most of my actions and decisions still, even now, are direct results of what he taught me. He taught me sports but, more importantly, he taught me about life and how to live, which is more important than hockey or anything else. He taught me how to accept everyone no matter his or her skin color, to be accountable for my actions and to choose family and friends over greed. The world was his classroom. My siblings and I learned through his many positive actions. Words mean nothing without actions. Bill Stewart, Jr. was a man of positive actions.

A favorite photograph of mine is one where I had just stepped off the ice after playing the Hartford Whalers in 1979-1980. With a black eye, of course, I was signing a fan's program and my dad stood wearing a fedora and sports jacket behind me with his hands on my hips and his face only half showing. The photograph is representative of Dad's life as a head coach. He never put himself first. He always credited his players first and worked to make their lives better while he stood in the background taking enjoyment in their successes. Seeing that photo and other small reminders, even at my age and almost three decades after his death, makes me think about how I wish I could still talk with him more than anything else. I loved to talk with my dad. I always wanted his advice. He was my best friend. He understood me. He kept me going.

My sister Pat recalled how I used to call my father and wake him in the middle of the night—sometimes as late as 4 a.m.—when I returned to hotels after playing or reffing games. My father always would tell me he was waiting for my call.

As a teenager, before moving back into the dorms at Groton one year, I trained at Boston English High. I was wearing brand-new Hyde Spot-bilt football low-cut cleats that my dad had just given me the money to buy. All the other kids wore high-tops and wanted low-cut cleats. Coming off the field after working out, my father asked me my shoe size.

"Nine," I replied.

"Let me have them," my dad said.

"What?" I asked. "I just got them yesterday."

"Take them off," my dad insisted. "Give me those cleats and don't say anything."

I did what he told me. We walked back to my father's office—me wearing only socks and dad holding the cleats. I dressed in his office where Dad reached under the desk, pulled out a large brown paper bag, placed the cleats inside, then left the office. He wasn't carrying the brown paper bag when he returned. I was curious but didn't ask him any more questions.

I again trained at English High the next day, but wore my old high-tops. Walking by Dad's talented running back, I noticed the boy had on my low-cuts. My dad gave my cleats to this boy because his family didn't have the money to buy any pair at all. Not long after, my dad bought me another new pair of low-cut cleats. Before he did, though, I learned a lesson about giving and appreciating what I had in life.

During one Thanksgiving Day football game, one of my father's best athletes, Bobby C., dislocated his elbow. Bobby was taken to Boston City Hospital. When the game finished, my father and I drove to the hospital, waited for Bobby to receive treatment, then drove him home to his family's apartment in an old walk-up at the bottom of Mission Hill and Huntington Avenue. I was only about eight years old at the time, and my father told me to wait inside the car while he helped Bobby up the stairs to his apartment.

After Dad was done, he and I drove home for Thanksgiving dinner. After dinner on Thanksgiving night, my dad's football players traditionally visited our house for cake. That year was different. My father washed out the turkey pan. He and my mother placed a giant portion of leftover turkey, stuffing, pie, and a couple of Coke cans in the pan. Then Dad looked at me and said, "I'm going back to see Bobby. You wanna go?" We hopped back in the car.

I helped carry the food inside. A single light bulb hung on a string in the dim stairwell. The interior of the apartment complex looked rundown, and I commented aloud about it.

"Keep your mouth shut and walk up the stairs," Dad replied. Bobby's mother answered the door. Bobby lay there on the couch. My father explained he had brought over dinner because Bobby's mother probably hadn't had time to cook while dealing with her son's injury. Realistically, his mother probably had little money to afford a turkey dinner because they were a low-income family and their living situation seemed hardly ideal.

"How will I return this pan to you?" Bobby's concerned mother asked.

"I'll stop by tomorrow to check up on Bobby, and I'll take it then," Dad replied.

This lesson about showing concern and compassion, while respecting the dignity of the other person, stuck with me throughout my life. My dad wasn't one to grandstand or sermonize, though. He just led by example.

Pat recalls how our dad let all four of his children and his athletes make their own decisions—but with his help. "Our father never forced it down our throats, like, 'You will do this' or 'You should do that.' He'd say, 'You can do it this way, or that way, or on the other hand, you could do it this way, too.'" By providing us several options, Dad made it seem like we were making our own decision in a tough situation when, in reality, we picked one of his many solutions, all good ones.

I've seen thousands of coaches in action. I reffed 1,010 NHL games. In my humble opinion, my father stands out as one of the best coaches ever at any sport, at any level, because he understood that coaching is selfless. What happened at Penn State with Joe Paterno is foreign to me because Paterno was the complete opposite of my dad, who always believed he worked in a noble profession. Coaches must put aside their own goals and personal issues and agendas. People and life are more important than wins—and my dad truly believed that. He inspired his family and his players to be the best they could be; not just the best athletes, but the best people. That is what a great coach does.

I even watched my father treat injured players. I remember this one three-hundred-pound Boston English bruiser, Rodney Burke, who once had blisters covering his feet. My dad sat there, washing each foot, one at a time. What I learned in my years of Catholic education was being demonstrated for me in real time. My father saw the service to others as part of his purpose in life.

Former Penguins coach "Badger" Bob Johnson reminded me of my dad. One night in Pittsburgh, I disallowed a Penguins' goal. From the time I left the crease to when I arrived at the penalty box, I knew I was wrong. Johnson stared at me and tilted his head. I could tell he was furious, but he didn't show it. He gave me the same type of look my dad gave when disappointed.

During the next television timeout, I skated near the Penguins' bench and pretended to kick some snow away. I quietly asked Johnson what was wrong. Nobody really knew we were talking. Johnson played with the sticks and quietly replied, "You're the best young referee we have in the NHL. That was not your best call."

That night I returned to the hotel and if I got five minutes of sleep, that was a lot because it bothered me so much I just couldn't sleep. If a coach is reading this and wants to take a lesson on influencing a referee in his thinking, especially for the next play, take this lesson from "Badger" Bob. Johnson gave me a positive and then a point that made me think. I became a better referee because of that moment with Bob Johnson.

I see a lot of young coaches trying to follow the Bobby Knight-style. So many called Knight "brilliant" but I never would have let Knight coach my children. My dad and Johnson—they were men I would trust with my sons. We need more "Badger" Bobs and fewer Bobby Knights.

Coaching, officiating, and everything my dad did had a higher meaning, a higher calling. He had no agendas or strategies to line his pockets. I love the saying, "You were happier when he arrived than when he left." I always thought that was a marvelous thing to say about someone. It certainly applies to my dad.

When you care for people like my dad did, they tend to return the same compassion. Not long before my father died, I stood in line at Boston's Logan Airport and noticed the late actor Leonard Nimoy, best known, of course, for his role as Mr. Spock in the original TV series *Star Trek*. He had been one of my father's students in high school.

"Just to let you know, whenever my dad sees you on TV, he elbows me and says, "Now that's an English High kid who did well for himself,'" I told Nimoy.

"Who's your dad?" Nimoy asked. I told him. He then asked if "Coach Stewart" ever told me how good an athlete he was.

"Now you're trying to find out if my dad ever exaggerated about you," I replied. "My father told me that you were a nice Jewish kid from Dorchester who was the son of a barber. You showed up to gym class on time, always wore your uniform, never bothered anybody, and were barely adequate at track."

Nimoy threw his head back and laughed, telling me, "Yeah, that's Coach Stewart, all right!"

He asked how my dad was doing. I told Nimoy that Dad was nearing the end of his life.

His smile faded and he pursed his lips, pensively. The actor then offered to write my dad a quick little message. I handed him one of my business cards. He scrawled: "Coach Stewart: It was always a pleasure, Leonard Nimoy."

My dad was as hard-working as he was selfless. Both my father and grandfather were men of many hats (coaching, reffing, scouting, mentoring). They taught me something essential at a young age: it's not how many hats you wear; it's how well you wear them. They took pride in performing all their jobs at the highest level possible.

Dad reffed college games each Saturday. He always was on the move. He officiated a football game at Cornell one sunny Saturday in the early 1960s when the Big Red had Pete Gogolak, the first soccer-style placekicker who later starred for the Buffalo Bills and New York Giants. I spent that afternoon chasing Gogolak's field goals and extra points. I always either volunteered as the ball boy or worked the chains. When that football game ended, Dad and I walked to the station wagon, opened the trunk, and pulled out the Coca-Cola cooler that came with us on every road trip. Inside were sandwiches and drinks my mother had packed. When we finished eating, my dad looked down at his watch.

"It's almost 5 p.m. We better get going," he said, throwing his football referee bag into the back of the car, then reaching in and pulling out his hockey bag. Putting on a different hat, my dad walked into historic Lynah Rink and dressed to ref the Cornell hockey game. I served as stick boy for legendary Coach Ned Harkness.

Being the son of Bill Stewart, Jr., I certainly lived an interesting, if somewhat unpredictable, and magical childhood in which I almost always was learning some sort of lesson in life or sports. I almost always stood three feet from my dad, soaking in those lessons while being the water boy at his football games, the stick boy at his hockey games, and the bat boy at his baseball games.

I chased foul balls for a nickel apiece during chilly spring baseball games. My life rotated from one sports season to the next, from stadium to arena, from baseball diamond to baseball diamond. Sports weren't something that happened after school. It was the Stewart family's way of life, passed down from generation to generation. Getting involved with, and learning about, as many sports as possible was what my family did. It was our family business.

My dad remained open to learning anything from anybody. He picked everyone's brain. After reffing a football game at UConn in 1964, he asked then-assistant Huskies coach, Lou Holtz, who went on to win a Division I national title with Notre Dame in 1988, to send him some film of the UConn offense. Tuesday morning, the film sat on my dad's desk at Boston English High. He watched it at home Tuesday night with me sitting beside him.

"You see this?" my dad asked me, pointing at the small projector screen, playing and rewinding the film time after time after time. "I'm going to put these plays into English's offense." A couple weeks later, English used an offense no other Massachusetts high school ever had seen before. Bill Stewart's English High boys clobbered the competition.

My dad taught me how to look at games in a certain way—to watch the whole field—which was an invaluable lesson that I used growing up playing football, hockey, and baseball, and eventually when I turned to reffing. He taught me to know all the assignments of every position. When we watched his team's game film together, he showed me exactly what certain players did wrong and what they did right. He always scribbled notes on cue cards and sometimes even stopped the film to test my knowledge.

"What did you think of that play?" he'd ask. He expected a specific answer—such as how the quarterback didn't see an open receiver downfield, but, instead, only looked right and threw right. He almost always analyzed games—no matter what level. He pointed out certain aspects and forms of great NFL players such as Nick Buoniconti, Gino Cappelletti, and Larry Csonka, telling me that was the way to tackle, block or catch. All his lessons certainly made me more astute and gave me an edge as I became more serious about sports—and along the way, his lessons shaped me into a confident person who knew the game.

My dad used to say that he taught to coach and he coached by teaching. Toward the end of his career, I commented to him, "Dad, you've got, like, six hundred sick days stored up. Why don't you take them?" He stared me down as if I had ten heads and replied, "Paul, I teach to coach. This is what I do. Don't you get it? These kids come to play for me."

My father's actions throughout his life shaped me, even while his body and physical strength deteriorated from Paget's Disease and psoriasis covering nearly eighty percent of his body. Even as his disease caused his back to hunch, he still made his way to Groton School to watch the sports teams play. He often visited Boston English practices without my mom knowing.

Many men and women have influenced me both personally and professionally. Binghamton Dusters owner Jim Matthews always showed me great kindness and the right way to treat others. Groton School coach Frank "Junie" O'Brien taught me leadership. Quebec Nordiques coach Jacques Demers, through his actions, taught me how to make others feel special about themselves. My officiating boss and mentor John McCauley, taught me friendship, compassion, loyalty, and everything about officiating.

But above all, there was my father. Of all the coaches I mention in this book, his name might be the most unrecognizable, but he truly was one of the greatest coaches of all-time. Coaching wasn't just his job; it was truly his calling in life. Through coaching, he shaped countless lives by teaching discipline, hard work, compassion, and loyalty. He didn't only teach sports, he taught life.

My dad's lessons throughout my childhood made me succeed. He is the reason I became such a go-getter. He is the reason I try to help out others when I get the chance. He is the number one reason I graduated from the University of Pennsylvania and made the NHL. He was the reason I came through cancer surgery and then survived chemotherapy and eventually beat colon cancer. In all honesty, he's the reason I'm alive, even though Dad died approximately eleven years before I even received my diagnosis. He was my Yoda. His lessons I now pass down to my sons, McCauley and Maxwell.

Two or three days before my dad died he told me, "I don't know how I'm doing. I know I am not doing too well. But I just want to you to know one thing: I don't owe anybody." He didn't owe anything to anybody.

But me? I owe my dad everything.

## CHAPTER 3: Skating With Ghosts

Do you remember where you were when you fell in love for the very first time? Maybe it was that first glance at that pretty girl sitting in the front row of your math class. Maybe it was the first time you walked into Fenway Park and saw the Green Monster. For me, my first love was the Boston Arena ice. I truly was enamored. I knew then and there that I wanted to become a hockey player and do it for my living. But like any love affair, my time at the Arena wasn't all wine and roses; I had a lot of learning and growing to do.

But also like that first experience with love, I remember my first time like it was yesterday.

I was five-years old in 1958 and hyperactive as usual when the morning of November 28 finally arrived. This day was a significant one in the Stewart household because conversations about football turned to hockey literally overnight. Thanksgiving is rivalry day in Massachusetts high school football. The turkey was difficult to digest in the Stewart house on November 27, 1958 because my dad's Boston English High football team lost a nail-biter, 26-24, to rival Boston Latin at Harvard Stadium that morning.

My family thought of only one high school—English High, Blue and Blue. It was in our blood and a fixture in our lives. Most Thanksgivings, we cleared the dining room table and then my grandfather, Dad and all of us men watched the game film from earlier that day in the basement. Boston English players, meanwhile, stopped by to have cake and coffee.

When everyone left, my dad took part in one final Thanksgiving ritual: he put his hockey skates in a duffel bag by the door. The focus suddenly shifted from football to hockey. Boston English hockey tryouts began early the morning after Thanksgiving at Boston Arena and my dad coached that team, too.

On that morning, I was brimming with excitement. I could barely contain myself. I was going to skate for the very first time at Boston Arena. My older siblings, Bill and Patricia, already had been skating before, and my parents finally told me I was old enough to do it, too. Boston Arena, however, already had been part of my life. I had been there several times to watch my dad coach and referee games.

"Look at the tiger!" my dad said, referring to me. He said this often. I had oodles of energy and power. It took a lot—a whole lot—to tire me. I often felt impatient and had difficulty focusing. I'm still hyperactive. Nobody ever knew about Attention Deficit Hyperactivity Disorder during the 1950s, but I'm pretty sure would have been diagnosed if there had been a test for it.

We drove there in Dad's blue Ford Country Squire station wagon, which had fake wood panels on the sides. My mother always insisted on buying either a blue or green car, and our family always owned automobiles with decorative wood on the sides because Mom considered it a classy look—a way to impress our neighbors. I sat in the backseat, probably leaning my head into the front near my dad as I usually did.

My older brother was there in the car with us. My mother wasn't. Years later, she said she wished she had a picture of me from that day. My family owned a camera but rarely used it. We may not have a photo, but the memory of that morning remains absolutely vivid in my mind. On that morning, I hustled inside Boston Arena after my dad parked the car. My parents gave me a dollar bill to have my blades sharpened. To the skate shop I went. The smell of singed metal is one with which I became quite accustomed.

My skates were hand-me-downs from my sister Pat. Yes, I was about to wear white figure skates with toe picks. No, I didn't care. Getting to skate with the older kids was all that mattered to me. After the skates were sharpened, I hustled to one of the locker rooms where my dad gave me a history lesson as he laced my skates.

"Your grandfather dressed in this room and the Bruins dressing room was right over there," my father said, pointing. "Did you see that panel at the bottom of the door? Art Ross kicked that panel in and broke it one night when your grandfather was reffing here."

At five-years old, I had no clue Ross was a former defenseman, the Boston Bruins' first coach and general manager, and greatly respected for designing a better hockey puck and goalie net. Not only didn't I know at that moment in time, I can't say I cared too much, either. I was five, and not only was I about to step onto any ice for the first time, but was about to do it with a bunch of Boston English hockey players at their first day of tryouts.

All the high-schoolers skated out when the Zamboni driver finished making new ice. I finally stepped out and took my first stride—and down I went. I stood up and then back down I went again. That pattern became repetitive. Before I had gone twenty feet, I felt cold, bruised, and soaked but also determined to push and glide just like the others.

Johnny Bishop, one of my dad's players, skated by, holding out his goalie stick and helping prop me up. I also managed to latch onto some other players' suspenders a few times. I received several tow jobs, being Coach Stewart's son, and those became fun. Twisting and turning, falling and rising, I finally made my way to the safety of the dasher boards. I held on for dear life and yet wanted to skate more.

My father angled by and suggested, "Try walking with small steps, keep holding the boards and get around the rink." The goal became to get around the rink once—and to stay on my feet for as many steps as possible. Something happened on that long, awkward voyage: I glided one time. Gliding on ice feels like hitting a golf ball or baseball just right. When you do it, you want to do it again and again. I remember the shuffling and falling and standing. By the time I got around, I knew that this was what I wanted to do for the rest of my life.

I tried skating between the blue lines, going from one side of the ice to the other as Boston English players did drills on either side during the rest of practice. My dad and brother came by to see if I still was alive when the practice ended and the team headed off. I was alive and excited. I wanted to skate more. It's obviously difficult to remember much about when I was five. But I remember that day clearly. I also still remember the smells of the arena—the smell of fresh popcorn, the old wood, and smells of dressing room showers—the ammonia and the brine—the distinctive smell of arena fries… All aromas that remained with me throughout my childhood. That day marked the beginning of a life-long love of the Boston Arena and all it symbolized.

With my first time on the ice happening right after Thanksgiving, Christmas was around the corner. I knew Dad didn't make much as a teacher and coach, and I never expected more than Pat's hand-me-down white figure skates any time soon. Dad said, "You can learn to skate in those. And when you learn to skate in those, maybe you'll get a better pair." Then, one day, maybe a few weeks just before Christmas, my dad's player John Bishop (who was running the skate shop at Boston Arena) said, "I need a favor, Paul."

I said, "What's that?"

He said, "My nephew's just your size. And I'm gonna get him this pair of skates for Christmas. Can you try 'em on?"

They were a pair of Hydes and they had blue skate tips on the end. I'll never forget them. I tried them on and they fit.

He said, "That's good. They should fit my nephew, too."

I took them off, reluctantly. Back into the box they went. I said, "Well, I hope he has fun in them." I remember running upstairs, a wee bit envious of John's nephew, to get a box of French fries from the bookie who ran the stand.

Christmas was a big deal in the Stewart family. My brother had gotten a train set, and there were all different types of toys that we unwrapped, along with the usual scarves and hats and scratchy stuff that we didn't even want to try on that our aunt sent us from California. All of the presents were unwrapped. My dad, leaning against the wall right next to the Christmas tree, said, "Paul, I think there's one more present." It was sort of tucked under the tree, but a little behind the couch; I couldn't really see it. I looked and it said, "To Paul, from Santa." I opened it up—it was those skates I had tried on!

I remember, after putting them on and clomping around the living room, looking up at my dad. He had his arms folded and a smile on his face. And he winked. My dad, my mom, they gave me the best present ever because those skates took me everywhere. But that night, my dad took me to the Arena to give the new skates a try. It was everything I had dreamed it would be.

Throughout my elementary school years, my father's team played games at Boston Arena on Tuesdays and Fridays, and Dad would be there other weekday nights, reffing high school games for five or ten dollars, or whatever the pay was in the '50s and '60s. I attended St. Gregory's Grammar School on Dorchester Avenue and constantly wanted to watch my dad when he coached and officiated games in the evening.

"You wanna go?" my dad asked. "Okay. Meet me there."

My dad gave explicit directions on how to take the bus, train, and trolley from St. Gregory's to Boston Arena. The train ride cost only five cents. Dad also told me where certain MTA (it later changed names to MBTA) information booths were located in case I had trouble finding my way. Going to the arena, I walked right by the key shop on the Massachusetts Avenue Bridge, which was an active bookie joint. Everyone knew that. At Boston Arena, a security guard named Harvey was often the first person to greet me. Harvey was an older man and a veteran of the Spanish-American War. He physically resembled tap-dancer Bill Robinson (AKA Mr. Bojangles), who co-starred with Shirley Temple.

"Oh, Coach Stewart's son is here," Harvey would say, patting my head while I ducked underneath the turnstile. "Don't put too much salt on your fries today," he'd admonish me.

When I grew older, I was given a key to the backdoor at Boston Arena and skated there during my free time. Whenever it snowed and school got cancelled—and most kids went sledding—I reached for my skates, headed into town on the trolley to the rink which was closed to everyone else because of the weather. I used the key like Rudy Ruettiger in the movie "Rudy" used the key that had been given him to access Notre Dame Stadium. The rink was dark, but I skated by the lights of the exit sign or what little light shined through the glass of the windows that have since been painted out. I grabbed my stick and puck and skated with the ghosts of games played long ago on that oval at St. Botolph Street.

I started my love affair with the Boston Arena back in 1958, but the rink had a storied history long before I entered the picture. Boston Arena, now known as Matthews Arena of Northeastern University, opened April 16, 1910. It's filled with sports history, although many are probably unaware of it. The city schools practiced and played games there. It is the world's oldest multiple-purpose arena still in use. Heavyweight champions Jack Dempsey, Gene Tunney, and Joe Louis boxed there. The NHL Boston Bruins played there from their inaugural season in 1924 until moving to the Boston Garden in 1928.

The Bruins' very first game was played there, a 2-1 Boston victory over the Montreal Maroons on December 1, 1924. Baseball Hall of Famer Babe Ruth, considered by many as the greatest hitter ever, played in hockey scrimmages at Boston Arena.

The Boston Tigers, a minor league professional team in the Canadian-American Hockey League from 1926-32, which also had been known as the Cubs, Tiger Cubs, and Bruin Cubs, played home games there. So did several college teams, including Harvard, Boston College, Northeastern, and MIT. Northeastern still does. It also was the Boston Celtics' original home and the funeral site of former Celtics All-Star Reggie Lewis, who died at age twenty-seven. Boston Arena's famous parquet floor was made from old scrap lumber used to build barracks and to ship war goods during World War II.

Old time pro wrestlers Wladek "Killer" Kowalski, Pat O'Connor, Steve "Crusher" Casey, and William "Haystacks" Calhoun performed at the Arena or at Boston Garden on a regular basis in shows promoted by Paul Bowser. Kowalski and others trained in the building attached to the Arena. I became buddies with Haystacks, who weighed more than six-hundred pounds. He loved to watch hockey and enjoyed sitting in the one penalty box where he kept the opposing players separated while they served penalties. The referees loved having him there because his girth kept the peace. He had another special spot in the stands. The cast iron arm-rests were removed so he could fit his six-hundred pound bottom on the wooden seats.

Even out of the ring, Haystacks wore massive jean bib overalls and plaid shirts. A horseshoe, which he told me he wore for luck, hung from a metal chain around his neck. He was gentle, kind, and a fantastic fixture in my life. When my father reffed high school and college games there, he often had me sit with Haystacks, who, many times, took me across the street to the Windsor Tap or Crusher Casey's Bar and Grille. I never starved when Haystacks babysat me. I would order one egg and a piece of toast while Haystacks ate like an entire army. It seemed like every time we went, he ordered four dozen eggs, two loaves of toast, two pounds of bacon, and a gallon of milk and coffee.

When we returned to the rink after eating across the street, he often ordered us French fries. Many people ask me how I grew to

6'1" when my mother was 5' and my father was about 5'6". I like to joke that it must have been the Boston Arena fries. Those fries were something else. The guy that sold the French fries was great. His name was Tony. He had two payphones of his stand, and when the phone would ring, he'd jump over the top of the counter. And he'd say to me, "Paul, mind the store." And I would hand out French fries for twenty-five cents, and he'd take a notebook out of his pocket. And he'd be writing notes. He was taking numbers for the horses.

If the French fries helped fill my stomach, the other experiences at Boston Arena filled my head and my heart with hockey knowledge, a tireless work ethic, and a visceral love of the game. I learned so much more at Boston Arena than just how to play hockey. I became Boston Arena's gofer boy. I made coffee runs for rink workers. If someone needed an extension cord, vacuum, or broom, I went upstairs to retrieve it. I helped make the popcorn at the concession stand and sometimes worked at the French fry stand. At seven years old, I learned how to lift goalie nets and move them. I was taught how to sharpen and stone skates at a very early age, too, and learned how to drive the Zamboni by age twelve.

"Cigar" Joe Sutherland from Whiskey Point in Brookline taught me a trick on how to set the post into the ice. We had a small can of forty-weight motor oil that he mixed in some antifreeze, then poured into the post holes. That mixture kept the posts from freezing into the ice. When we took the posts out, we stuck a rag in the hole soaked in our oil mix. We never had to drill to get the post holes from freezing.

Like a sponge, I soaked in everything. I learned the meaning of hard work. I helped the ice crew stir in the rock salt for the brine tank that circulated in the pipes. There were hundred-pound bags of salt. We'd stir with a wooden paddle to make the brine that created the chill to make the ice and use the light spray of the hose when we first started to lay down the ice. Patience and rubber boots were a must.

If someone wanted to give me a hockey history lesson, I listened attentively. This rink, after all, was where the Boston Bruins and old-time hockey were born. It is where Dit Clapper and Eddie Shore played. It remains a cradle of hockey history. That knowledge was instilled in me at Boston Arena.

I also learned inside that rink that no job was too big or too small for me. This is a lesson that has reverberated throughout my life. My life hasn't been easy at all. I've struggled at several different times to make ends meet. I've performed many jobs, including managing a laundromat, selling cars, cleaning grave stones and decorating the plots to make a living. But I also have been fortunate to accept several different jobs within hockey after my playing career ended and then, again, after my reffing career ended, because of my extensive knowledge of the game.

Someday, I will be one of those ghosts skating around Boston Arena in the dark, but for now, I live on and still wonder the reason God has allowed me stay in this life. I feel my life has some purpose. I'm just not sure yet why I was saved.

# CHAPTER 4: A Kid From Dorchester

A lot of people assume that because of my father's and grandfather's backgrounds, that a path to pro hockey was paved for me. Nothing could be further from the truth. Just because they couldn't pave my way, though, doesn't mean that they didn't give me the tools I needed to make it on my own. They did. Their perseverance and work ethic, which passed down to me, were actually the only reasons I had the career I had. More times than I can even count, I have had to fight and claw my way through life, in hockey and beyond. I have fought battles at every step of the way, and my family's history makes me wonder if it wasn't just the lot I was born into. Many of my fights have been by choice, but many others have not. I don't think I was born with a chip on my shoulder as much as other people have mistaken my ambition and exuberance for querulousness. If I was cantankerous, it was because I felt I had something to prove.

My sister, Pat, recalled that when I was a child, "He was a little runt and they made fun of him. And he had freckles all over. Paul looked like one of the 'Our Gang' kids. He was a tough-looking boy. He wasn't an altar-boy type. He always had a growl on his face."

If my scowl was so off-putting, you'd think I'd have been in fewer fights! But maybe my outer appearance reflected my inner struggle: I was coping with lots of uncertainty and change. I was fighting to establish my own identity and my own place in the world and maybe some of my peers just got caught in the cross-hairs.

My family initially lived in a two-family house in Mattapan, then moved to a single-family house in Dorchester. We finally moved to my grandfather's Jamaica Plain home in June 1964, four months after my granddad died. My parents inherited the house that Grampy built with his bonus money from winning the Stanley Cup. On the surface, this was probably a lifestyle upgrade, but moving to Jamaica

Plain was difficult. I left all my friends I'd grown up with and spent every day with—buddies such as Mikey and Billy Carroll, who taught me to fish and brought me on their family camping trips. My father was a fabulous coach and friend but didn't know anything about camping and fishing. For me, it was a different part of life. I actually enjoyed it.

My Dorchester neighborhood was very blue-collar, consisting of teachers, bus drivers, bartenders, firemen, policemen, and the like—not that I knew or cared about their jobs back then. My Jamaica Plain neighborhood, on the other hand, consisted of approximately fifty percent working class who lived in double- and triple-deck houses or the projects, and fifty percent upper-class who lived in the big houses on Moss Hill. Our new house was on Moss Hill where all the judges, physicians, lawyers, and politicians lived. As a white Irish-Catholic boy and the third child of a modest high school teacher/coach, I quickly learned the definition of haves- and have-nots. I knew that we weren't what they called "lace-curtain Irish."

When we moved, I transferred grammar schools from St. Gregory's to St. Thomas. I was entering the sixth grade and going through puberty. I began to look at girls my own age differently. All of these changes happened and I hardly felt like the happiest kid in town as I searched for my identity. I, for sure, didn't have a clue who I was or who I should be. I knew nobody and felt like an outsider. This feeling would find me again as I matured and found myself feeling alone at other critical junctures in my life. It would drive certain decisions in my life that were motivated by the desire to fit in. Despite my lack of certainty, my identity in school and life began to emerge: I was the tough kid who played sports. That became my comfort zone, my niche.

I played Pee-Wee hockey in Brookline, Massachusetts, a town adjacent to Jamaica Plain, for coach Eddie Kirrane. Coach Kirrane took me aside and told me to tell people I lived in Brookline if anyone asked. I felt like an outsider playing for Brookline, too. But it was there my identity as a tough kid began to develop. A few years later, after I made the team and a Brookline kid didn't, his parents went to the town and complained that I shouldn't be allowed to play as I wasn't from the town. So, I had to leave and play somewhere else. Good lesson for a twelve-year-old on seeing politics prevail over merit.

Ironically, as an adult, Brookline Youth Hockey chose me, someone who never lived a day in Brookline, to deliver a speech representing all who played for its program at a rink dedication honoring Ed Kirrane's brother, Jack Kirrane, captain of the 1960 United States hockey team, a gold medal winner in the Winter Olympics, and a longtime dedicated Brookline firefighter.

I was one of many tough boys who lived in Jamaica Plain and who attended St. Thomas School. I eventually became friends with the kids in my new neighborhood and at my new grammar school, although it fairly common for friends to fist-fight. I fought opponents during Pee-Wee hockey games. I fought friends on ponds during shinny hockey games. If someone slashed someone, the two friends dropped their gloves and duked it out. I developed more courage and fierceness from fighting in the neighborhood because it happened often. We'd fight over something inconsequential such as attending different schools. Ten minutes after the fight, the problem was resolved and we were friends again. It was somewhat like fighting in the NHL, although I obviously was unaware of it back then as a kid.

Once, I duked it out with a friend, Nicky Fish, on the rotary circle at the Arborway and Centre Street in Jamaica Plain. The Costello's Tavern owner's wife, with her Irish accent, called my mother to warn her about my street brawl. My mom walked down to observe the goings-on but didn't stop the fight.

She picked up my lunch box and coat off the sidewalk, then stood and watched us beat the snot out of each other. Fish was as tough as anyone I ever fought on the ice. Some people pulled their cars to the side of the road to watch us. Some of the Poor Clare nuns walked outside of a nearby convent to watch. As I returned home disheveled, I asked my mom the reason she came down to the fight. I felt embarrassed that she had. In typical Helen Stewart fashion, she told me she wanted to make sure nobody stole my coat.

In my neighborhood, fighting didn't typically end friendships. It often strengthened them. And each street fight prepared me for a career in hockey. So did the boxing clinics my dad enrolled me in at twelve years old on Saturdays and Sundays at a gym near the Boston Garden. Boston English High junior varsity baseball coach Bill Duffy taught there. Duffy taped my hands and taught me several fighting techniques on how to block punches, move my feet, and turn my hips to use my weight. He then pitted me against other boys two and three years older than me who were much taller and weighed more.

The most important tip Duffy gave me was this: A fighter must be willing to take a punch to give a punch. All hockey fighters should understand that. I always could take a punch.

I also attended classes at Mattson Academy of Karate in Boston as a teenager. I didn't advance very far in karate, but I learned technique. Everything helped and prepared me. Years later, during college, I hired a 2nd-dan black belt to teach me the Japanese grappling art of aikido. He helped me understand how to feel the energy of an opponent and then turn their energy against them.

"If the opponent's going a certain way with his power, let him go with it and counter it," the aikido expert instructed me.

From martial arts, I learned that hockey fighting is a lot about pushing when pulled and pulling when pushed. Once, an instructor fired a roundhouse kick at me during one of our many workouts. I blocked it, then threw an elbow and caught him in the side of the head. The blow knocked him to the mat. It was the only I time I knocked him down. Years later, hockey legend Gordie Howe hit me with the same type of elbow right in the face, sending me falling to the ice. History has a way of repeating itself.

It happened the first time I played against Howe when the Hall of Famer was playing for the New England Whalers of the World Hockey Association and I was on the Cincinnati Stingers during the 1977-1978 season. Earlier that game, I told him, "Mr. Howe, I just want you to know how much I've always admired you. I even named my dog after you." While I was in college, I had a dog that I named Gordie. After the elbow, I skated by him and joked, "I'm gonna go home and strangle that dog!"

Howe replied, "Welcome to the pros, kid."

My father told me that someone would always be tougher than me no matter how tough I considered myself and so to fight smart and pick my battles. When he offered this advice, I'm pretty sure he didn't have Gordie Howe in mind, but it was still sage advice. However, my job on all my professional hockey teams was to fight, so I couldn't pick all my fights. But if I couldn't choose my opponents, I could at least plan my strategy.

As a professional hockey player, I planned strategies on how to fight opponents well before arriving at the rink each night. Sometimes, though, you can't even do that; circumstances can catch you off-guard no matter how well-prepared you may be.

Caught off-guard in a fight was exactly how I felt when I started the prestigious Groton School. I was not a White Anglo-Saxon Protestant like most everyone else I met there. I talked with a different accent. I didn't pronounce my "Rs" like a Boston Brahmin did. I became aware of subtle discrimination and real-world issues. Before I went there, I thought a WASP was an insect. I was about to learn the difference after I started Groton.

Groton is a five-year private Episcopal institution and the alma mater of Franklin Delano Roosevelt, the thirty-second president of the United States. I took the Secondary School Admission Test to gain admittance there and did okay on the math section but earned a perfect score on the English portion. I loved to read, even at an early age, but Groton's admissions office didn't believe I could score so high so it retested me. I earned another perfect score. I underwent further testing, being asked to put together puzzles and partake in timed tests. I'm surprised I did so well because of what I know about myself now and my likely undiagnosed ADHD. Staying on task remains difficult for me to this day.

The morning finally arrived when I moved into the Groton School dormitories. When then-headmaster Rev. Bert Honea told parents to say goodbye to their children, I had tears in my eyes. The idea of living away at a prep school never scared me; I liked being on my own. Even during summers at Groton School, I caddied and lived at Hyannisport Club in Hyannis Port, Massachusetts. We caddies lived in *M*A*S*H*-style tents, eight of us per tent on the golf course. (These many years later, I have been a member of that very same club for the last thirty-eight years. It has one of the most beautiful views in the world should you happen to be near Hyannisport and The Kennedy Compound). But it was still hard to say goodbye. My dad and I shook hands. My mom wished me good luck. No hugs or kisses were exchanged. That just wasn't the way my family did things.

I didn't quite fit in. I met so many cultured classmates, some who spoke multiple languages, and that amazed me. I introduced myself to Jim Cooper, who went on to become a Rhodes Scholar, eventually studied at Oxford and Harvard, and now serves as a U.S.

Representative for the 5th congressional district in Tennessee. I also met Nicholas Vreeland, now a monk who works with the Dalai Lama. Classmates hailed from Long Island, Oyster Bay, and several other wealthy cities. Meanwhile, when someone said, "Brooks Brothers," I thought they were talking about the two guys who invented cough drops. I didn't know it was a men's clothing store. I got an education in many ways when I started out at Groton.

All of it, however, became part of my education and a big part of my life. It prepared me for the real world. I went through a sort of social and lifestyle metamorphosis. Being the tough kid from Boston was my identity. Whether it was a good or bad tag, it was my tag. Everyone knew me that way. While in awe of my classmates, I didn't feel like one of them. I never did. My classmates looked at me differently. Some liked me, others didn't. It was a struggle and a challenge to live and survive in a vastly different environment than I was used to. Many at Groton like my friends Larney Fowler, Nicholas Vreeland, and my advisor, Dave Rogerson, treated me as equals. Some of the others in the school acted polite but distant. I could feel the distance, some of which was so extreme as to be comparable to hazing. Sometimes classmates and teammates invited a group to their family house for a weekend. Many times, I wasn't one who got asked.

I often contemplated why I was good enough to play on their teams and study at Groton with them but not good enough for the other parts of their lives. There were two different worlds and different levels in the caste system. It's okay now, but life lessons can be difficult on the young and optimistic. These are some of the battles you never choose to fight and you can't really prepare for. They inflict the deepest wounds. But that doesn't mean you can't fight back.

I recall when an upperclassman, Carll (two lls) Tucker III, told me that I wouldn't last beyond December of my second form, eighth-grade year. He didn't know me very well. He, and others, misjudged me. They didn't understand that I didn't know the words "quit" or "failure." Since I first put on skates, I have possessed a determination and a sense of urgency. I can feel the fight inside of me. For example, I went to a hockey tryout in Hyde Park as a young boy. Coach Eddy Dalton had us skate around one of the circles clockwise, then counter-clockwise. I had difficultly skating clockwise so Dalton put me at the side of the rink with the weaker skaters. That week, I went to Ulin Rink in Milton, a public rink with a chain-link fence. I jumped the fence when nobody was there and skated around and around clockwise until mastering it. A lot of falling and some hitting the boards happened. But during the next tryout, I showed Dalton how I could skate clockwise and he sent me to the side with the better skaters. I had to prove myself to Dalton and I did. I showed I deserved to be there.

Likewise, I fell a few times at Groton, but every time—whether in the classroom, field, or rink—I always got back up quickly. I certainly had a great deal of help from teachers and friends who gave me their time and effort. Carll and others misjudged me upon first glance. It was a bad feeling, but it also helped shape me into the person I am today.

Thankfully, not everyone was as pompous as Carll and his ilk. Classmate Larney Fowler and I probably should not have been friends at all, but life, being what it is, made us best friends. Fowler commented, "I was from the Upper East Side, a preppy from New York City and Paul was a down-in-the-street sort of combative, fighter-type from Jamaica Plain. I don't know what it was. We hit it off right away. He just had a way about him. He had a sense of humor and charm that far surpassed what, early on, one might have thought was his rough ways. He always said what he meant and meant what he said. By no means was diplomacy one of his strong suits. He could say something really silly or uncouth or off-the-cuff and you couldn't help but like the guy." Fowler added, "Paul was 'rough around the edges' when he arrived at Groton."

"When we were at Groton, we would have what was called 'Fac Supper,'" Fowler recalled. "Fac" was short for faculty. On certain occasions, you'd be able to go to either the headmaster's or one of the other master's homes and they'd have donuts and cupcakes and you'd have milk or soda, and you'd get to know the (master's) family. It'd be a lot of fun. We were at the Brooks House at evening study hall. We were in the third form, which is the ninth grade, and I remember Charlie Sheerin, who was the teacher, said, 'Time for Fac Supper for anyone who wants to go.' And Stewy piped up, as a ninth grader, and said, 'Mr. Sheerin, which of the faculty's wives are going to be there?' I'll never forget it. Sheerin said, 'Stewart, you are a barbarian.' He was serious but tongue-and-cheek at the same time. The place just cracked up and that was Stewy. There was really no one else in our class of thirty-five to forty boys who was like him. He marched to the beat of his own drummer."

Fowler and I were drawn together by a mutual love for hockey. His favorite team was the New York Rangers and his favorite players were Eddie Giacomin, Jean Ratelle, and Rod Gilbert. Fowler served as the Groton hockey team manager. He helped me with schoolwork and brought me to New York City to eat meals at his mother's house. His mom was the epitome of elegance. I never had been to New York City before Fowler took me there to visit.

We often went to the outside rink at Groton late at night, especially during senior year. We'd turn on the lights. Fowler stood behind the net passing pucks to me, one after another, and I'd fire slap shots on net.

"We did that many times for hours," Fowler recalled. "I remember one time, I think it was the night of what might have been a prom. We were not a co-ed school back then but maybe some girl schools were coming over. Stewy and I, we didn't really care. We didn't have any dates so we went to play hockey. And Mr. Paul Wright, who was headmaster then and was a wonderful old-timer, came over and caught us playing." Wright wasn't mad. He just stared at us in a certain way that we knew to stop playing and return to our dorm right away.

Years later, in 1976, I went to training camp with the New York Rangers and played in an exhibition game at Madison Square Garden against the Philadelphia Flyers, fighting Steve Short. I gave Fowler the jersey I wore that game when his Rangers won the 1993-94 Stanley Cup. He was born to wear it and has been a great friend for all these years.

Classmate Nicky Vreeland, who I mentioned now is a Buddhist monk who works with the Dalai Lama, also always treated me kindly. Maybe this isn't surprising, given where his life took him. He taught me photography and took me skiing for my first time ever at Mount Sunapee. I borrowed skis from classmate Dick Storey, a boy from Chicago. Our teachers often asked us students our plans for winter and spring vacations. I'd always tell them I was going to watch my dad referee the ECAC hockey tournament at the Boston Garden, or some similar event. Others had more elaborate plans, such as vacationing in Aruba and skiing at Lake Tahoe. I never had skied in my life before Vreeland invited me to go with him. I had always thought skiing happened only at the Blue Hills in Milton, Massachusetts, and it wasn't something my family did because we played hockey.

Despite my resolve not to let the naysayers at Groton define me or my time there, there was one occasion where I almost did quit. Thankfully, before that happened, a great man stepped in to provide me with the proper vision. It occurred during my senior year at Groton and that man was Frank "Junie" O'Brien, who had a profound influence on my life and the lives of many others.

At a hockey game, a St. Sebastian's fan blew cigar smoke in my face, then spit on me during a game. I got so angry that I deliberately wiped out the entire front row with my hockey stick, just like a scene from the movie "Slap Shot." Coach Jon Choate justifiably suspended me for the next game against Nobles, but, at the time, I didn't feel like the punishment was a just one. I had been eager to play against Nobles because I heard some college recruiters were attending. I went to the rink, picked up my skates, and left campus without any thought of ever returning. As I walked down Farmer's Row, away from the school, Coach O'Brien pulled his Jeep up alongside me.

"Where are you going?" asked O'Brien, who was the former Groton hockey coach, but still my baseball coach at the time.

"I'm outta here. I'm leaving," I replied. "I'm going to catch a bus to Boston."

"It's cold," he responded. "Get in. I'll give you a ride to the station."

O'Brien obviously never considered letting me board a Boston-bound bus. We ended up at an ice-cream stand, eating hamburgers and drinking frappes.

"You're the assistant captain of the hockey team and what you did was wrong," he said later. "Accept your punishment and set a positive example by showing your teammates you're not a quitter and you won't give up on them. If you're as tough as you think you are, then you won't quit."

Coach O'Brien attended the Groton/Nobles game with me and stood beside me the whole game. When the game ended, he told me to go into the locker room to tell my teammates they did a nice job. Reflecting back on it, I didn't get to play and referee in many games that I wanted to or should have played or worked throughout my career. But the lesson I learned from Coach O'Brien that day—not to quit and to do the right thing even when you are frustrated or angry—stuck with me just as so many other lessons learned at Groton, for better or worse.

A couple years ago, I used O'Brien's lesson with my son, McCauley, who attended Dexter School, an independent boys school in Brookline. McCauley received a one-game suspension from the coach of the Dexter Middle School team for being late to practice several days in a row. McCauley came home and told me he wanted to quit. I gave him Junie's talk, then stood with my son at the next game and told him to congratulate his teammates when the contest ended. Like farming, some seeds take a little longer to sprout than others. Coach O'Brien's was a lesson that stayed with me.

Hockey might have been my bread and butter, but I excelled in every sport I played. Some say I was a better football and baseball player (catcher and cleanup hitter) than a hockey player. I was all-league in both football and baseball, including being all-league in three different positions for football during my junior and senior years. On offense, I played quarterback, then was moved to halfback, then fullback, then end before winding up at guard. I also played defensive end and on every special team my senior year. I played every minute of every football game my junior and senior years, and I loved to hit.

We played my dad's Boston English football, hockey, and baseball teams, and I felt a little extra pumped for those games. Fowler recalled my football game against Dad's English boys: "It seemed like his tackles were harder than they were against St. Mark's or Middlesex. There was a different feel about it. He could relate to it because he was the kid from Boston. Those kids were probably used to someone like Stewy, but they weren't used to seeing him on the pastoral fields of Groton."

I played quarterback as an eighth grader, and I was pretty good at running plays from all the lessons I had learned growing up as Coach Bill Stewart's son. I competed for the quarterback position during freshman year with Bill Larkin, a big kid from Manhasset,

New York, the hometown of former NFL star running back Jim Brown. Something must be in the water in Long Island because Larkin, like Brown, was naturally big. In his early teens, Larkin looked like a twenty-five-year-old man. He could grow a beard in, say, five minutes. He was a superior athlete in football, basketball, and baseball or anything he wanted to play. He had a considerable size and strength advantage over me.

Even though I competed hard against him and wouldn't back down, he easily won the starting QB job. The coaching staff moved me to fullback. But the competition between Larkin and me continued when both of us wanted the PAT/field goal kicker duties. We had a Charlie Brown/Lucy van Pelt moment at tryouts with me kicking and him holding. I went to kick the football and he pulled it away.

I went flying down to the ground, then got up and threw a punch at him. All I could hear was Coach Jake Congleton, yelling, "Don't hurt your hand, Bill! Don't hurt your hand!" We had our helmets off and we were whacking each other. My hands obviously weren't as critical to our team's success as Larkin's. Larkin earned twelve varsity letters at Groton, passed for 2,616 yards, rushed for 1,348 yards, and was named All-New England Quarterback and Offensive Player of the Year in 1971 by *The Boston Globe*.

As my time at Groton continued, my identity as that scrappy, tough kid from Boston was only enhanced. During my junior year, we played Milton Academy and on the first play from scrimmage, the Milton Academy 235-pound fullback, a kid named Sheptek, knocked our middle linebacker, 220-pound Hench Ellis, to the ground, separating Ellis' shoulder. My coach replaced Ellis at middle linebacker with 190-pound me. When Sheptek came through the line on the next play, I showed him he couldn't bully my team. I drove my helmet right into his cup. I gave him a little extra, right in the balls, when we both stood.

That took a little bit of the steam out of him for the rest of the half. It wasn't the right thing to do, but it seemed okay to me at the time, and a little bit of the enforcer I became in hockey had started to become a part of me and my game in prep school. I started to use my toughness for a purpose. I started to stand up for my teams. My fights began to have meaning. That continued during the hockey season when Groton played Hudson High from Hudson, Massachusetts one cold New England night. Some of our players from Oyster Bay and Long Island seemed unprepared for Hudson High's rough, public school style. Hudson is a mill town. I skated by one of the Hudson players and told him to cut the crap.

"If you don't, I'm going to smack you," I added.

"Oh, you're a tough preppy, huh?" the Hudson player replied.

That was all I needed to hear. I dropped my right glove and punched him in the face. I looked at the other Hudson High players and said, "Anyone else want to try the preppies? Anyone else want to try me? Let's go!"

Coach Choate and my advisor, Coach Dave Rogerson, and other spectators looked horrified. The next day, Headmaster Mr. Paul Wright summoned me to his office.

"I was at the game last night," he said.

"I figured that's why I'm here," I replied.

"I understand why you did what you did," Wright remarked. "I appreciate your enthusiasm for our school, but fighting shouldn't be something we do during a hockey game. We don't fight here at Groton." As I was walking out of his office, Wright looked into my eyes and added, "But I must say, you did hit him with a marvelous punch!"

I wasn't as talented a hockey player as many of the other kids in the Prep School league but I was tough, big, could skate, and was versatile.

"It was just a rougher game and a rougher bunch of guys," Fowler recalled about the Hudson High team. "When you play people like that, they want to show up the preppies. And I remember Stewy leveling some pretty nasty body checks in that game. I think he got several penalties. He just wasn't going to let anyone besmirch the Groton name. He would sort of be the defender of the team."

While defending my team and my teammates felt to me like something of a noble calling, not everyone agreed. Some of my enthusiastic and flashy style often rubbed some teammates the wrong way, although I didn't always realize it until later. My junior year, I visited Canada with a New England Prep School team. Another player, our captain, and surprisingly a teammate from Groton who had gone on the trip the year before, did not want me to go on the trip. He told two of the Prep Star coaches I wasn't good enough to play with the team. He had been our senior team captain and I thought he was my friend. That was the first time I saw petty jealousy and true meanness. I took the spotlight off him and I think that's why he didn't want me on that team. He ended up matriculating at Dartmouth and never skated a single stride there.

In hindsight, he didn't really have what it took to make it in hockey. He was clever, talented, and strong physically, but he also was very heavy. He was successful in prep school with a big shot, but the graveyards are full of so-called "talented players." It's the same thing I tell my sons about some of their teammates—they aren't in shape. And that's not good because hockey is a marathon, not a sprint. It doesn't matter who has the fastest and hardest shot. All that really matters is working and trying to improve day after day. The hockey players who live by that code are the ones who end up making it.

During the trip to Canada, we played in Calgary, Edmonton, and Winnipeg. In Calgary, I scored my team's first goal of the tournament, jamming it in at the front of the net. I showed an aggressive style my Canadian opponents didn't expect and one of them tried to fight me. I obliged. It wasn't the first time I fought in a game, but it was the first of many on this trip. In Edmonton, an opponent dinged me with his stick and cut the corner of my eye. I hustled into the dressing room, received eight stitches, returned to the ice, found the delinquent who had swatted me, and clipped him with an elbow right in his face. I was becoming the player I eventually became in professional hockey.

In Winnipeg, I found a fight not on the ice, but off it. I was billeted at an opponent's family house with a couple of my other teammates. The father of the household berated the United States at the dinner table. He told me that my countrymen think they are the best at everything and have the best military. This man was sour and also bragged about how Canada owned hockey. I didn't see it that way and still don't. I understood that Russian and Czechoslovakian players, as well as some players from the United States, were equally as talented as the Canadians. That was the first time I experienced anti-American sentiment. I argued with him, grabbed my luggage, left the house, and checked into a hotel. I refused to acquiesce to his anti-American opinions. He verbally abused my country and I didn't approve of his behavior. I have a lot of national pride, but I do respect diversity and culture. My grandmother was Canadian for God's sake. So, what? What's the difference?

I didn't necessarily like some teammates, either, but they probably disliked me, too. Our priorities and goals didn't always align, but all these lessons were learned and stored. I eventually returned to Edmonton, Calgary, and Winnipeg with different teams as a professional hockey player, and then as a NHL referee with a different perspective and reason for being there.

My senior year at Groton, I again made the New England Prep School team and, this time, we traveled to Europe. We played in Switzerland, Italy, and Czechoslovakia. Facing the Italian Junior National Team, an opponent cross-checked me square in the mouth and cut me. I started a fight. The fans went nuts, yelling and barking at us. The games were well-attended as we made our way across northern Italy and through the Alps.

Although we had some talented players who went on to play hockey in college, some of the guys weren't as focused. Such as in Prague, where three teammates, after a few too many beers, began a fight and dumped a pitcher of something, likely urine, on me. That prompted me to take on these three so-called "tough guys" simultaneously. The police arrived and broke up the mayhem. It was three-against-one so, despite the language barrier, the police knew and let me return to the hotel without arresting me.

I wasn't a troublemaker. I went to Europe to wear the USA jersey and not to disgrace myself, my country, or my family. I wasn't really, in any way, like some of my juvenile, drunken, semi-courageous teammates who got braver in packs and by the drink. I was in awe of being able to play in Europe and didn't want to reflect badly on our team, yet I just wasn't going to accept anyone's indiscretions either, especially those given to me by my own teammates.

We had a few guys who couldn't handle their booze. Some teammates appeared more interested in drinking and chasing women than playing hockey and representing the United States in Europe. Several cinderblock-headed teammates tipped over a dumpster when we were in St. Moritz on what was my nineteenth birthday. After my birthday party dinner, I had spent the night sightseeing, including viewing a B-17 that had been forced down in World War II and was on display in a city park. I then returned to the hotel and fell asleep. At approximately 4 a.m., the police stormed into the hotel, shined a flashlight in our faces, and told us to get up, get on our bus, and leave their village immediately. I came to find out, the dumpster that our eggheads tipped had hit a car as it crashed down the hill. As a result, we had to sleep on the bus. But the experience, (like each one in prep school), for better or worse, helped mold me even more and showed me my own path.

I realized I didn't wanted to be one of those guys without any maturity, purpose, and direction. I wasn't going to be just another idiot party animal in college. I'd have to keep my eye on the prize: making the NHL. I knew I needed to stay focused.

I survived Groton with a diploma. I did okay academically, played three sports, served as the Dining Room Prefect, received a score of 1150 on the SATs, and survived and prospered so much that, when I was handed my diploma, I received a standing ovation from my classmates. Thinking back on Prize Day, maybe I just surprised a few who didn't think that I would make it through. I remember wearing my school blazer on graduation day and thinking about how that phase of my life was finished and a new one was about to begin.

You know what, though? Nowadays, I look back on Groton with gratitude. I learned a lot while I was there, about myself, about life, and about people. I had great teachers and coaches. Junie O'Brien was always in my corner, among others. I made some lifelong friends. Even the not-so-happy memories were learning experiences.

At the time, I was poised to attend Boston College. In reality, though, I didn't want to go to school there because I dreaded the idea of living at home without my independence and dealing with my difficult relationship with my mother, Helen.

My mother was a closet drinker. Her alcoholism gave strong reason for my dad to leave his equipment bag near the front door. As soon as the time came for him to referee or coach a game, he left our house quickly and received a needed break from my mother's often destructive behavior.

Do you know the Alan Jackson and Jimmy Buffett song, "It's Five O'Clock Somewhere?" It always was 5 p.m. somewhere for my mom. She never waited too long to begin drinking. She started with vodka and switched to scotch. She became mean when she drank. She arrived late to family events and nitpicked everything we did or said. She sometimes stood over the kitchen sink or washer machine just staring into space.

I don't think my mom was ever happy in life. She had a dysfunctional relationship with her sister and mother. Her father died when she was a young girl, something that had a lasting and saddening effect on her. I don't think my mom had too terrific a relationship with any of her four children either. And yet, my father likely never thought about divorcing her. His life revolved around coaching, officiating, and family, particularly his kids. He wasn't the type of man to make a drastic life change and so he stayed loyal and stayed with my mother, for better or worse. I don't feel my dad's decision to stay with my mother was the wrong one, although I've been divorced twice and I realized I wouldn't continue to live the rest of my life in a relationship that didn't make me happy. I'm not sure if any of us are completely happy with our lives and our relationships, but we don't always have to be either. On the flip side, staying a relationship that makes you miserable is beneficial to no one.

With all of these considerations weighing on my mind, I needed to formulate a plan that seemed a better option than Boston College. I actually thought about joining the United States Marine Corps instead. But since I was a kid, I had dreamed of attending an Ivy League school. I also had just spent five years at one of the most intense prep schools in the nation and knew that I could hold my own there. With Harvard, Yale, and Princeton not quite within reach, I explored other options. Like W.C. Fields, I found out that things might be better in Philadelphia.

# CHAPTER 5: The Weirdo At Penn

If I am being completely honest, it wasn't only the academic rigors of an Ivy League college that intrigued me; I wanted to play hockey there. No guaranteed spot on Boston College's hockey squad was waiting for me. It wasn't guaranteed anywhere else, either, but at least I'd have half of what I wanted.

In trying to gauge my prospects at BC, I had spoken with then-Eagles coach Len Ceglarski. Ceglarski had recently been appointed to replace John "Snooks" Kelley, a legend, who coached BC from 1932 to 1942 and 1946 to 1972. Ceglarski told me I'd have the chance to make the team as a walk-on. I certainly wasn't a shoo-in. I wasn't a smooth, crafty playmaker who recruiters identify as a blue-chipper. Fate took its course that summer when Jack Kelley (the father of television writer/producer David E. Kelley), resigned as head coach at Boston University after winning back-to-back national titles and became the head coach and general manager of the New England Whalers of the fledgling World Hockey Association. Kelley's longtime assistant, Bob Crocker, wasn't promoted to head coach despite years of loyal and solid service at BU, but Crocker did land the head coaching position at the University of Pennsylvania, the southernmost university in the Ivy League.

Crocker had known me since I was a baby. He was friendly with my father, who knew most everyone on the local athletic scene. My dad heard Crocker was recruiting players to fill out his roster, so he contacted him and assured Crocker I was capable of doing the academic workload and determined enough to play Division I hockey. Crocker took my dad's word for it. He scheduled an interview for me with Penn's admissions staff for late August '72. He and I drove to Philadelphia together for it. I actually drove Crocker's car because he had the stomach flu, and so we hit several rest stops on the way to Philly.

The interview with Jim Nolan, Director of Undergraduate Admissions, went well. Without even touring the campus, I boarded a plane home to Boston, paying my own airfare. When my dad picked me up at the airport, he told me someone from the university had called to let me know I had been accepted. Being a lifelong history buff, I felt like Benjamin Franklin, transplanting from Boston to Philadelphia to make my mark on the world, although my several jobs in Philadelphia weren't nearly as prestigious as Franklin's. Franklin actually attended Boston Latin High, the rival of my dad's English High. Franklin didn't graduate, but went on to become the founder of the University of Pennsylvania.

My first day on campus wasn't different from any other day of my life. I've always considered myself a go-getter and someone who doesn't think any job is too small or too big for me. Remember how I was the rink gopher at Boston Arena? Same thing at Penn, too. First day on campus, I applied for and received work at Class of 1923 Arena doing several odd jobs. I also worked in the Penn Athletic Department under Assistant Athletic Director Dick Corrigan and athletic director Fred Shabel (the UConn men's basketball coach from 1963-67 with a 72-29 record), conducting group sales and uncovering a counterfeit ticket ring at the Penn Relays.

I cut pounds of ham and broke hundreds of eggs two at a time at the athletic training house on Saturday mornings, letting the eggs slide down a cutting board into a big pot for the athletes playing in Saturday games. You name it, and I did it. I stuffed envelopes. I painted the numbers on the 65,000 seats at Franklin Field—1, 1, 1, 1, 1, 2, 2, 2, 2, 2, etc.—all the way up and down the stands with a spray can and stencil. I worked the Penn Relays, cleaned toilets, painted dressing rooms, refereed intramural and youth hockey games on campus, drove the Zamboni, and sharpened skates. I even sold every advertisement in Penn's annual "Friends of Hockey" book one year. "Give me that job," I told Crocker. "I guarantee I can sell all those ads." I made ten percent of the book's revenue when I did sell them all. Crocker remarked, "Paul could sell refrigerators to Eskimos."

I also was a bouncer at Mike Doyle's New Deck Tavern, an Irish pub and restaurant in Philadelphia, and Smokey Joe's, owned by the Paul Ryan family. I worked at Smokey Joe's the longest of anywhere. I'm honored to be one of a few former Penn hockey players whose photo still hangs on the wall there. A legendary campus bar, many call Smokey Joe's "The Pennstitution." I occasionally tended bar there and also at the New Deck Tavern. The cooks, especially Lily at Smokey Joe's and Carey at the training house, fed me well. Carey was the first person I introduced to my parents when they visited me at Penn freshman year. She was a terrific friend and sometimes even made me a picnic basket lunch to bring to football games. I'd bring the basket and a date, and I'd sit in the stands eating fried chicken, deviled eggs, or whatever Carey packed. Not once did I buy a meal ticket in four years at Penn thanks to Carey and Lily. When I ventured off campus to eat, I ordered the local specialties. I acquired a taste for scrapple, Philly's breakfast time mystery meat. Or I'd go to South Philly for a hoagie or perhaps over to Pat's King of Steaks for a cheesesteak. None are exactly "training table" foods, but all are delicious.

Rarely did I ask my father for money because he didn't have any to give. He couldn't afford an Ivy League tuition after helping to pay for my five years at Groton School. To support myself, I worked forty hours a week in addition to a grueling class load and playing Penn hockey and baseball. I have always considered myself a hard worker. I've always found ways to make a buck. I caddied at the Hyannisport Club during my summers. And after caddying there all day, I either helped in the pro shop, picked the range, washed clubs, headed to Wimpy's in Osterville to wash dishes, or stayed at the club to work in the kitchen. I think of those soapy moments now as I eat at the club with my family. I became a member of Hyannisport in 1980, another boyhood dream realized.

To keep me company at Penn, I had my dog, Gordie. He was a beagle-golden retriever mix. I had him with me every morning to work at the training house during my freshman and sophomore years. Other days, I drove my ten-speed bike from one job to the next.

I played on Penn's freshman hockey team and then made varsity my sophomore year. On varsity, I was a member of the fearless grinder line. At right wing was Rick Murphy from Winchester, Massachusetts, who had been a tremendous lacrosse player in high school. He came from a wonderful family and now works as a lawyer. Johnny Harwood, from Pawtucket Rhode, Rhode Island, played center on our line and was two years ahead of me in school.

We called him "The Rocket." Harwood greeted me with three hard elbows around the net during a scrimmage my freshman year. We were friends from that moment forward. We still are. We were in each other's weddings. Johnny even handled one of my divorces. Now that's a friend indeed.

Harwood, who starred at Mount Saint Charles Academy in Woonsocket wasn't huge, but he was a street smart, scrappy kid from a three-decker neighborhood. His dad worked as a laborer for Gilbane, Inc., a real estate development and construction company. His mother, Helen, had beautiful blue eyes and always had a meal and smile waiting for me when I visited.

Both smooth and smart, Johnny also played baseball at Penn. He graduated from Penn's prestigious Wharton School and earned his MBA at the University of Miami before receiving a degree in law from Boston College. Harwood later served in the House of Representatives from 1980-2004 and was Speaker of the House in Rhode Island from 1993-2003. Like Murphy, Harwood is a lawyer so I had two lawyers on my line. The way I played hockey, I needed them.

Early during sophomore year, I established my gritty style by fighting our captain Brian Jacks, a tough-as-nails, red-haired kid built like a young Terry O'Reilly. Our practice was going badly. We were in the midst of an intrasquad scrimmage and there was no energy whatsoever. Coach Crocker enlisted my help to get the team going.

"So I went by Paul and said, 'Hey, Paul, you've got to get these guys going. We're falling asleep out here.'" Crocker recounted. "So, on the next face-off, Paul takes the face-off with Brian Jacks. We dropped the puck and Paul dropped the gloves and started to punch Brian Jacks. So I said, 'Paul, I didn't have that quite in mind.' But it did get us going. That's a story I'll never forget."

I never will claim to have won or lost the fight with Jacks. No true tough hockey player brags about winning a fight and it doesn't matter, anyway. But Jacks and I both happened to be at The Deck together at the same time later that evening and he walked over to me and handed me a beer. I like to think I earned his respect. That fight helped me establish myself with the upperclassmen.

My sophomore year went fairly well. We played Michigan Tech and Boston College in the Great Lakes Tournament at the old

Olympia in Detroit during Christmastime in 1973. Many of our players were skillful but lacked toughness, and they struggled against a more physical Michigan Tech squad. My team also seemed overwhelmed by the competition and large venue. With us trailing by several goals, I wanted to show Michigan Tech that Penn hockey wasn't a punching bag. When the opportunity arose, I ran over Michigan Tech goaltender Jim Warden when he skated behind the net to field a puck. I buried him and started a war between the two teams. We needed to do something to get some life back in us. A few punches were thrown, a few high sticks flew, a few taunts were voiced—and there appeared to be a few surprised onlookers that a Groton boy had acted so uncouth.

"You sure stir it up for a preppie," former Brown coach and then-New York Islanders scout Jim Fullerton said to me after the game.

"Keep that in mind because the Islanders could use a guy like me," I replied bluntly.

Crocker agreed with Fullerton's assessment. Years later, he said of me, "Paul was a physical guy, he played physical, he ran into goalies, he ran into the defensemen… He played through everybody. He was tough in the corners, along the boards, in front of the net. Sure, he might have had a couple of little altercations with goaltenders," Crocker added. "Paul played that style of hockey that, if the puck was there, if it was between him and the goaltender, he had no limitations of playing through the goalie or showing his physical prowess in the tough areas of the ice."

Crocker felt that my game was more suited for professional hockey than the college game.

We played BC the next night in the consolation game. Penn graduate assistant Peter Yetten, who'd played for Crocker at Boston University, had a brother Ned Yetten, who started in net for the Eagles. Ned tickled me with his stick in the back of my knee, more likely in the cup, when I skated near his crease. Thereafter, I waited for him to leave the crease. When he finally did, I ran an elbow right into his face. Don't forget: I had mailed my deposit to BC, so I had some extra motivation to stir things up against the Eagles.

Yes, I received a few penalties, and yes, I enjoyed stirring the pot and pushing the limits. That was my game and my style. I played aggressively and I played hard. I have no regrets. Ned Yetten challenged me to a fight at the Howard Johnson hotel after the consolation game. We never actually fought but no love was lost. I saw some of those players again in professional hockey.

We also played at University of New Hampshire one night during my sophomore season. The Wildcats, one of the country's top-ranked programs, featured star Gordie Clark, who averaged 54 points per season with UNH between 1971-1974. Harwood, Murphy, and I played against Clark's line and shut them down. We out-skated them, bodied them, and antagonized them to the point where UNH's Dave Lumley (who went on to play for the Montreal Canadiens, Edmonton Oilers, and Hartford Whalers) leaned out over the boards and hit me with a two-hander directly in the face. He not only knocked me out cold, but he also knocked out a couple of my teeth and broke my nose.

Four years later, during the 1977-1978 season, Lumley and I crossed paths in the American Hockey League when he played for the Nova Scotia Voyageurs and I played for the Binghamton Dusters, then an AHL organization. I saw him during the pregame skate. He looked familiar, but I wasn't quite sure I knew him, so I asked our trainer, Peter Millar, for Nova Scotia's roster. Immediately upon seeing Lumley's name listed, the recollection clicked in my mind. I skated directly over to Dusters coach Larry Kish and told him he needed to put me on the ice against Lumley's line.

Kish fulfilled my request. I skated next to Lumley and sucker-punched him. I then leaned over him and asked, "Do you remember me?"

Nova Scotia's Pierre Roy, a 6', 172-pounder who played with me on the Dusters the next year, came off the point to fight me in attempt to protect Lumley. I smacked around Roy, too. Then 6'6", 205-pound bruiser Gilles Lupien, who eventually played for the Montreal Canadiens, Pittsburgh Penguins, and Hartford Whalers, skated after me, and the two of us fought. I got kicked out, but I had paid back a guy that thought he got away scot-free that night in Durham.

Things went well sophomore year until we played Merrimack College. I received a hooking penalty after a forward slipped by our two defensemen. Merrimack scored on the power play, and Crocker benched me immediately. He thought it was a needless penalty and I could have checked the guy legally. Maybe I could have. I don't know.

I don't think I played much the rest of the season. Crocker clearly was mad at me. People haven't always had much patience for me, and maybe some of that is my fault.

The bulk of my problems at Penn didn't start until junior year, however, when Crocker recruited a new batch of stars. A few weren't actually stars on the ice, but believed themselves to be. I found them to be immature teenagers with inflated senses of entitlement.

This group mostly enjoyed drinking beer excessively and regularly cutting class. They played, nevertheless, despite displaying poor attitudes and no respect for the school or the hockey team. Penn dropped the hockey program not too long after. It bothered me.

I got cut during the second day of training camp my junior year. Crocker was more excited about those incoming freshman recruits. He thought they would make the team better. I called home feeling devastated and wanting to hear my dad's opinion, which I so highly valued.

"If you quit, they win," my dad told me. "If you can skate, you'll find a team to play for. Last year you were playing in the Great Lakes Tournament and you were one of the best players on the ice. This year, something has happened and you don't fit on this team. But keep skating and get your education. Get by this year and things will happen for you."

I did what my dad instructed. I was so far down on the depth chart I couldn't be found with a bloodhound, but I never quit. I still attended practices and all home games, and I played on the club team.

One night, an announcement blared over the loud speaker during pre-game warm-ups at the Class of 1923 Arena: "Paul Stewart, report to the dressing room."

"Maybe Coach Crocker's going to put you in," said Jan Weaver, my fiancée at the time, while she sat beside me in the stands. I excitedly hustled downstairs, hoping Jan was correct. Devastation set in, however, when I arrived inside the dressing room. Crocker didn't need me to play in the game. Rather, one of his hot-shot players needed me to sharpen his skates.

I felt like someone had punched me in the stomach, but I never showed my devastation or any emotion. I sharpened the skates, returned to my seat beside Jan, and watched the game. By then, my Penn teammates had already destroyed part of my spirit, but I hadn't lost sight of my long-term goal of making it to the NHL. I always kept believing in myself because people like my dad believed in me.

I was not a world-class scholar or a highly skilled hockey player by any means, but one thing anyone had to admit about me was that I cared, and I was willing to do whatever it took to better myself. I worked very hard on the ice to improve my game and was a gung-ho, never-say-die player in the locker room and on the ice. Apart from my interest in martial arts and boxing, I worked out hard in the weight room in an era where many players dismissed it as just a big bore.

All of these things were enjoyable to me, but they drove a bigger wedge between my Penn teammates and me. I would come to the locker room and no one would talk to me. I was ostracized as the "weird guy."

Back in those days, though, the two-time Stanley Cup champion Philadelphia Flyers used to practice at Penn's Class of 1923 Rink. I was a rink attendant for them, and a gofer for their head coach, Fred Shero.

Without Fred Shero—and many of the players on the Broad Street Bullies-era Flyers who practiced at the Class of 1923 rink—I probably would not have had a subsequent career in this sport. The way that Shero and players on the team treated me at that rink was different from the way I got treated by some members of my own team.

The Flyers guys were pros. These guys were in the NHL. These guys were Stanley Cup champions twice, and guys like Shero and Barry Ashbee and Dave Schultz could not possibly have been nicer or more helpful to me.

Like a sponge, I absorbed all I could learn from watching Shero. I noticed the way he made every member of his team feel valued and got them to take pride in their role on the team, whatever that role may have been. He got his "non-skill" tough guys and checking liners to take pride in what they did and also to challenge themselves to want to continue to work on their skating, their puck handling, and their decision-making.

Everything—and I mean everything—was team-first with Shero. He put his players in position to succeed rather than setting them up to fail. He knew how to get players to recognize and maximize their areas of strength and to treat the not-so-strong areas of their game as opportunities for improvement rather than as weaknesses.

Shero knew hockey strategy and team coaching better than anyone I had ever seen. I was extremely fortunate to be able to watch him at work, and he generously shared his knowledge with me after sending me up Walnut Street to get him a few long-neck Schmidt's beers and maybe a sandwich.

He'd invite me to sit down as he chain-smoked his cigarettes and popped open a beer or two while he did preparations. Sometimes, he'd sit in silence for a long period of time and then suddenly blurt out something like, "So, do you think we should try out Schultz on the power play next game?"

At first, I didn't know if I was supposed to be like a potted plant in the room or if I was supposed to answer. But I soon realized that Shero was a perpetual collector of ideas, which he would then synthesize through his own unique prism.

Additionally, he was someone who was extremely generous with his time if you asked him hockey questions. Asking questions is something many young hockey players—and referees and linesmen—are afraid to do, but they are only cheating themselves by not tapping into the knowledge and experience that is available to help guide them.

I have never been afraid to ask questions. I wasn't afraid then and I'm still not afraid now. As a result, I always feel like I'm learning new things. Back in those days, I hung on every word that Fred Shero told me about the art and science of what he did.

To this very day, by the way, I employ specific things that Fred Shero taught me. For instance, my method of teaching skating to young officials—how to keep their heads up properly, which lanes to skate in and avoid—was directly adapted from things I saw Shero doing while instructing his Stanley Cup winning team.

Shero always stressed to me the importance of self-critique as a player (which I also later applied to officiating). Understand why you get the ice time you get. Understand why you are used in the situations you are used, and work to be the best player you can possibly be in that role. In the meantime, never quit on working on other parts of your game, too, because a time may come when you may be able to step into a bigger role.

Look at what Shero did for role players like Bob "The Hound" Kelly and Don Saleski. The Hound never played a single game in the minor leagues, and it wasn't because he was the most talented player on the ice. He just understood his role and performed it with big-time gusto. Look at Saleski, who started out as "just another agitator and fighter." Over the years, he worked his way up to be a penalty killer who also scored 20-plus goals in three straight years. Those guys would be quick to tell you that none of that would have been possible for their careers if they'd had a lesser coach than Freddie "The Fog" Shero to guide them and lesser team leaders to show they had confidence in their abilities.

Although I never played in the Flyers system, I did learn and benefit from Shero's teachings because I was around the rink and his team. I learned from guys like Schultz treating me kindly and making me want to work even harder for a chance to someday pull on an NHL sweater and find my own little niche.

When Freddie the Fog was finally posthumously inducted into the Hockey Hall of Fame, there was a certain long-ago rink rat from the Class of 1923 rink who rejoiced. Thank you, Fred Shero, from the bottom of my heart.

Philadelphia Flyers left wing, "The Hound," provided a similar boost that kept my spirits high. Bob told me Crocker had made a decision about me that resulted in me being cut, but I had to make a decision about Crocker's decision.

Honestly, that advice has been useful at many junctures in my life; people have often made their decisions about me and then it was up to me to decide if I was going to accept their assessment of my abilities or rise to prove them wrong. When all was said and done, junior year was a difficult and emotional wrench, but it served a purpose; it became part of my growth and path to the NHL.

"The Hound" gave me another piece of sage advice. He told me to buy a copy of *The Hockey News* and to search through it to find the lowest level league in professional hockey. He told me to call the worst team in the worst league and ask for a tryout. "Start there and work your way up," he added. I did what Kelly said soon after he had suggested it. I called Steve Stirling, who played at Boston University under Crocker, and Rich Hart, who played at Boston English High for my dad and then played at Boston College. Both were playing for the Binghamton-Broome Dusters of the North American Hockey League (the "NAHL"). And both told me their coach, Wayne Clairmont, was short on players and would give me a tryout if things at Penn didn't pan out that season. They needed some tough players in Binghamton, they told me.

Kelly wasn't the only Flyers player to buoy my spirits. "Don't quit kid," Flyers defenseman Barry Ashbee told me. "Hang in there. It took me a long time to get here." Ashbee waded through the minors for twelve years before earning a promotion to the NHL. I heeded his advice and kept with it.

I watched Ashbee and other Flyers, such as Schultz, Terry Crisp, and Joe Watson during their team practices at Class of 1923 Arena. They all inspired me and kept me motivated because they didn't boast oodles of talent. Many of those "Broad Street Bullies" made the NHL solely because of grit, hustle, toughness, and determination.

I helped at Flyers practices as much as I could during my time at Penn. I made ice when they needed it made. I cleaned their dressing room. I retrieved items from players' cars and poured Alka-Seltzer and Pepto-Bismol for others. I got the players their dentures when they had to do media interviews. I helped Philadelphia Flyers trainers, Frank Lewis and Jim McKenzie, pack and unpack bags.

General Manager Keith Allen visited the rink several times. He had known my grandfather and so I talked with him any opportunity I had. He was a stately and kind-hearted man with encyclopedic hockey knowledge. He could also get tough when he needed to.

Flyers owner, Ed Snider, whose son Jay later attended Penn, also visited the rink on many occasions. I always greeted him and chatted with him whenever possible. Years later, Mr. Snider walked by me in the Spectrum hallway when I reffed a game there and he remembered me from Penn. He always treated me well. I appreciated it.

The Philadelphia Flyers did more than just build my confidence; they helped build the conditioning I'd need to join their ranks in the NHL. They had a heavy bag and I pounded it. I did Apollo resistance-training exercise routines and lifted weights with Flyers players. I hung over the boards during their practices, soaking in all the information I could. I skated with them sometimes.

Flyers center Rick MacLeish, a 50-goal scorer one season, had me drop pucks so he could practice face-offs and batting the puck out of the air. He could skate like the wind, was clever with the puck, had quick hands and a longshoreman's wrists. He offered me an extra ticket to Flyers home games whenever he had one. Rick passed away a few years ago.

Ashbee—who, sadly, died of leukemia at age thirty-seven back in 1977—spent more time with me than any other Flyers player did, helping me with my game. He taught me to block shots and worked with me on my positioning and technique. I now teach my children what he showed me. He was a straight-up tough guy, but also extremely kind. I see my sons play and I hope they someday will possess the same intelligence and grit as Ashbee did. I wrote him a letter when he became ill and spoke with him over the telephone before he died. He told me he had heard I was playing professional hockey now and he was glad for me.

"I hear you're tearing it up," he said.

"Not like you did," I replied. "I don't know if I'll ever make the NHL."

"Don't worry. You will."

I didn't like the Flyers orange uniform color and their wool socks, but trainer Frank Lewis—a jazz musician who played the saxophone—gave me Dave Schultz's entire rookie year uniform as a gift. And Flyers public relations director Joe Kadlec, a delightful man who has been involved in hockey in various capacities for sixty years, gave me two tickets to a Frank Sinatra concert after the star made his comeback in 1973. I sat two rows from the stage, right near comedian/actor Jack Benny.

The "Thrilla in Manila" between heavyweight boxing star Muhammad Ali and Philly hometown boy Joe Frazier was broadcasted on the big screen at the Spectrum and I went, thanks to Schultz and his brother Ray, who had an extra ticket to the event and asked me to come with them. Ray played for the Philadelphia Firebirds and styled a big black afro. Ray died of cancer in 1994 at just forty-six-years old. He dressed like a "Slap Shot" character with a leather jacket, bellbottom pants, and platform shoes. I remember Ray as being very honest and sincere.

Dave Schultz, meanwhile, was the toughest of the "Broad Street

Bullies." The Flyers lost some of their fearlessness when they got rid of him. I went into the corner with him once when he played for the Buffalo Sabres and I played for the Nordiques. Everyone expected me to fight him. I instead glanced at him and said, "Hey, Dave. How's it going?" He said something nice back and we continued playing. I wouldn't have fought him because nothing was to be gained by doing it. I didn't need to prove myself to him, and he was tired of fighting by that point. He knew me and I respected and liked him.

The Flyers certainly treated me well, and I worked hard for them at the rink. When I made my hockey preseason debut as a New York Ranger, it was against Philadelphia. Funny how things come full circle like that.

I also met heavyweight champion Joe Frazier while I went to Penn. I worked out and boxed at the same gym where he trained. I got to know Frazier and his son, Marvis. Joe had such a thick neck, sort of like Tie Domi's, and he worked out like a machine. He made the jump rope sound like a sewing needle and the speed bag sang a rhythmic tune.

Despite my kinship with some of the Flyers and a handful of Penn players, the lack of acceptance from my teammates still ate at me. I had a girlfriend, Jan Weaver, but felt alone in my innermost thoughts. This period, however miserable it felt at the time, wound up being transformative. I had my key to Class of 1923 Arena from working there, and I used it wisely.

I skated when everyone else partied, drank beer, and slept. I skated from midnight to 1 a.m. I sometimes even slept on the training table and woke early in the morning to skate again before the team showed up there. I felt I had more to me than what others thought. I had more to give, but did anyone want it? I laugh when I think back to those difficult days, but the memories still sting a bit.

Seeking to alleviate this aching loneliness, I married Jan at the end of junior year. Her family had a summer cottage on a lake in Northern New Jersey. I trained that whole summer entering my senior year at the cottage. I developed to a muscular two hundred pounds and I could fight. I also was skating well. My preparedness for the physical demands of the game did little, however, to prepare me for the personal struggle that still lay ahead.

As bad as my junior year had been, my senior year at Penn

turned out even worse. I clashed with the underclassmen. My aggressive style turned them off.

Of the strained dynamic, Crocker said, "We had several Canadian kids and the two sometimes didn't mix as well as they should. Paul was the toughest kid on our team. And sometimes he comes across as a braggadocious type of guy. But he's really not. He's just a guy who loves to talk and expound. And some of the Canadian associates might have taken a little offense to it."

Crocker didn't recruit many players from the United States or prep schools. And they hardly understood my natural playing style, which included flash and flair. I also dressed like a preppie, had an over-the-top personality, and played all-out all the time because I knew that was the only way for me have a shot at playing in the pros. When I had been an underclassman, some called me "The Convener" because I always tried to do things as a team and group. I worked hard constantly, maybe too hard. They felt I was grandstanding, and it angered certain teammates.

Some teammates and I had personality clashes that resolved years later. A few became friends. Other just simply weren't very nice people. A couple of Flyers players made the All-Star Game and had kept their All-Star uniform sweaters in their Class of 1923 Arena dressing room. Some Penn players snuck in and stole the sweaters. I found out who did it and made them return them. At first, these teammates told me to screw myself. But I threatened to call the police and to beat them up myself if they didn't return the sweaters.

Training camp began that fall and started well. I pumped in a couple goals during some early scrimmages and felt I was playing better than ever. We played the U.S. Olympic team and I played well. But I should have seen the handwriting on the wall. Every players' name appeared on the back of their sweaters besides mine. Then came the beginning of the end for me at Penn.

One teammate—who I think had spent the summer digging graves and had grown to a robust one hundred sixty-five pounds—hit me from behind. He wasn't tough enough to challenge me from the front, and his cheap shot was like digging his own grave. It happened as I stood in front of the net during a team scrimmage. This guy was from Toronto. He cracked a stick right across the back of my neck. I suffered such spasms that I had to receive a shot of morphine at the hospital.

I had cracked my third cervical vertebra and was placed in traction. Equally painful was none of my teammates visited me at the hospital, nor did anyone pick up a phone to ask about my condition. I remained in the hospital for a week. I returned to the ice wearing a brace a few weeks later against my doctor's recommendation. This "hero" walked by me in the dressing room before that first practice back.

"Why did you hit me from behind with your stick?" I asked him. "You know you put me in the hospital. What did I ever do to you?"

"I'm not here to be friends with you," my teammate replied.

That was the wrong answer. I hit him with a clean body check during practice that day while scrimmaging. He came around the net with his head down and two-hundred-pound me stepped off the left wing directly into him. I put my shoulder through his chest, driving him back into the dasher. He separated his shoulder and broke his clavicle.

*C'est la guerre*. Have a nice day, I remember thinking after the body-check. Off to the hospital he went. His mom visited him from Toronto. She stopped by the rink and gave me death stares and waved her finger at me. Nowadays, I wonder if he remembers me when it rains and his shoulder aches.

I fought a couple other teammates who challenged me during a scrimmage the next day at practice, and when done, I then yelled, "Anybody else want to try me?"

I cried alone later that day in my apartment. I never had felt so unhappy. Being the outsider feels terrible for those who want to be a part of a team. But just when I thought things couldn't possibly get worse, they did. Crocker told me before the season opener that I wouldn't skate a minute that season, I went to the bus station that very night and bought a $14, one-way ticket to Binghamton to try out.

The next morning, I left Philadelphia for the pros. I might never have looked back, either, except for another twist of fate. The University of Pennsylvania closed for nearly three months on December 12, 1973 due to the Arab oil embargo.

That allowed me enough time to take my shot in professional hockey and make it back in time to Penn after the pro season ended to fulfill my credits to graduate that spring. I eventually found out, although Crocker denies it happened, that several senior Penn teammates—my classmates—had gone to him and told him they didn't want me to play on the team. Again, I had several nice teammates whom I cherish to this day, but the team also included a small clique of guys about whom I prefer not to talk and will not mention by name.

Just as with Groton, though, today I am very proud to be a Penn graduate. My bachelor's degree is in Asian History. I wasn't a great student or the smartest kid, but I worked at it and loved to learn even though it wasn't the "cool" thing to do. Besides, I like to joke that I graduated first in my class in knocked-out teeth and broken noses. My graduate studies were at the School of Hard Knocks.

During the bus ride to Binghamton (which we Dusters called "Bingo"), I had a clear perspective on how things turned out at Penn and what I needed to do to be successful in professional hockey. Many years before, I had read Stan Fischler's book *Up from the Minor Leagues of Hockey*, which my parents had given me as a kid. I knew I needed to pay my dues in the NAHL. That would be my first step on my own way "up from the minors." I was ready to go.

## CHAPTER 6: Life Aboard The 'Iron Lung'

"The Shave" was a rite of passage, a sort of freshman initiation for all new Binghamton Broome Dusters players (and every other professional player everywhere). The veterans grabbed the newcomer, taped him to the trainers' table, cut off his clothes, and then shaved half his head, one eyebrow, and his pubic hair before lathering his skin with a mix of Vaseline and Bengay. Like pallbearers, the veterans carried the trainers' table—with the player tied to it—to center ice, leaving him there to fight his way free.

There I was, completely naked and taped down with a sock shoved in my mouth with several cleaning women chuckling as they swept up popcorn and plastic cups in the empty stands. I still was strapped down there when the Maine Nordiques, scheduled to play the Dusters that night, skated onto the ice for their morning skate. The late Johnny Cunniff, a South Boston native and former Boston College star, was the player/coach for Maine. I had known Cunniff for years. We later roomed together before he coached the New Jersey Devils. He cracked a few jokes before finding a pair of scissors and cutting me free.

Some might consider "The Shave" vulgar and immature. It was, for sure. But it was a ritual and part of an acceptance into a group of vulgar, immature fun guys known for crazy antics. I actually looked forward to the ritual. It was like cutting your finger as a kid with your best buddy and becoming blood brothers. It was a rite of passage and a benchmark, a part of the lore of making it as a pro. I so much wanted to be a part of that life. It had been my dream. So a terrible haircut did not seem like a big price to pay to finally be considered a pro.

Many people will read this and say, "How immature. How stupid. That's hazing!"

It was a different time and a different mindset. "Political correctness" hadn't been invented yet. With that haircut, I now belonged. Remember, I had not belonged among my Penn teammates just weeks earlier. Penn was so far in my rear-view mirror. I was now focused on becoming more skilled at my trade and eventually making the NHL. I learned a lot about myself in my first year of professional hockey. I had tons of *Slap Shot*-type fun, but I also learned about professionalism, not only from some teammates and opponents, but also from classy Dusters owner, Jim Matthews, an incredibly generous man who became a loyal friend for life.

Shortly after my bus from Philadelphia pulled into Binghamton, I visited the arena and met with Broome Dusters GM Paul Brown who asked me to skate with the team that very day at a practice at Grippen Park, an outdoor rink. A professional hockey team practicing at an outdoor rink sounds insane, but that was life in the North American Hockey League, where the word "luxurious" was never spoken.

"So, you think this is pro hockey? Okay, Kid, welcome to the pros," said right winger Ken Davidson, a former Dartmouth star from Sioux Lookout, Ontario.

We named our team bus "The Iron Lung." When the driver had difficulty gaining traction driving up an icy hill, we players ran from the rear to the front of the bus to help the wheels gain it. The bus then often fishtailed as it started up a hill, so we'd run back to the rear to level it. The bus' accelerator spring broke one cold night so we tied a few hockey laces together and used it as a chain from the accelerator all the way around the bus and through the broken window by the toilet. We pulled the lace harder to help our driver accelerate speeds.

My second day with the Dusters, we practiced inside Broome County Veterans Memorial Arena before our morning skate and then we played the Buffalo Norsemen that evening. A few hours before the game, I wrote Bob Crocker a letter on Dusters team stationery to thank him for giving me a chance to be part of his team and the ability to study at an Ivy League school. I felt no bitterness toward him.

The Broome County Veterans Memorial Arena not only was rocking on May 26 and 27 of 1977 when Elvis Presley played concerts there: it was also rocking every time the Dusters took the ice. Binghamton residents loved their team and always packed the arena, which seats slightly under 5,000 for hockey games.

The rink was built small and tight. Organist Bob Moppert played the Dusters' theme song, Jim Croce's "Bad, Bad Leroy Brown," with energy and enthusiasm. Moppert was in his early thirties and he was a big fan of the Boston Red Sox, even though he lived in New York. He worked as the New York State Director of Economic Development and also played the organ at Binghamton Mets baseball games. Moppert also was a part owner of the Mapes Mayflower Moving Company in Binghamton. As I would later learn, playing, packing, and moving were all grouped into the same sentence in pro hockey. I would get to know Bob and The Mayflower Moving Company quite well within the next few years. For now, though, I was absolutely jacked and feeling good about my hockey career for the first time in a long time, maybe ever. I had arrived.

When I stepped onto the ice against the Norsemen, Brown and I still had not negotiated a contract. I still was in the tryout stage. But I was in heaven anyway.

Pierre Belanger refereed. During the game, I fought Buffalo defenseman Wayne Morrin. I hit him at least twice and then he clipped me with a left hook and cut the corner of my right eyebrow. I didn't go down, but I was bleeding profusely. Our team doctor, Joel Schnure, told me he didn't know if he could get me back to the game in time if he stitched me so I told him to forget about it.

"Just butterfly it and get me back out there, Doc," I told him. "This could be my last hockey game ever. I kinda want to finish it."

I fought Morrin again during the last game of the season on St. Patrick's Day, and a picture of it ran in the newspaper. That was a nice feeling.

After my first game, Clairmont approached me and told me that he liked how I had played tough. I had played hard as usual that night. I recorded an assist, made some nice passes and body checks, blocked a couple of shots, and fought Morrin. Most importantly, our team beat the Norsemen. Clairmont told me I hadn't looked out of place for that league, but he and Paul Brown still wanted to see me play more before committing to a contract.

A couple of nights later, the Johnstown Jets visited Binghamton. The *Slap Shot* movie was based on Johnstown and their players' antics. The Jets had two of the three Carlson brothers, Jeff and Steve, as well as legendary Dave Hanson. Dave was a 6'1", 195-pound, scraggly bearded defenseman from Cumberland, Wisconsin who compiled 311 penalty minutes in sixty-six regular season games in 1975-1976, and then fifty-four more minutes in penalties in nine playoff games.

My dance card was full that night, and my wallet got fuller after the game. Well, fuller at least by my standards at the time. The Dusters signed me to a lucrative $250 a week contract. Jan and I lived at the Skylark Motel for $100 a month. We ate most of our meals at the Skylark Diner out in front.

That first Christmas, with my wife in tow, having left our apartment in Philly with that small Christmas tree still up, I thought I was rich, and the fun had just begun.

My sister, Pat, and other family members visited South Yarmouth to watch the Dusters play against the Cape Codders. Pat recalls our bus driver as having droopy hair and not all his teeth.

"They're all getting on the bus and they all looked like they needed to go take a shower or go to a car-wash in a convertible," Pat said. "Here we are, coming to see Paul, and it's Christmas. We gave him a chocolate cake with white frosting and a Santa Claus on it and he puts it on the bus with all these escapees."

I don't think the cake lasted more than a few moments.

Our team bus had bunk beds. Everyone used a sleeping bag, which we bought with our own money (I still have mine) so we didn't suffer from frostbite from the freezing air blowing in through a broken window. I can't remember the window ever being repaired. I always went for one of the beds in the middle of the bus away from the rear where the broken window was located and a repulsive smell emanated from a tiny bathroom. Most players despised the top bunks because they were so high, leaving approximately three inches between a player's head and the ceiling. I've never slept in a bunk in the torpedo room of a submarine, but it was probably similar to that. I actually preferred the top bunks, though. It felt warmer up there being farther from the windows. The top bunks also were more peaceful. Players often bumped, fell onto, and spilled beer onto the lower bunks.

Many teammates were heavy smokers and drinkers who spent most of their free time playing cards. Many of the best fights happened not against opposing players, but between us on the bus when someone stole a teammate's beer or too much Jack Daniel's got mixed into the beer, like a kind of boilermaker on the sly.

One night in particular, teammate Bill "Goldie" Goldthorpe went after Peter Millar, our trainer, for whatever reason. I never knew why. Going after a peaceful and dedicated guy such as Millar was a real no-no. Within seconds, Larry Mavety, Gary Jaquith, and Billy Orr had Goldie pinned to his seat about to do more bodily harm than could have been imagined. Cooler heads prevailed. It wasn't a first and certainly wouldn't be the last time someone acted up or got ruffled on "The Iron Lung."

I found out a lot about myself out on the road. I realized I wasn't a big drinker because these guys were heavyweights in that department. I played cards although I never learned Euchre.

Almost everyone on the Dusters team smoked. Boys will be boys, right? I didn't know any better and wanted to fit in and so I started smoking, too. Nobody knew the extent of the serious health risks in those days. I think back on it and realize that we all were influenced by the culture and subtle advertising. Ah, the bliss of youth! When I later quit, I never missed it.

On my way to accumulating 273 penalty minutes in my first year in Binghamton, I became a better fighter thanks in some part to breaking my right hand with about two and a half months left in the season. A slap shot struck me in my right hand and the force knocked my glove off. I played the remainder of the season despite having a broken hand, although I didn't know it then. Instead of hitting opponents mainly with my right fist, I was forced to use my left fist, too. I became equally as strong or better with my left punch as with my right one.

I waited until the season was over to finally have my hand x-rayed. The doctor asked me if I knew I broke my hand. I hadn't. In a small way, I felt some pride, like I had my Red Badge of Courage. I had played the game with the same guts as Bobby Baun, a Maple Leafs defenseman who played in the 1964 Stanley Cup Finals against Detroit with a broken foot, which he sustained during Game Six while blocking a Gordie Howe slap shot. Baun returned to Game Six despite the break. He scored the game-winning goal in overtime and then helped Toronto win Game Seven to hoist the Cup. I hadn't given in to the pain either. I had played each game through it. Later in my life and in my career, I would have to do it again.

A broken hand was hardly the worst injury I suffered during my days as a Duster. In a game against Erie, eight of my teeth landed on the ice one night. Chicklets galore. I needed sixty-four stitches to seal the gigantic gash on my face. I also suffered a broken jaw. All that resulted from one hit, a cross-check to the face from Erie left wing Rick Jodzio in a game during my second year with the Dusters in 1976-77. I sustained a concussion, but I remained in the game. That was the standard practice in those days; if anyone knew better, they certainly never mentioned it to me.

Larry Kish, who took over as head coach after the firing of Wayne Clairmont, was furious that Jodzio had not been called for a cross-checking penalty. Between periods, Kish took out his frustration by grabbing me as I sat in the medical room in my underwear dripping blood, and pushing me at referee Al Goodman, yelling, "Look at his face, Al!" Goodman, put his hands on my shoulders—his hands also came up toward my face—and he pushed me back at Kish. I didn't know whether to shit or wind my watch I felt so out of it. I landed back on Kish and then I jumped toward Goodman and instinctively threw a punch at him. I broke his nose, or least I'm told I did, because I don't even remember him being the referee or much about what happened at all that night.

I rode back on the "The Iron Lung" in the freezing cold from Erie to Bingo in absolute agony. By the time, we arrived in Binghamton, my face had swelled so brutally that all sixty-four stitches split and popped out. I got admitted to the hospital in Binghamton almost immediately upon my return. Doctors stitched me again. The hospital also brought in a plastic and oral surgeon to work on my face and rewire my teeth. Initially, in Erie, my teeth had been picked up off the ice and wired back into my gums. I was pretty messed up physically. Even now, my teeth still bleed when I brush them because of what happened to my lower gums.

The league had to discipline me for punching Goodman. There was talk about a lifetime ban. League commissioner Jack Timmons knew me pretty well. He had reffed college hockey with my dad. John Mitchell, the Johnstown Jets Executive Director and General Manager at the time of the filming of the movie *Slap Shot*, had attended the game in Erie and he knew my family, too. Johnstown had lost their team. Dusters owner Jim Matthews was such a good guy; he brought John Mitchell to Binghamton as a special advisor and assistant GM for the club. It was a job that was an example of a true caring man helping another man whose entire life had been spent involved with hockey. Mitchell being left in Johnstown without a team would have been a cruel way for a hockey man to end his career.

Matthews fixed all that by bringing Mitchell to Bingo. As it turned out, John had spent a long career in the NHL and he had reffed games with my grandfather. I'd sit in the front of the bus with Mitchell, a living library of hockey history.

So, on this day, Mitchell drove to the league office in Buffalo with me for the hearing. Mitchell explained that I had been in a dazed and confused state of mind. Mitchell also argued that Kish had acted wrongly by pushing me into the referee.

"I don't think Paul knows to this day who he hit," Mitchell told Timmons. I didn't. I already had called Goodman to apologize, telling him I didn't know it was him I'd punched. Timmons asked me how long the doctors said I'd be sidelined.

"About ten games, until my face heals," I replied.

"Okay, then, I'm going to suspend you for eight games," he said. The league also fined me approximately $5,000, which was silly because I only made $250 per week. I paid the fine, and literally, a day later, the money appeared in cash sitting in my locker, courtesy of Matthews. I never would have hit a referee in the right state of mind considering my family history (both my father and grandfather officiated) and the respect my dad always taught me to show for the game and its officials. Matthews, among a few other men throughout my life, always showed me great kindness and the right way to treat others. He reimbursed me money more than once and he showed me the ultimate humanity. He's one of the men who shaped me into who I am.

It didn't take long for Matthews to take a liking to me. He taught me professionalism by making me sign autographs at Boy Scout troop meetings and every community event they had in the Binghamton area. He also had me do the same for fans after home games. Matthews even gave me a job at his car dealership one summer.

"You're a college kid. Whether you play or not, you have a chance to really make a career for yourself," he reminded me on more than one occasion. "Have patience." He always believed in me. Sadly, we lost Jim to cancer. We lost a good man that day.

My time in the North American Hockey League was an experience like no other. I played against players I had known about and respected such as Blake Ball, Cleland "Keke" Mortson, "Gypsy Joe" Hardy, and Ted McCaskill, then the Mohawk Valley Comets head coach. Once in a bar after a game, Ted McCaskill asked if I would come play for him.

"I can make you the most feared man in hockey. I'll teach you how to use the stick," he said. I had one thought: "This is pro hockey?" Billy Gratton and some other teammates introduced me to Tom & Marty's (a bar on State Street in Binghamton) a few days after I arrived in town. As we sat there, Gratton turned to me and said, "Hey kid, we all like the way you come at it. But if you think you're going to make it as a goal scorer, you have another thing thing coming. You'll have to become a better fighter."

I used the opportunity in Binghamton over the next year or two to grow as a player and learn as much possible about the game and the style I had to play for the best chance to make the NHL. It didn't take long before I began to believe playing hockey was my life calling. I had never felt happier. My mission became to make my mark at each level of the minors and then the NHL. Some have called me a "goon" for always fighting, but I always did it the right way. I never stuck anyone with a stick without them coming at me with one first. Nor did I ever jump anyone from behind. I never went after any skill player. I always fought other enforcers, fought the right way, and respected the rules and the "Code." I fought because I did it well and fighting was my ticket to the NHL when I lacked the skill and experience of most NHL players. I'm a fighter in more than one sense of the word—and you know what? I actually love a good fight. But I like a fight that follows the rules of fighting.

Not everyone feels that way. Some people, like Goldthorpe, sought out fights even when they served no actual purpose and were well beyond the scope of the unwritten rules of fighting. To that end, trainer Peter Millar was not his only unwilling opponent with the Dusters.

I first met the Goldthorpe, sporting his giant blond afro, a "Saturday Night Fever" wardrobe and the same propensity as Uruguay soccer striker Luis Suarez to bite his opponents during the Binghamton Dusters' 1975 team Christmas party. I'm sure you remember Ogie Ogilthorpe, the character from *Slap Shot*. The Ogilthorpe character, played by Boston native Ned Dowd (who was the real-life inspiration for the movie's "Ned Braden" character), is based on the real-life antics of Goldthorpe.

Goldthorpe, in my humble opinion, missed his movie when they shot "One Flew Over the Coo-Coo's Nest" without him. Not long after Wayne Clairmont was fired as Binghamton's head coach and replaced by Coach Larry Kish, Goldthorpe was traded to the Dusters from the Erie Blades. Kish and then-general manager Paul Brown acquired Goldthorpe as competition for my role.

Stories about Goldthorpe are legendary. About most guys, I'd chuckle and think it has to be hyperbole. I can attest, though, that he was a wild man off the ice as well as on.

The 1975-1976 season marked my first in professional hockey, and my college hockey career had just ended in disappointment. We were in a bar in Binghamton celebrating the Christmas season with a nice spread of food set out for us, and some teammates played pool. I sat chatting with other teammates and drinking beer at the bar when Goldthorpe walked in. I didn't notice him until he approached me, tapped my shoulder, and asked, "Are you Stewart?"

I extended my hand to shake.

Goldthorpe had something else in mind.

He sucker-punched me square in the face, knocking me flat off the barstool. After I dropped to the floor, teammates pushed Goldthorpe away from me.

"Who the hell is this guy?" I asked, picking myself up.

Goldthorpe kept trying to get at me like a vicious animal that had just escaped captivity, so I agreed to go outside to fight him there. Team captain (and *Slap Shot* movie stunt double) Roddy Bloomfield turned to me and cautioned, "If you don't think you can beat him or don't want to fight, stay here."

I laughed as I removed my watch and handed it to Bloomer.

"Let's go!" I said.

Goldthorpe tried some taekwondo-like fighting technique on me, trying a high kick intended for my jaw. I intercepted his leg when he went to kick me, and flipped him up, holding him near my head. He weighed about thirty pounds less than I did. People surrounding us screamed for me to throw him through the bar's glass window.

Someone yelled to throw him into traffic. I didn't know what to do with Goldthorpe so I just flung him down and jumped on him. We wrestled a bit, then he did something that caught me totally off guard. He bit my cheek!

"What are you doing, you crazy bastard?!?" I said (or something to that effect) as I jumped to my feet. At the time, I still didn't even know why we were fighting. Second, I excepted a "normal" fight with fists, not a biting match. Unwisely, I attempted to walk away with my back turned. Goldthorpe jumped on me and bit me a second time, this time on my back.

Instead of enjoying a nice time at the Binghamton team Christmas party during my first year playing for the Dusters of the North American Hockey League, I ended up at the hospital around midnight receiving a tetanus shot and stitches. Peter Millar, our trainer, also had his party ruined as he went with me to help me get my shot. I said above that the fight had no real purpose, and to my mind it didn't, but, in fact, Goldthorpe had acted like a rabid Labrador Retriever and Mastiff mix when he met me because he wanted to try to put me in my place. He wanted to be known as the toughest of the Dusters players. He disliked the attention I received, and probably also disliked that I was a college kid. And an American one at that.

I thought it was over after our Christmas party brawl. I was wrong. Goldthorpe skated at me, looking to pick a fight the next day at practice.

I was ready for him this time. I smacked him with my stick and knocked him down on the ice. It was about to get life-and-death. Teammate Gary Jaquith grabbed Goldthorpe and banged him off the glass. Jaquith was a very big and very tough guy. He looked like a mix between Hulk Hogan and The Hoxton Creeper from the *Sherlock Holmes* movies. He had both a huge head and body to match. He wasn't a terrific skater but possessed as much power as any hockey player I've ever met. Jaquith grabbed Goldthorpe, threw him into the dasher and yelled at him to leave me alone. I sat in my stall after practice and eyed Goldthorpe when he walked by me at the end of practice.

"You can come after me again, but, next time, I'm going to club you with this stick," I told him as I held my hockey stick in front of me. "I'm going to club you and I'm going to kill you. I don't really care. Try me!"

My wife and I later drove together to the Chrysler dealership Matthews owned. I told Matthews about the biting incident at the Christmas party and what had transpired with Goldthorpe at practice.

"I don't even know this guy," I said. "All I know is I came here to play hockey for you and for this team and to prove myself and to make a living. Do I have to club this guy to death? What do you want from me? How do you want me to handle this?" Matthews told me to let him handle it. He did do something because Goldthorpe laid off me thereafter.

I never really liked Goldie because I never came to trust him. He seemed unhinged. I didn't think he was too courageous, anyway. A lot of what he did was bluff and bravado. One night, he stepped in as a third man when I was fighting Dave Hanson in Johnstown. I didn't need his help. I thought he jumped in to let everyone think he was the big guy helping the rookie. It was completely unnecessary and a sign of disrespect.

Some teammates liked Goldie, but many did not. Goldie grew up in Thunder Bay, Ontario, the same hometown as "Wild" Willie Trognitz, a little bit of a nutty character, too. But I liked Trognitz, who played with me on the Cincinnati Stingers of the World Hockey Association during the 1977-1978 season. Trognitz is the one who clubbed Archie Henderson in the head with his stick back in 1977 and subsequently received a lifetime ban from the International League. Maybe it's the water, but those two were some of the real "unique" types I ran into in the North American League.

While Matthews made Goldthorpe leave me alone, the goon continued to incite others. He angered several teammates after a well-known Italian businessman from Binghamton—who we knew was a "made man" in the Mafia—told the bartender at Tom & Marty's that he wanted to pay for our drinks and meals. Goldthorpe decided it would be a good time to act the tough guy. He looked at the man, then slapped some mustard on the lapels of his suit, telling him we didn't need his money. Veteran teammate Larry Mavety broke a beer bottle off the bar, held it up at Goldthorpe, and told him to get the hell out of the bar and not to come near him anymore.

"You just made a big mistake," he told Goldthorpe. After a stunt like that one, Goldthorpe could very well have been found in the bottom of the Chenango River with a cigarette machine tied to his leg. After that incident, things sort of changed. One of my teammates probably talked some sense into Goldthorpe, who had to apologize to the connected businessman. After that, things settled down a bit with Goldthorpe who only played nineteen games for the Dusters before signing with the WHA Denver Spurs/Ottawa Civics.

Author Ed Willes noted in his book, *The Rebel League: The Short and Unruly Life of the World Hockey Association*, that Goldthorpe claims to have been shot and wounded while trying to protect a woman, and then his father died while he was in the hospital recovering from the gun wound. He went back to school for accounting and computer-programming after being let out of the hospital and works as a construction foreman in San Diego.

I saw Goldthorpe at a bar in New Brunswick years later. He stood there and looked at me. I just put my back against the wall. He didn't say anything to me. I said nothing to him. I didn't want any trouble, but also didn't want to talk to him. Goldie later wrote a book and said I was always talking and bothering him. My version is that I kept my distance and made sure he did the same.

Anyway, I have heard Goldthorpe is doing well and found religion. I hope that is true. I doubt we'll ever be friends, but I wish him no ill will.

The team drama and antics were undeniably a part of the experience of playing for the Dusters, but the real reason I went to Binghamton was to become a pro hockey player. I stayed out on the ice after practices to work on my skills that weren't yet in my toolbox. I had learned to put in the extra time at Penn from Flyers players and Shero. They told me I had to be the first one on the ice and the last one off it. They urged me to practice the things I couldn't do, learn to flip the puck and take the puck in the feet as well as to work on passing and shooting, increasing my physical size, and getting tougher. I signed up for a membership at a gym in Binghamton. My plan was to play for the Dusters for a year or two at the most and then advance to the American Hockey League. We had plenty of hard workers in our dressing room who never made the NHL, but I stayed determined. People didn't necessarily give me a shot. Nobody really thought I would make it, except maybe Matthews, who was a very proud team owner.

Matthews told me many years later that General Manager Paul Brown, and head coach Larry Kish wanted to trade me on several occasions. But Matthews saw something in me and didn't let them do it. Matthews and I sat at the diner together many times eating omelets, drinking coffee, and smoking cigarettes until all hours of the morning. We drank beers together.

He always kept an eye on me. Matthews was so successful as a businessman, but he valued loyalty and integrity above all else. He took care of his family, his workers, and me. Matthews told me once that he had several arguments with management about players, including me. It wasn't Matthews who wanted to bring in Goldthorpe. Kish and Brown acquired him. They probably figured, by signing Goldthorpe, they could then release me, but Matthews never let it happen even though other teams had offered to trade for me.

Toward the end of my first season in Binghamton, I sat with some teammates at Thirsty's Tavern, drinking beer, eating pizza, and watching the New York Rangers play the Atlanta Flames. Rangers defenseman Dave Maloney cross-checked Flames left winger Curt Bennett in the back. Bennett took one stride, turned, and fired a punch at Maloney, knocking Maloney out flat and cold. Nobody on the Rangers retaliated. During a televised post-game press conference, I watched as then-New York Rangers General Manager John Ferguson, the former Montreal Canadians enforcer, shouted about how he would find himself a tough guy. He guaranteed he would not allow another opponent to walk into New York and bully his players.

The next morning, I wrote a letter to Ferguson, describing myself as the tough guy he needed. Within the week, the Rangers contacted me and put me on their negotiation list, which meant they owned my NHL rights. When I returned to the University of Pennsylvania to finish out my degree, I was technically a member of the Rangers organization after Binghamton's 1975-76 season ended with a 27-45-2-0 record and no playoff berth.

I only needed one course to graduate, and so I signed up for French Literature, took it pass/fail, and passed the class. I was there wearing my cap and gown as members of the Penn Class of 1976 received their diplomas.

Chief Justice Warren E. Burger delivered the commencement speaker at the 1976 Penn graduation. Years later, by happenstance, I sat next to Burger on a plane. I introduced myself, telling him that I was a member of the senior class he spoke to at Penn in 1976.

"Do you remember much of the speech?" he asked.

"Frankly, I remember only a bit," I replied. "I remember that I was happy that it was short and to the point. I do remember that you challenged us with carrying on the responsibility of keeping the world fair. So I've gone into your trade and that's what I've done."

"Are you a judge?" he asked.

"Yeah, I'm a judge," I said.

"Where do you sit?"

"I go to different places all over this country and Canada, too, like a big circuit court," I replied.

He looked at me, perplexed.

"Yeah, I'm a referee in the NHL," I continued. "A big difference between your job and mine is you take three months to make a decision and I take three seconds. And when you make a decision, you have eight friends to sit there and support you. When I make a decision, I have no friends and get pizza and beer thrown at me."

Burger laughed.

In the Philadelphia Civic Center in 1976, as I listened to Burger speak, I was a long way away from becoming a referee and had no idea that was my true path in life. I was a New York Ranger or so I thought. Little did I know that my hockey journey would lead me back to Binghamton, hockey's most "major" minor league town, before I eventually made it to the NHL, first as a player and then as a referee.

## CHAPTER 7: Battling To Be A Blueshirt

The letter I wrote in 1976 to Rangers GM John Ferguson was cocky. I tooted my own horn because I didn't have an agent to toot it for me. I told him he didn't have to look any further than Central New York for the fearless enforcer he was seeking. I was right there in Binghamton and would fight anyone at any time. Ferguson was a tough guy looking for tough guys. The match seemed perfect, like Bob Hope and Bing Crosby, but it occasionally turned volatile like Batman and the Joker.

The Rangers replied with a letter approximately a week later. The Rangers added me to their negotiation list, meaning they owned my NHL rights. I was thrilled beyond words. Ferguson later called me on the phone and invited me to his New York City office in spring 1976. I visited both Ferguson and Bill Jennings, then the president of the Rangers.

"Funny, you don't look like a Groton grad," Jennings said to me.

"A year in the North American League and growing up in Dorchester will do that to you," I replied.

I didn't tell Ferguson that I had admired his style and persistence as a player. I just got right down to business.

"Nobody who puts on a pair of skates will intimidate me, ever," I assured him.

Without seeing me skate, but likely having gotten the word of my limited skill set, Ferguson told me I needed to become a better skater. He was right, though, and I agreed to do whatever he had in mind for me. What he had in mind was Huron Hockey School in Centralia, Ontario, near London, which was where I spent most of the summer of '76. Centralia was an old Royal Canadian Air Force WWII training base used to train pilots during World War II. The Rangers paid for my flight, and all of us players stayed in the old army barracks. We were in the middle of nowhere. All we did was skate, drink beer, and eye the local women.

Every team, it seemed, was sending their tough, young players who needed to improve on their skates. The Montreal Canadiens sent Gilles Lupien, Rick Chartraw, Doug Risebrough, and Pierre Mondou, although Mondou really flew on his blades. Perhaps Montreal wanted to expose him to the tough side of the game, too. The Atlanta Flames sent Harold Phillipoff. The Rangers sent Nick Fotiu and me. There were a lot of penalty minutes in that room!

Billy Mahoney, who later coached the Minnesota North Stars, ran the camp. The instructors didn't let us fight; that was their first rule in our initial meeting. They knew we were tough, but we weren't there to prove our grit, they reminded us. We were there to learn to skate—using our edges, turning, stopping, and starting. I left Huron Hockey School a better skater. Many techniques learned there I used throughout my playing and refereeing careers.

The early portion of the summer, before I headed to Rangers training camp, was spent with Jan at her family's cottage in New Jersey on all the weekends. Allowing myself little downtime, the cottage served as a makeshift training facility while I was there. Prior to graduating from Penn, Coach Crocker had given me the heavy bag from the gym at Class of 1923 Arena as a gift.

"This will be your ticket to the NHL," Crocker said.

I appreciated him giving it to me. I hung the bag underneath the cottage's screened porch. The house and porch shook as I pounded the bag for hours. Nobody could relax on the porch while I trained. I shot between 200-400 pucks a day, did a couple of hundred pushups, and lifted free weights. I bought the *Rocky* soundtrack album for inspiration, constantly playing it as I hit the bag, jumped rope, did pushups and sit-ups until I couldn't do any more.

Meanwhile, I helped frame and paint houses to earn extra cash. Admittedly, I wasn't a very good painter.

I was in the best shape of my life. I went for long runs around the lake each day. I already had become a smarter fighter since leaving Binghamton. I had spent the rest of the spring semester at Penn training in aikido. I was building strength and power with my weight training, agility and leverage through aikido. I was going to the NHL prepared for the fight of my life.

Still, I felt a lot of anxiety—possibly even some panic attacks—that summer. I was nervous because I so badly wanted to make the right impression with the Rangers and earn a spot on their NHL or AHL affiliate. Despite my hours of daily hard work, I always felt I hadn't done enough when it came time to go to bed. That's an unsettling feeling. I've always been a nervous guy.

Years later, I read how the actor, Yul Brynner, before the last of his 4,625 different performances of the Broadway play, *The King and I*, was seen pacing with the script, rereading his lines. When asked why he seemed so on edge, he responded by saying that he knew there were audience members who had never seen him perform. It was a fear that he would make a mistake. He always wanted to be ready so he practiced. I would bet that all top-flight performers have that butterfly feeling inside of them. That isn't a bad thing as long as it doesn't turn into a fear of performing. Being on edge just before he goes on may be the secret to his success. It's then, when the light comes on, the music starts to play, and the first contact in that moment happens, a true champion emerges to give his best performance regardless of the stage or venue.

One day, while I was training at the cottage, former Penn teammate Johnny Harwood called me. He already was a practicing attorney and playing in a hockey league in Smithfield, Rhode Island. The league consisted of both college and minor league players. Former Providence College star Ron Wilson, who went on to play 177 NHL games and coach 1,401 NHL games, played in the league. So did Billy Bennett, the brother of Curt and Harvey Bennett.

"My team is going against a bunch of tough and experienced skaters," Harwood told me. "We need your help."

"Yeah, Johnny? What's in it for me?" I asked Harwood.

"I'll take you out for Chinese food and a couple of beers," he replied.

That's all I needed to hear. I packed my skates and equipment. Off to Rhode Island I went. I am not a tough negotiator.

The game got chippy. John Sleaver was one of the referees. Sleaver played twelve games for the Chicago Blackhawks during the 1956-1957 and scored one goal, his only goal in thirteen NHL games. The Copper Cliff, Ontario native also played on several minor league teams from 1951-1971. He was a right-shooting center for the Providence Reds from 1966-1969.

If memory serves, Zellio Toppazzini was one of the referees.

Toppazzini, ironically, is a Copper Cliff, Ontario native as well. He played in 123 NHL games and posted forty-two points and also is considered one the greatest players in the history of the Providence Reds. His brother is the great Jerry Toppazzini, a right wing who recorded 407 points in 783 NHL games, combined, between the Boston Bruins, Chicago Blackhawks, and Detroit Red Wings.

I must have given Sleaver and Topper quite the headache that night.

"The other teams were not very talented, but they were total goons," Harwood recalled. "To make a long story short, they were street kids and they were tough kids, no question about it. Well, they picked the wrong guy."

One of the goons elbowed Harwood. I wasn't pleased and shouted, "Hey, man, we're paying like ten bucks to play so what is your problem?"

I don't remember his reply, but even if he had apologized, he wasn't getting away with elbowing my friend. I punched him until he dropped to the ice. His teammates came to his rescue. Eventually, I was throwing punches left and right.

"I just remember three guys getting their butts kicked," Harwood said. "Paul gets the first guy and kicks the living crap out of him. The guy's down on the ice... and the second kid jumps on his shoulder. Paul grabs him with one arm and beats the hell out of him, too. Now there are two guys down on the ice. The other kid's hobbling to get back up. A third guy hops in and Paul annihilates him."

Sleaver just shrugged and pointed to the gate.

I enjoyed the game and team and decided to continue to play in the Rhode Island league each Tuesday evening throughout the summer. Since I was in New England each week anyway, I also decided to play in Hockey Night in Boston and the New England Pro Am Chowder Cup in Quincy, which is the same league I now administer for officials.

I played in Falmouth on Fridays against pros who lived on Cape Cod. After those games each week, I'd drive back to New Jersey to stay with Jan at her family's cottage through Tuesday morning. I'd spend Tuesday, Wednesday, and Thursday nights at my parents' house in Jamaica Plain.

My dad recommended I ask ex-welterweight boxer Vinny Marino to train me. Marino owned the South Side Gym in Roslindale

Square where Marvin Hagler had trained. I worked with Marino on Wednesday and Thursday afternoons. Marino ran me tirelessly in the heat and challenged me to train harder than I already had been. He noticed I was vulnerable to left hooks and showed me a better way to protect my face from them. He also taught me to put all my momentum into each punch. It's possible to kill someone if a fighter gets the right power behind his punch.

Summer of 1976 was stressful, but also a dream come true. I felt on top of the world. The New York Rangers paid all my expenses: gas, tolls, and hockey fees. September arrived and I was off to New York Rangers rookie camp in Point-Claire, Quebec where I literally brawled with almost every player there because I knew it was the only way to make the Rangers' NHL roster.

Dave Farrish, Mike McEwen, Don Murdoch, Danny Newman, and Nick Fotiu all were at camp with me. I roomed there with Fotiu, a Staten Island native and one of the toughest hockey players I have ever seen.

I made a request to room with Nick because they told me was the toughest one there and I needed to size up the competition, even though I had known him a little bit. He previously had served as an enforcer for the Cape Codders of the Northern American Hockey League as well as the New England Whalers of the World Hockey Association. When I met Fotiu, I told him I'd be rooming with him, shook his hand, and then challenged him to a fight there in our hotel room. We didn't fight then, but he and I both knew that it would have to happen eventually. We fought out on the ice twice.

He had been the Police Athletic League boxing champion and won all three bouts against me. The "score" in two of these fights wasn't even close. Every punch he threw stung. He was a muscular 6'2", 210-pounder and was a year older than me. Funny thing, though: we quickly forged a friendship off the ice. Nick was a guy with a big heart, almost as big as his hands. We remain friends to this day.

Forbes Kennedy, who played center in the NHL during the fifties and sixties, was one of our coaches at rookie camp. Kennedy was extremely friendly, loved puffing on cigars, and maintained a tough persona. He was tough as nails, once fighting nearly all the Boston Bruins while playing for the Toronto Maple Leafs . "Forbie" earned the respect of every player on the ice.

But Forbie had one little secret. While not afraid of men, he was petrified of mice. While we all were eating out one night, I had a waiter bring a platter over to the table and open it in front of Kennedy. There under the silver cover I had planted a fake rubber mouse on a huge bed of lettuce.

"Oh, my God!" Kennedy screamed. He jumped up, tipped the table over and ran out of the bistro with us howling as he fled. Several hundred dollars later in reparation, we finished our meal. Kennedy and I both were from Dorchester, although he was from Dorchester, New Brunswick. Kennedy and the other coaches must have liked me for more than my practical jokes because I was ultimately invited to the main Rangers training camp in New York.

One night, during rookie training camp, we were playing an exhibition against Trois Rivieres of the Quebec Major Junior Hockey League, a team coached by Michel Bergeron, who went on to post a 265-283 record as the head coach of the Quebec Nordiques and New York Rangers from 1980-1990. Officially, it was Jean-Guy Talbot Night at Colisée de Trois-Rivières, but, by the end of the third period, it had turned into Paul Stewart Night.

The coliseum was packed. The fans were rowdy. It was just like the previous season at Binghamton's Broome County Veterans Memorial Arena. It was exactly the atmosphere I fed off.

Late in the game, I checked an opponent in the corner, and then three of Bergeron's boys came skating at me like they wanted to rip off my head. They ran me into the dasher and my head smashed against the glass. I was one of many players in those days who didn't wear a helmet. No Chris Nowinskis, of course, existed in the 1970s to educate young athletes about the long-term dangers of concussions. The culture of the NHL at the time was such that wearing a helmet would have been seen as a sign of weakness, or lack of commitment anyway. In those days, regardless of the injury, players were encouraged to play through whatever injuries they suffered. It was a badge of honor. I suffered at least twenty-seven concussions during my hockey career, and this was one of them.

Feeling woozy and lightheaded, I wobbled up ice trying to clear my head. I was barely aware of anything happening, but I did clear my head enough to see one of three players who had drilled me into the dasher looking back over his shoulder for a pass. He was skating up the ice in my direction. A pass was sent to him, a real sucker pass as we say in the trade. He caught it and that's when I stepped into him with everything: two hundred-pounds of power, stick, shoulder, knee, and chest. I hit him so hard he folded up like an accordion. The whistle blew. And the rink erupted with everyone focused on destroying me.

My target was down and writhing in pain with a broken leg, as we later learned. He had to be carted off the ice. Before that happened, it seemed like every standing Trois Rivieres skater flew at me, wanting to kill me or worse—if there is a worse. They surrounded me like a pack of hungry wolves. Our goalie, Gilles Gratton, also skated toward me to lend his protection. I grabbed Gratton's stick swinging it like a machete, fending off Trois Rivieres players from all sides. I was able to use the goalie stick to hack a path to the bench. I went through and into the dressing room, escaping the crowd and finding a somewhat safe haven.

That's where Nick Garen, a longtime NHL trainer with the Chicago Blackhawks, New York Rangers, and New York Islanders, rested me on his table. As Garen stitched me, Rangers General Manager and Head Coach, John Ferguson, walked into the room. Extremely groggy and confused, I thought Fergy was a Trois Rivieres player there to fight. I jumped off the table and stuck my stick right in Ferguson's face, nearly gashing out one of his eyes.

"Get away from me!" I yelled.

"No, no, no, it's me!" Ferguson shouted as he backed off from my advance. That's one of my favorite Fergie stories, and there are plenty of them to tell. Attending Rangers training camp and being a part of Ferguson's organization was a thrill considering I grew up admiring him greatly. My main purpose there was to show Ferguson and the Rangers I belonged. I wanted Fergie to know I was the tough, gritty player he was seeking, the player I had described to him in my handcrafted letter.

I had watched plenty of professional hockey throughout my childhood and teen years. I had seen Ferguson play many times on television. I saw him take on everyone, no matter who. His fight against "Terrible" Ted Green in Boston was indelible in my mind. He's the reason I wore number twenty-two. He was one of my idols, even though he had been an enforcer for the Montreal Canadiens and I was a Boston boy at heart.

Ever since my mother had given me Stan Fischler's *Up From the Minor Leagues of Hockey*, I found Ferguson and his personal account the most fascinating. I saw many parallels between his story and mine. Ferguson grew up in love with hockey and did anything to earn ice time, including working long hours at the rink in his native Vancouver. As Ferguson explained in Fischler's book, he was part of a group called "rink rats" at The Vancouver Forum, the Canucks' home arena. Ferguson wrote about the pre-Zamboni rink rat group, "We were local kids who couldn't get enough ice to skate on to satisfy us, so what we did was work at the rink, cleaning and scraping it in return for the privilege of skating on it."

Ferguson eventually became a stick boy for the Canucks. He unpacked bags with the team trainers, polished skates, and ran across the street to have skates sharpened. His early life at The Forum reminded me of my early days at Boston Arena and also my college days at the University of Pennsylvania helping out the Flyers players in any way possible.

His NHL playing career, of course, was lengthier and more successful than mine. Ferguson scored 145 goals and added 158 assists (303 points) in 500 NHL games. He also recorded 1,214 penalty minutes, including an NHL-leading 177 penalty minutes in 1966-1967. But I don't think Ferguson was a better hockey player than I. He just was more experienced and he got the chances that I never seemed to for whatever reason. He had played more games growing up in Canada and that's a point that shouldn't be forgotten. He was given more of a chance to succeed in the NHL than I was given. That's just the way it works sometimes, especially as an American trying to make it in the 1970s.

Even with all that, nothing came easy for the 5'11", 190-pound Ferguson, a left wing. I admired his determination. He worked his tail off to make the NHL. He played three years in the Saskatchewan Junior Hockey League, one year in the International Hockey League, and three more years in the American Hockey League before ever making it to the NHL with the Montreal Canadiens during the 1963-1964 season at twenty-five years old. He was a mere thirty-eight-years old during his first year as head coach and GM of the New York Rangers in 1976-77.

I'll always feel grateful for the opportunity Ferguson gave me.

He gave me the chance to establish my career and exposed me to the world's largest sports market. I considered him a friend. But our relationship was rocky at times. I never wanted to take his eye out with my stick like I almost did accidentally, but I did want to punch him in the face a couple times. Friction is part of the game.

Ferguson also gave me the opportunity to play for the Rangers in two NHL exhibition games. One was against the Philadelphia Flyers. We played the Flyers at Madison Square Garden and John McCauley officiated. McCauley eventually became my mentor when I turned to officiating. I named my first son after him. I spent hundreds of dollars for ten tickets to the game. I invited Coach O'Brien from Groton, my brother, parents, my wife and her family.

During training camp, I roomed with Danny Newman, who eventually spent time in the NHL with the Rangers, Montreal Canadiens, and Edmonton Oilers. We took the train to the game against the Flyers from Rockville Center, Long Island. Sitting across from each other, I saw his short dress pants revealed his white socks.

"What are you, a farmer?" I asked him.

"Yeah, I am a farmer," he replied. He looked as serious as can be when he replied, but he probably was only trying to make me sweat and eat my words. He was from Windsor, Ontario, a southern Canadian city not known for growing anything.

My line started that game and I was there on the ice during the national anthem. Nick Beverley was paired with me on defense. I had watched Beverley play with the Bruins. Nick was prematurely grey. If he hadn't been grey, the first shift with me would likely have turned him ash white after the anthem finished.

Most all the Flyers players knew me from my days at Penn. They all were asking me how I was doing. Bob "The Hound" Kelly, the Flyers' left wing, who had given me the prescient advice to ask for a try-out with the lowest level professional hockey team I could find years earlier, might have regretted sharing that tip. That first shift included me firing a shot on net and battling with Kelly in the corner. I hit him with a clean body check.

Flyers' left winger Steve Short gave me a stick to the back. He was a big kid, about 6'2", 210 pounds. The Flyers had selected him in the eighth round of the 1974 draft. I punched him two or three times, dropping him to the ice right in front of the net. I then reached for the back of his sweater and tried to pull him up by the collar. Instead, I got a handful of his hair. Not good. Pulling someone's hair was a gross misconduct penalty, one the NHL had recently implemented. Pulling hair wasn't my style anyway. I typically grabbed sweaters during fights, either pulling on the back or pulling up the front over my opponent's face.

The shift ended with me getting ejected by referee John McCauley. Unfortunately, I lasted just eighty-one seconds in that game. My early exit made me available for an interview with play-by-play man Marv Albert between the first and second periods. We talked about the Flyers and my Boston background. The Rangers radio network gave me a speaker-phone as a gift for going on the air with Albert. I had received free white, high-heeled Saturday Night Fever shoes in Bingo and then a free speaker-phone in NYC. Life was looking up!

After the game, I took my large contingent of family and friends to eat at Toots Shor's and I paid the bar bill. It was not only an expensive night but one I reflect on with some disappointment, regret, and wonder. I often ponder what could have been if I had lasted more than eighty-one seconds. Maybe I could have forced the Rangers to keep me because of my grit and effort. I could have showed them I was a better hockey player than they had thought.

One highlight from training camp was having dinner with Hall of Famer Rod Gilbert at Il Vagabondo on 62nd Street between 1st and 2nd. Rod is still my friend, as is his beautiful wife, Judy.

The day after my fight with Short, I was optioned to New York's AHL affiliate, the New Haven Nighthawks coached by Parker MacDonald, a native of Sydney, Nova Scotia who didn't seem to like me or any Americans. He had some veterans on the team, including Doug Jarrett, who already had played in the NHL for Chicago. MacDonald simply just wasn't in the mood to keep me. I received wind that MacDonald planned to option me to the Richmond Wildcats of the Southern Hockey League. I didn't want to play there and wade through another league so I, instead, returned to Binghamton.

I saw the writing on the wall, anyway. Fotiu was their man and deservingly so. He was a hometown boy who brought both grit and size. But maybe if I had played more and shown more of my ability and the versatility to play wing or defense as needed, the Rangers also would have seen something more in me and kept me. Fotiu became a valuable player to the Rangers and later for some other teams, including the Hartford Whalers and Calgary Flames, because he was a good checking role player in addition to being an excellent fighter. He went on to play 646 NHL games.

Within two weeks of my return to Binghamton, I received a tryout from the Edmonton Oilers, then a World Hockey Association team. The Oilers were looking for an enforcer and so I went there for a tryout to be just that. I was there with Frank Beaton and Ted Scharf. We basically were all trying out for one spot. Beaton and Scharf had more of a reputation than I did. They had spent more time in the minors. Beaton ended up winning the job. He played in sixty-eight games and compiled 274 penalty minutes for the Oilers that year. I would see both of these guys again, though not as teammates.

I lasted just two games with the Oilers. One game was against the Minnesota Fighting Saints and the other was against the Calgary Cowboys. I didn't receive a single shift during the Calgary game and received just one or two shifts in the Minnesota game. However, I skated one of those shifts with left wing Glen Sather, who is in the Hall of Fame as a builder. So there's that.

I received one penalty while with Edmonton for elbowing Craig Patrick in the head. I went to body-check him and missed. I clipped him with an elbow. Patrick, of course, went on to become an assistant coach under head coach Herb Brooks for the 1980 United States gold medal-winning Olympic team. He was inducted into the Hockey Hall of Fame in 2001 as a builder. His grandfather had been a coach of the Rangers when my grandfather reffed and coached. Both his dad and uncle were stars in the NHL during the '40s and '50s.

Veteran goalie Dave Dryden and his wife drove me to the Edmonton airport the day I left. Dryden's younger brother was former Cornell goalie, Ken Dryden, whom I had watched many times play in college when my dad reffed his games. Dave and I worked together again years later when I was a ref and he was on the equipment committee for the NHL. I was in Edmonton for all of one week before returning to Binghamton.

Back in Binghamton, I played sixty games and recorded four goals, thirteen assists and 232 penalty minutes. That was forty-one fewer minutes than the year before, probably because fewer opponents wanted to fight me. Plus, a lot of the opponents I had fought the year before had advanced to the WHA.

Maine Nordiques player Alan Globensky was quite a character. He skated by the Dusters bench after smacking one of my teammates. I hollered, “Why don’t you try me?”

“I will if you ever get on the ice,” he dryly replied.

I jumped over the boards to fight him and he hit me while my feet were still about three feet from the ice. I went flying back over the boards and fell into my team’s bench. Globensky and I both were sent to the penalty box for fighting, him for punching and me for receiving.

“So, you got me,” I told Globensky. “Too bad because now you’re going to have to get me again.”

I don’t remember if I actually fought him again that game, but would in subsequent games. Alan and I became good friends and roommates a few years later when we were both with the Cape Cod Freedoms. Globensky was a player and later became assistant coach for the Freedoms. I also played on that Cape Cod team with coach John Cunniff, one of the best men that South Boston has ever produced. Globensky, meanwhile, later told me that he never was afraid of me, but he knew if he picked a fight with me, he would have to fight me a hundred more times. He told me that I used to tire him out.

When I attended 1977-78 Rangers training camp, my goal was to win a job on their AHL New Haven affiliate. Things were looking promising. I was told I was playing in an exhibition game against the New York Islanders and was ready to make a better impression this year. I was scheduled to play with the Rangers regulars, including Kenny Hodge and Phil Esposito.

Johnny “Black Cat” Gagnon, a former NHL player-turned Rangers scout, visited my hotel room the night before the Islanders games. “Black Cat” Gagnon was an old-time French player who knew my grandfather. He was a Quebec native who had played for the Montreal Canadiens, Boston Bruins, and New York Americans. Gagnon told me the Rangers planned to option me to Port Huron of the International Hockey League instead of New Haven. I was obviously upset.

I didn't want to wade through another league. Gagnon also told me the Providence Reds were going to be an independent team in the AHL and suggested I contact their general manager, Ross Brooks. The Rangers owned my rights for two years so I either had to accept their assignment or sign with a team not affiliated with an AHL franchise.

The Providence Reds seemed like a perfect fit. They were in the AHL and close to my native Boston. The Boston Bruins and Harry Sinden had expressed interest in me. Sinden and scout John Carlton had tossed around the possibility of me playing for the Bruins' AHL affiliate, Rochester. But Rangers GM Ferguson would not release me, and so I couldn't join my hometown team. That greatly irked me.

There in my hotel room, Gagnon and I called Brooks together.

"I'll play the game against the Islanders and then see what happens," I told Brooks.

"Well, if things don't work out, then call me and you'll have a spot here in Providence," he said.

Ferguson approached me the next day following my morning skate and told me to meet him at 3:30 p.m. in the locker room. "We'll negotiate your contact," he said.

I arrived back to the rink before 3:30 p.m. eager to sit down with Fergie. But like an undesirable date, I was stood up. I still was waiting there for him at my dressing room stall at 6 p.m. I was tired and frustrated. During training camp, players skated and ran each morning. For those playing in an exhibition game that night, they would take the afternoon off to rest. But I had been in that dressing room all afternoon instead of in a comfy bed. Ferguson finally walked in, well after 6 p.m.

"I've been waiting for you," I said. "Did I make a mistake on the time? I thought we were supposed to meet to talk about my contract?"

"Put your gear on and go out and play," he replied. "I'll sign you when you I want to sign you."

I came out of my stall toward him like a bull on Red Bull. I was furious. "You bluff people and you push people around," I told him. "Why don't you take that contract and stick it right up your ass?"

"Why don't you take some of that toughness and see what you can do tonight," he fired back. "Show me you can play hockey."

He pointed his lit cigar at me like he was daring me. I recorded two assists, fought three opponents, and earned a game misconduct. Ferguson came into the dressing room afterward. He pointed his cigar at me and said, "Now I have myself a defenseman!"

"Now you've got shit," I replied. I turned and walked away.

I returned to the Holiday Inn and called Brooks, telling him I would be in Providence the next day. In the meantime, it was almost like the Magical Mystery Tour happened. The Providence owner sold the team that night to Andre Veilleux, who moved the team to Binghamton.

Yes, Binghamton again. Bingo was a magnet to me.

The North American Hockey League had folded. Veilleux had owned the Beauce Jaros and a part of the Quebec Nordiques. He was the first overall selection in the 1965 draft but never made the NHL. He always wanted me and liked my style and heart. I received a call from the new Binghamton Dusters GM, Paul Brown, the next morning when I was ready to head to Providence. He informed me that the NAHL had folded and Veilleux wanted to sign me. They wanted me at the press conference.

Veilleux called me from Binghamton and asked if I was under contract yet with the Rangers. I wasn't, so he told me that they would sign me to an American Hockey League deal. He asked me if I could come to Binghamton that day.

I went to Long Island Arena to collect my skates. While there, Frankie Pace told me that Fergy wanted me to come to Manhattan. Shortly thereafter, I went to Madison Square Garden to collect my equipment and other belongings. Ferguson was there.

"I'm sure we can work something out," he said.

"Are you prepared to sign me to a contract right now?" I replied.

"No, I'm not," he said.

"Okay, then. I'll see you later."

Back in Binghamton for the third straight season, Brown got cute and instead of a contract, he offered me a twenty-five-game tryout. My pay would have been voided if I got hurt, but my salary increased to $500 a week. I signed the deal.

I was psyched to be back in Binghamton where I had 505 penalties in minutes in two years, made my name, and finally was playing in the AHL. People knew me there. Soon after I arrived, I went to Jim Matthews' dealership and bought a Chrysler Cordoba with fine Corinthian leather, just as Ricardo Montalban had promised. Matthews gave me another great deal like he had in the first year when I paid him $100 a month for a Plymouth Duster. Yes, I was a Duster driving a Duster.

Around Thanksgiving, Binghamton played at New Haven where I saw Ferguson before the game, as I got off the bus. "I'll get my pound of flesh tonight and you'll be sorry," I told him.

He laughed and told me to get lost.

My parents had driven down from Boston to watch, too. It was a perfect night and I had perfect motivation to show my stuff. My first shift, I fought a tough kid, Eddie Johnstone. He stood up and fought with me, punch for punch, blow for blow. As I made my way to the penalty box, I skated by the New Haven bench. One of the New Haven players was leaning over and yapping at me. I slapped him. I didn't punch—but, instead, I just slapped him.

"Why don't you sit down," I told him. "You're the guy who took my spot. You'll get your shot against me." I pointed at New Haven coach Parker MacDonald and said something to the effect of, "I ought to come over those boards and kick your ass for what you did to me, you stooge."

The referee tossed me after my next fight. I didn't even make it to the end of the first period, which was okay because we were in New Haven where there are several delicious pizza parlors. I took a shower and, with the game still in progress, my parents and I went to dinner. I enjoyed some pizza and Chianti before returning to rink where the game had just finished. Coach Kish came walking up to me and asked me where I had been. I told him I had gone out to eat with my parents.

"We've got to talk," he said.

I thought I was in trouble. We went into the office in the visiting dressing room and there was a man sitting there.

"Hey, Paul Stewart," the man said with a bit of a French accent. "I've seen you play before. You put on a good show tonight."

"I had a special reason," I told him. "I had some business to take care of." He handed me his card. It read, "Flo Potvin, Chief Scout, WHA Cincinnati Stingers."

"So what can I do for you?" I asked, staring at the card.

He told me that Cincinnati, a team in the WHA, needed an enforcer like me. He told me he would give me a three-game tryout.

"That's not good enough. I want ten games." Potvin agreed to the ten-game tryout in which I would earn $500 per game. From there, I hopped onto the bus with my Dusters teammates and returned to Binghamton with the sandwiches and cake my mother and father had given me for me and my teammates. The next night I played my final game for the Dusters and scored a goal.

Stingers GM Jerry Rafter was in the stands and signed me to a contract, even though it was now just a five-game agreement worth $500 per game. But I was guaranteed the money in writing. The Rangers only owned my NHL rights for two years; by the end of the 1977-78 season, I was done with Ferguson and the Rangers.

Ironically, in Fischler's book, Ferguson stated, "I study these kids today, and I can see that they are bubbling over with talent, so much talent that it's hard to believe. On the other hand, they don't always take advantage of what they have. When practices are over, they're gone; they're the first ones off the ice when they could be doing more for themselves by staying out and improving their style. Part of their problem is that they never had the benefit of minor league experience, and they don't really respect work."

Maybe it sounded good at the time, but Ferguson was not true to his word. You would think that if hard work and minor league experience were truly important to him, I'd have been one of his favorites. But he pushed me, of all people, around—the kid who stayed after practice and had oodles of drive to make the NHL. Yes, I respect Ferguson and his path to the NHL. It was a truly inspirational one. If only he had given me the same chance he had once received, I would have respected him as a GM, too.

# CHAPTER 8: Livin' On The Air In Cincinnati

The Thanksgiving Massacre, as it was dubbed, happened on Thanksgiving Day in 1977 between the Cincinnati Stingers and Birmingham Bulls.

Robbie Ftorek, Del Hall, Jamie Hislop, Ron Plumb, and Barry Legge started for the Stingers. Gilles "Bad News" Bilodeau, Steve Durbano, Frank Beaton, Serge Beaudoin, and Bob Stephenson started for the Bulls. Within the first thirty seconds, three fights had broken out: Beaudoin versus Ftorek, Bilodeau versus Hislop, and Durbano versus Plumb. Of course, Ftorek, Plumb, and Hislop—three skill players—had zero chance against the other three bruisers, but, strangely, referee Peter Moffat gave the Stingers extra penalties, causing Cincinnati coach Jacques Demers to throw sticks on the ice and go after Bulls GM Gilles Leger, as Ed Willes described in *The Rebel League*.

After that game, Cincinnati team leader Rick Dudley, a left wing, demanded the Stingers add an enforcer. Little did I know the background story when the Stingers head scout, Flo Potvin, offered me a tryout contract after the game in New Haven. I was the enforcer the Stingers recruited to join their team, and, thus, "one of the more interesting careers in hockey was born," Willes wrote.

I was nothing if not brazen in those days.

My first game for the Stingers, we played Indianapolis and I didn't receive a single shift. I just sat there on the end of the bench. I was looking at coach Jacques Demers like he had two heads. Why were they paying me $500 a game and not playing me? I went into Demers' office after the game holding a roll of toilet paper.

"I don't mind getting crapped on, but I need toilet paper when it happens," I told my new coach.

"We didn't need you tonight," he said. "But we're playing Birmingham tomorrow. You'll play."

We left for Birmingham to play the Bulls the following morning. The WHA was a whole different world from the North American Hockey League. To my pleasant surprise, my equipment bag already was packed and put in the storage compartment under the bus when I arrived at the arena to board the bus that shuttled us to the airport.

After we checked in to the hotel in Birmingham, a few of us walked to a bar across the street from the BJCC Coliseum. I struck up a wonderful conversation there with a Farrah Fawcett lookalike. She was impossibly curvy, had tall hair, and a heavy southern drawl.

"Gilles Bilodeau's going to kick your ass tomorrow," she told me.

I told her that I liked her spirit, among other attributes. I didn't know Southern belles knew words like the ones she used in response.

I ran into Bulls owner John Bassett while walking into the rink the next morning. He was with his then ten- year-old daughter, Carling Bassett, who eventually became a professional tennis player. She was named after her grandfather, John Carling, who owned the Carling Brewery.

"You should go get a box of tissues for your dad," I hold her, "because I'm going to make your daddy cry tonight when I beat up his whole team."

Carling looked horrified, as you might expect. I meant it, though. Sitting in the dressing room before warm-ups, I thought about which Bull to fight first. Perhaps I'd do it in alphabetical order.

Beaton and his boys knew why the Stingers had signed me. They let me hear about it during warm-ups. It was the NAHL all over again, just in a larger arena. Not even a minute into the game, Beaton charged at me and gave me his stick. Then, we dropped the gloves. The scuffle happened right after I went to field a puck. Beaton brought his stick up and sort of crossed-checked me. I threw several hard punches at him.

He got twisted and spun around the wrong way with his leg getting caught in a rut. He either broke or twisted his ankle. He couldn't stand. He needed to be helped off the ice. Serving my five-minute penalty, Gilles Bilodeau skated by the box and said, "You're a [bleeping] dead man."

"Well, Beaton was first and Bilodeau is next," I replied. "I'll be right out."

Alphabetical order? Well, not quite. Alphabetical would have been Beaton, Beaudoin, and Bilodeau, but hell, Beaudoin's name started with "B" and I was in the heat of the moment. Can you blame me for disposing the order despite my Ivy League degree?

While fighting Bilodeau, I stepped on a hockey stick and began falling backward. But I was able to keep my balance and I sprang straight up and popped Bilodeau with a strong upper cut. He went over backward and down to the ice. His eyes glazed over slightly. That was the end of fight number two. Bad News wasn't so bad after all. I only wondered how the Farrah Fawcett-clone from the bar was handling her hero's wooziness. Back to the box I went for five minutes when Dave Hanson skated by and issued a challenge.

"I'm only fighting the Bs tonight Davey.," I shouted. "Sorry, you're not on my fight card. Tell Beaudoin he's next."

Beaudoin, was big—about 6'3". He charged at me like Bilodeau did. Boom! We fought and I was given a game misconduct. My Stingers debut ended early. A Yankee, Paul Stewart, had invaded the South. Dixie hockey would never be the same again.

Before that game, I was saddled with the nickname given to me by Hank Nowak, my ex-Binghamton teammate. He had always had called me "Stewkid." Nowak and other Binghamton teammates had written "Stewkid" on my underwear in permanent marker. I didn't especially care for that nickname. But after the Birmingham game, teammate Pat "Whitey" Stapleton told me that I sprung up as quick as a cat while fighting Bilodeau and if I got hit, all I did was blink without a flinch.

He nicknamed me "Stewcat." He and other teammates even gave me some coffee creamers to accentuate the nickname. Meow! Of course, I was thinking that life was great.

I played sixty-three games in two seasons for the Stingers. Well, I dressed for sixty-three games but didn't always skate. I scored three goals, six assists, and recorded 286 penalty minutes. I reflect on my days in Cincy with fondness—and a bit of a laugh and wry smile. My time there was simply fantastic. I was one of the guys. I think acceptance was what I sought the most even going back to Groton and Penn, both places where I'd felt I like an outsider.

Sure, I had been accepted in Binghamton, but in Cincinnati, I was playing in the WHA with superior players, earning a much more lucrative salary. The players, coaches, and front office treated me like I was major leaguer. I gained their respect because I had persistence and did everything I was told to do so I could stick with the team. Turning the old Groucho Marx joke on its ear, I was thrilled to finally gain acceptance from a club that wanted me as a member.

Much of life and hockey for me was purely psychological. When I was challenged, I wouldn't go down. I couldn't go down because I never let myself go down. Still, I felt anxiety. I worried about not doing the job well enough to keep it.

A couple days after our game in Birmingham, we flew to Hartford to play the New England Whalers. It was just after Christmas. I was psyched because it was the closest WHA city to home. My parents and brothers drove from Boston to watch. New England Whalers GM Jack Kelley was friends with my dad, so he had known me for many years. Kelley had coached Boston University and Colby College.

"Be careful with my player, Jack Carlson," Kelley cautioned me before the game as I walked into the arena. "He's the best fighter in the league. He can hurt you."

I thanked Kelley for his advice, looking at him like my Dutch uncle. Deep in my gut, I was thinking Carlson better watch out for me. I wasn't afraid of anyone and Kelley's warning made me more eager to fight Carlson, who had nearly everyone intimidated with his big helmet and his connection to the movie *Slap Shot*.

Jack was the only Carlson brother I hadn't yet fought. The Carlson brothers were talented fighters because they were tall, built strong, and had tremendous range. They also had everyone convinced they were a bit crazy. But was anyone crazier than I was after what I had done to get to the WHA? I was ready, willing, and able to play, and that included fighting Jack Carlson.

John McKenzie, Dave Keon, and Gordie Howe were just a few of the big-name players on New England's roster, but Carlson was my dance partner, for sure. McKenzie tried to hook me as teammate Rich Leduc and I broke in toward the net on my first shift. I shucked McKenzie with a quick elbow to get rid of him and off me. Leduc took a shot, and the rebound came to me. I snapped it past goalie Jean-Louis Levasseur for my first WHA goal. Life couldn't have been grander until I examined the puck. How cheap were the

Whalers? They gave me the puck, but it didn't even have a WHA logo on it. It looked like a practice puck. But it still meant a lot; it still does.

I skated to the bench and gave it to trainer Tim Ringler, who served as a trainer with the Toronto Blue Jays in his later life. Demers motioned for me to stay on the ice. I looked at the Whalers bench and Carlson jumped over the boards after Coach Harry Neale tapped him on the shoulder. Everyone knew what was about to happen. Carlson was upset about the elbow I threw at McKenzie. He lined up next to me. I backed off a little because I didn't want him to jump me and get an edge.

Referee Bill Friday dropped the puck and I began skating, but I could feel Carlson coming at me. I turned and threw my gloves in the air instead of throwing them straight down. I threw the first punch. Carlson and I then grabbed each other. The crowd roared, but it seemed to suddenly turn quiet. All you could hear was BOOM, BOOM, BOOM, BOOM, THWACK, THWACK, THWACK, THWACK. Carlson hit me and I hit him. He hit me again and I hit him. We traded shots with no one bothering to block any punches. No rabbit punches were thrown. No grabbing sweaters. There was no hiding or ducking. I had lived my whole life for this moment. There was no way I was going down.

We didn't remove our helmets and I'll never know how they stayed on us. Probably twenty to thirty punches apiece were thrown, switching hands, punch-for-punch, toe-to-toe, left-for-left, right-for-right. We were throwing haymakers, right out of the "Donneybrook" from the movie *Quiet Man*. Every punch he threw, I countered. I stayed right with him. The fight was right near the red line just at center ice between both benches. After a few punches, you could hear a pin drop I was told.

Maybe the crowd had figured Carlson should have flattened me and were amazed I still was standing. Not on that night; I stayed punch-for-punch with the toughest tough guy in the league, or at least that was the reputation that preceded him.

Carlson clipped me just above the left eye and sort of stunned me a bit. I winced. He came in for the kill, but I nailed him with a short left and straightened him up. I knew then that I had him but also felt exhausted. It was time to end it.

I had earned a moral victory and the fight needed to stop. I grabbed him by the sweater near his throat and pulled him in tight. No cat-calling or cheap talk happened between us. There was only respect. We held on and stared into each other's eyes.

Bill Friday told us it was the greatest fight he had ever seen. I have no idea whether Friday was telling the truth, but it definitely was a good fight. No, it was a great fight, a tremendous fight. We went into the box and Carlson leaned over the partition toward me. No glass stood between us—just the off-ice official.

"You know we have to go again," Carlson said.

"It's your building, your barnyard," I replied. "I'll be ready. No problem." Five minutes later, we skated out of the box and straight to our benches. The next shift we both returned to the ice. The face-off was down by the corner. The puck dropped and was sent behind the net. Carlson bumped the Stingers goalie when he went to field the puck, and I skated right to Carlson, checked him, dropped the gloves, and we began to fight again. Round Two was entertaining for the fans, but it didn't live up to Round One. Fewer punches were thrown. It wasn't a punch-for-punch battle either. It was maybe three or four punches for each of us and then we held on to each other's sweaters. We both still felt exhausted from Round One.

Nevertheless, I had made the moment count and had proved my point. I was as tough as anyone in the WHA. I had earned my spot in the rankings of being the "Best."

"What have you guys been drinking, green beer?" Friday asked us. "You're both crazy."

Friday often used that green beer line after breaking up fights. People have asked me how I did during the second fight against Carlson. I usually tell them that I don't know but Carlson didn't ask me for a third fight, so I think I did OK. Thinking back on that night, going from there, Jack and I rarely ever saw one another. We never fought again. He went on with his life and I went on with mine. Regardless, while we may not be friends, I like to think that we respect each other. I liked him, I liked his brothers and Dave Hanson. Without them, I would never have been known so widely for being "tough." Besides, everyone knows them from *Slap Shot*—and that is a bit of pride for me, too.

Dave Hanson wrote in his book the reason everyone didn't like to fight me was because I bled too much on their sweaters. Haha. I didn't bleed that night in Hartford. I see Big Dave around these days in Pittsburgh where he runs a rink. Nothing but the greatest respect exists between us. There was no question about whether we feared each other. That was not even in the equation. There was never fear for me or him or any of the others who I fought. It was our job and we knew what we had to do to continue our hockey careers. We took pride in it. I know I did.

Coach Demers summoned me to his office after the Whalers game and Bill DeWitt, Jr., the Stingers owner who now owns the Major League Baseball St. Louis Cardinals, was sitting there, too.

"You had quite the game," Bill said to me.

"Good or bad, I'm here," I replied. "I've got two games left in my tryout and I've enjoyed being with this team. By the way, I know your father used to own the Reds. My grandfather was an umpire in the National League. He always worked Opening Day in Cincinnati. He used to buy a couple of Palm Beach suits and hats in Cincinnati. He said that he always enjoyed Cincy."

"I didn't know that," DeWitt replied. "Well, Cincinnati enjoys having you. We want to sign you for the rest of the year." DeWitt offered me $20,000 for the rest of the season. I turned it down right then and there. I told him Carlson likely earned twice as much and all three Birmingham Bulls who I fought also were making more than $20,000.

"I want $20,000 for the rest of the season, a $5,000 signing bonus, and a car to drive around while I'm in Cincy," I said.

"You've got a deal!" DeWitt said, handing me $1,000 in cash right there on the spot. Funny, eh? My first paycheck in Binghamton was for $250 or $193.47 after taxes. Is it all about the Benjamins? Maybe for some, but for me it was about the respect that I had earned. The money was a sign of the respect that this man, this coach, and this team had for me. I didn't have an agent and didn't want to push it too far. I ended up driving around a Jeep that Ftorek lent me. It was a long way from my Duster.

Ftorek is a wonderful guy and still my friend. I don't know if he got anything back from DeWitt for lending me the Jeep, but he asked me to dinner at his house and he gave me the keys. The veteran guys on the team got a kick out of watching me because I'd run through the boards or do whatever had to be done to receive more playing time. I'd stay out on the ice after practice and worked hard. I did a lot of push-ups and sit-ups, and I hit the heavy bag nearly every day.

I even did a promo for the Stingers TV, sort of a *Rocky* take, hitting the meat with my shirt off, my hands taped like a boxer, telling the fans they should come to the next Stingers game because there might be some action. After the commercial aired, I received approximately fifty letters from women telling me they liked my chest. They sent photos of themselves for me to inspect. It was a big difference from what hockey was like in the minors, where riding buses and eating at all-night diners on the thruway was the norm.

Jamie Hislop and I taped all the pictures of the women we received to the back of our lockers. It was an amusing diversion that became a bit of a contest between us to see who received the most interesting fan mail or just who received the most letters from gorgeous women.

Jamie had played at the University of New Hampshire and was easily one of my hardest working teammates I ever played alongside. He also was one of the best-conditioned athletes I have ever known. But he was a skill player; he wasn't the guy on the team to fight. Within my first week with Cincy, St. Paul-native, Dave Langevin, who played for the Edmonton Oilers, rammed Hislop's face into the glass and then just sort of wiped him across the dasher. Hislop's face hit the stanchion and he dropped to the ice. He broke his nose and was knocked out cold.

I stood up on the bench and yelled to my teammates, asking if anybody planned to do anything about what had just happened. Nobody said anything. They all just sat there. I asked Demers to put me out there, but he didn't. When the period ended, I walked down the runway into the dressing room and berated my teammates for their passive style. Some of them were just standing there, smoking cigarettes.

Center Hugh Harris asked, "Why don't you do something?"

"I can't do something from the end of the bench!" I shouted. "How am I supposed to do something from the end of the bench? You guys are all playing." I tipped over a table and Demers rushed into the room to find out what all the commotion was about. "Why don't you put me on a plane and send me somewhere else, because this team has no jam?" I told Demers. "Our most honest player, a kid who's not a fighter, just got his face smashed in and we're losing 4-0. And all your heroes have got nothing in them to protect this guy."

I started pointing at certain players. Hugh Harris, who always smoked a pipe, sat there with his pipe in his mouth and challenged Demers to put me in the game. I loved Hughie; he said exactly what needed to be said. Demers obliged him.

My first shift out there, when Langevin came near me, I threw the gloves off and hit him like you wouldn't believe. I took him from one end of the rink to the other to the point where he was shielding himself from my punches. I was beyond insane, and I went to the box and took a seat. I have the video in case you think I am exaggerating. Oilers left wing Dave Semenko skated over and had a few words for me. I jumped right back onto the ice after him so I was tossed from the game in the matter of seconds.

My teammates rallied back to tie the game. "I did my job," I said to Demers and then walked away. As for Langevin, if you're a tough guy, then you don't take on Jamie Hislop, you take on me. It's that simple.

I had my run-ins with the Edmonton Oilers more than once. One night in Cincinnati, Oilers coach Glen Sather mocked me, so I skated over, took off my helmet, and I threw it at him as hard as I could. He ducked and the helmet hit Sparky the stick boy, then bounced into the stands. Another time, Demers had indicated I would dress against the Oilers in Edmonton but then told me I wasn't playing during pregame warm-ups. Angry, I hijacked the Zamboni near the open gate. I'd at least do something productive if I wasn't going to play. I began cleaning the ice right there and then in my uniform. Sather looked stunned and furious as I drove by the Edmonton bench. He was making out his lineup card and I beeped the horn and smiled at him.

After a while, all the WHA teams understood my message: My team wasn't going to be bullied. After I got to Cincinnati and made my way through the WHA once, that pretty well ended all those teams taking runs at the Stingers. I went right through Quebec and took on all of them—Wally Weir, Steve Sutherland, Bob Fitchner, Curt Brackenbury, Paul Baxter—I took on every tough guy on every team. It seemed like the right thing to do.

I fought Winnipeg's Kim Clackson. Everyone talked about

Clackson's toughness. I fought him to a standstill in Winnipeg. We only fought once. After that, we would both sit on the end of our benches and wave to each other. There was no chance of getting on the ice when Winnipeg had Hull, Hedberg, and Nilson on that ice, anyway.

We all began playing more like a team, and I ended up loving them all like brothers. I look back on that 1977-1978 team as one of the best times in my life. I enjoyed having that opportunity. The camaraderie was tremendous. I had seen several of my teammates play before joining Cincinnati. I respected them and knew their capabilities. Having an enforcer like me allowed the Stingers to settle down and play hockey. I think that was when the opportunity for me to develop my skills should have happened, but it did not in any real way.

Coach Jacques Demers, Whitey Stapelton, Butchy Deadmarsh, Hugh Harris, Barry Melrose, and several other veteran players took a liking to me and worked with me on developing my skills, but I didn't get to play a lot, which was both curious and frustrating. Still, I made my mark doing the thing I was hired to do. I did it well, and I did it with pride.

Rick Dudley, the Stinger whose demand that his team add an enforcer ultimately led to my employment with their organization, was a fierce and tough competitor. He was solid, wiry, and strong. He was a thinker, too. I've gotten the chance to know him better throughout the years and he has one of the best minds in hockey. Everywhere he goes, he puts together a successful organization and team. I had earned his respect and I appreciated it.

"Paul Stewart was as tough as any player I've ever seen," Rick Dudley said in *The Rebel League*. "I did it for a purpose, but he actually liked to fight. He'd fight anyone, anywhere, at any time, and you had to admire him for that."

Well… not everyone…

One night in Hartford, Ftorek hook-checked the puck off Gordie Howe's stick, making Howe look somewhat foolish. Ftorek turned and passed the puck right away up to linemate Jamie Hislop, who then took off down the ice. Everyone was focused on the puck and Hislop. Meanwhile, Howe took one look around and made sure he knew where the referee was and then he cut Ftorek with his stick from Ftorek's nose almost to his eye. Peter Marsh was on the bench sitting next to me and asked me if I had seen what happened.

"You gotta go get him!" Marsh said.

"What? Are you shitting me? That's Gordie Howe!" I replied.

There was no way I was leaving the bench to fight Gordie Howe. I knew my place and I knew Gordie's. Besides, at 49, Gordie could still ragdoll me and likely anyone else on skates. That wouldn't have been fun. Contrary to popular perception, it wasn't like I always was looking for a fight, but I always was trying to let people know that I wouldn't avoid one, either. Except against Gordie, of course.

The following season, 1978-1979, brought on more changes, challenges and, of course, fun. That season saw the addition to the Stingers roster of seventeen-year old Mark Messier. He was a big, solid strapping boy. I could tell immediately he was extremely gifted. After one of his first practices with the Stingers, I took him to the bar, Sleep Out Louie's, for lunch. He was wearing a pair or work boots and bib-overall blue jeans with a T-shirt that showed off his muscular arms. We walked inside, where legendary Cincinnati Reds player Pete Rose was sitting at the bar. I had known Rose from participating in charity events in Cincinnati.

I introduced Rose to Messier. When Messier went to the restroom, Rose grabbed me and said, "The kid looks like he just fell of a tractor."

"Yeah, but he's going to be an excellent player," I replied.

I knew almost everyone in town. I had hung out with Bengals' tight end Bob Trumpy and Cincinnati Reds' players Pete Rose, Tom Seaver and Ray Knight, as well as Reds' manager Sparky Anderson. They all called me "Cat."

I told Sparky that he'd made me cry when his Reds beat my Red Sox in the 1975 World Series. I had hoped he had would have tripped over the white foul line on his way out to the mound when making pitching changes. It was his thing to step over the line, never touching it. And it also was his thing to make pitching changes. That's how he received the nickname "Captain Hook." Anderson frequently guest DJ'd at Lucy In The Sky, a Saturday Night Fever- style bar on the top of the Holiday Inn. When I went there to party with him, I wore my platform shoes and my black leather jacket with the bell-bottom pants. Who didn't dress like that? After all, we all thought we were John Travolta.

I even introduced Ray Knight to LPGA golfer Nancy Lopez.

They were married for several years and have three daughters together. While at a charity golf tournament at Kings Island, I was playing pool with Lopez and she saw Knight across the room and asked me if I knew him.

"He plays for the Reds," I said. "I'll go bring him over here."

Stingers owner Bill DeWitt and the front office members treated me sensationally. They were classy people. The NHL rejecting DeWitt was a huge mistake. He would have added a lot to the league. Just look at what he's done with the St. Louis Cardinals, which is one of baseball's top franchises.

Skip Smith was one of the minority owners of the Stingers. He was a stockbroker with Merrill Lynch and a big wheel with them. He took a liking to me. During the summer, the owners flew me back to Cincinnati to play golf with the big wigs at Procter & Gamble, headquartered in Cincinnati. I also was on the Stingers' season ticket campaign. They brought me back during the off-season, and I sat in an office for two weeks making phone calls to sell tickets. I went out and met with groups and sponsors, I made speeches.

When you examine my career points compared to my career penalty minutes, you'd probably just think I had a cinderblock for a head and, even then, as far as cinderblocks go, was not too smart. But I had a real appreciation for what I was doing and who I was doing it with (teammates and opponents) and who I was doing it for (the owners of my teams).

## CHAPTER 9: Me And Mrs. Paul

My roommate in Cincy was Bill Gilligan from Bevery, Massachusetts and Brown University. We certainly had fun together. We shared an apartment in the winter of 1978. One day at practice, he asked me for the water and I squirted him with it. Infuriated, he punched me. He wasn't too big, about 5'11", 170-175 pounds, but he was a competitor. I had to stay to do extra work as always after practice. I asked our trainer Timmy Ringler where Gilly was when I got done with the extra work.

"He told me to tell you to go screw yourself and find your own way home," Ringo responded. I called Gilly on the pay phone at our practice rink at Cincinnati Gardens and told him it was all well and good to be mad at me. Cell phones were well into the future.

"But how am I going to get home?" I asked. "We live ten miles from downtown."

"Okay, I'll come getcha," he replied. What a guy! He made his point, I guess.

Gilly played at Brown, where he holds the program records for scoring and assists. At the end of the 1978-79 season, as the WHA was folding, Gilligan sat there in the apartment listening to tapes in German, trying to learn the language because he planned to head overseas to play in Austria or Switzerland. He ended up playing in Switzerland and stayed for a lengthy time, playing for five years and then coaching there. He was the head coach of the Swiss National Team from 1992-1994, then came home to be assistant coach at UMass Amherst. Now he has young kids, is married to a beautiful woman, and was the assistant coach at Merrimac College.

Despite all the great times in Cincy, there were times when I knew I should have played more. I knew I was capable of playing well, I was just not getting the chance or the ice time I needed to get better and gain confidence. It was the one aspect of playing for Demers where I felt he could have helped me more. Even though I had started to improve my skills at practices, I began dressing less and less frequently because teams weren't taking runs at the Stingers as much anymore, thanks in part to me. As I said, teams were starting to play hockey against Cincinnati, and Demers didn't need me as much. If you tell a normal working-man he has the day off, he is pleased. He will play golf or relax in front of the television watching a football game with a six-pack of beer. But I hated it. I can't stand idle time even to this day. I always want to be doing something and that was especially the case back then as a professional hockey player. I looked at my time as a player like it was gasoline—time and gas were slipping away. I was burning daylight and not yet playing as much as I would have liked.

Further, my second year in Cincy wasn't as nice as the first. Floyd Smith took over as head coach. He liked veterans and Canadians. I was neither. He brought in Dave Forbes, who played dirty but wasn't a particularly good fighter. Forbes had showed his true self when he stuck Henry Boucha in the eye with a stick. I don't like stick guys; never have and never will. When Forbes joined the team, he was a Christian athlete who had gone through a sort of metamorphosis. He was nowhere near capable of handling the role of enforcer. With Forbes now filling my role, albeit poorly, Smith sent me down to the AHL. I actually played for four teams that year: the Stingers, the NEHL Cape Cod Freedoms, the AHL's Philadelphia Firebirds, and the AHL's Binghamton Dusters.

My return to Philadelphia was not a happy homecoming. It was a funny team and a funny time in my career, more in the bad sense of the term than the good.

The Firebirds played their home games at the now-extinct Philadelphia Civic Center, a horrendous facility located on the perimeter of my collegiate alma mater. My old stomping grounds, the Class of 1923 Rink, was a stone's throw away.

However, I was in no *Welcome Back, Kotter* frame of mind at the time; I wasn't exactly singing along with John Sebastian's song on the .45 player at my temporary home in Voorhees, NJ.

Quite frankly, I wasn't happy to be a Firebird. For one thing, I had been sent there from the WHA's Cincinnati Stingers under adversarial circumstances, and the American Hockey League was a downward step on the professional ladder. For another, it was a terrible team because it had affiliated with the NHL's lowly Colorado Rockies and much of the roster was filled with gutless players who would not even have been considered prospects on well-run NHL teams of the time.

Had I played for the Firebirds a little earlier in my career when I was literally fighting my way up the professional ladder one rung at a time from the North American Hockey League, it might have been a better experience for me.

The Firebirds were originally a team in the North American Hockey League and were a good team at that level. Actually, if their NAHL club been my starting point in pro hockey, I'd have been ecstatic. They won the championship (the Lockhart Cup) during the 1975-76 season, which was my first season with Binghamton.

When the entire NAHL folded, the Firebirds were accepted into the AHL. They still had some good holdover players from their NAHL teams. Players such as Gordie Brooks, Bob Collyard, and goalie Reggie Lemelin all spent some time in the NHL as well as the minor leagues. The club also had my friend, Steve Coates, a small but feisty checking forward who had a brief stint in the NHL with the Detroit Red Wings and later became a hockey broadcaster.

Searching for an NHL affiliation, the Firebirds were only able to strike a deal with the Colorado Rockies. That pretty much doomed the club to having subpar talent. Most of the Rockies-affiliated players were not just mediocre in skill (even at the AHL level), they also lacked work ethic and were a bunch of pansies on top of it.

The Firebirds were owned by millionaire Edward Piszek and his son, George. The family had made its fortune in the frozen food business as the owners of Mrs. Paul's fishsticks and related frozen fish items sold in grocery stores nationwide. Later, they took a bath financially when they bought the Arthur Treacher's Fish and Chips fast food franchise with the intention of selling more of their products. They ended up selling the franchise for a fraction of what they originally paid for it.

The Piszeks were nice enough people on a personal level, but they were too cheap to merely be called frugal. Even by minor league penny-pinching standards, they cut corners and it started to have a negative effect. The team consistently lost money.

Let's just say that I hope the quality control at the Mrs. Paul's plant was better than the quality control of their hockey team. During the franchise's NAHL championship days, the Firebirds actually developed a nice little cult following in Philly. They did it partially by riding the coattails of the Flyers' being at the zenith of their success and partially because they were a winning and tough team. From there, however, the product went downhill and the attendance at the Civic Center got sparser and sparser.

During the 1978-79 season, the Firebirds were coached by the late Armand "Bep" Guidolin. He was eccentric, but he was a good man without an enemy in the world.

Bep was a hoot. He lived in a hotel while he was coaching the Firebirds and was shocked and dismayed when he was presented a bill. He somehow thought the Firebirds were going to the foot the bill. I doubt it ever got paid.

Guidolin was far from the best strategic coach I ever saw. Getting outcoached by Fred Shero in the 1974 Stanley Cup Finals was one of the reasons why Bep's Bruins were upset by Philadelphia. Preparation was not his strong suit, nor was running his bench. By the time he got to the Firebirds, Bep paid little attention to things like which players had just come back to the bench at the end of shifts and who should be going out with whom for the next shift.

I decided to have a little fun with it and get myself some extra ice time to boot. Sometimes, when coming off the ice after a shift on the wing, I would exit the ice on the side of the bench where the defensemen sat. Then I'd go right back out as a defenseman since Bep wasn't paying any attention.

My teammates caught on and would laugh about it. Bep either never figured it out or decided it didn't matter since our team was so bad.

On a personal level, Bep was easy to like in an oddball uncle sort of way. Bep was not exactly a snappy dresser. He used to coach wearing a windbreaker on game nights and was otherwise prone to wearing mismatched clothes. The teasing rolled right off his back. He used to say odd and funny things to crack us up on the bench and on the team bus.

For example, one time Bep hollered at Coatsie to come over to the bench before a faceoff. Going over some strategy, perhaps? Nope.

Bep was pointing out an attractive and shapely woman in the stands whom he was convinced was flirting with him.

I reported to the Firebirds on the day of the team's Christmas party, which was held at Coates' house. Back in those days, the team holiday party was usually a players-only event but Bep was there. Later, I found out that Bep had invited himself and shown up three hours early!

There was one thing that would get Bep riled up. He read the team the riot act a few times in the dressing room for the lack of moxie that many of the players showed. That was the one thing that genuinely did bother him—and me—about that Firebirds squad.

The fighting duties were left to me. In 16 games, I scored a pair of goals and had 92 penalty minutes. I wasn't too happy about it, either.

One night in Portland, we were playing the Maine Mariners, the Flyers' affiliate. They were a tough team filled with guys who fought regularly. I tried in vain to fire up the team by stirring the pot before the drop of the puck. Big, big mistake.

I got jumped by a gang of Mariners and was left all alone on the ice to get my butt kicked. I fought with six different Maine players, including Jim Cunningham, Glen Cochrane, Al Hill, and John Paddock. I was a bloody mess but screamed at the Maine players to keep bringing it on. They did—mercilessly. By the end, both my eyes were swollen shut and I was still standing with my fists cocked, my own blood streaming. I could only swing blindly by that point. When it was finally over, Coates helped me off the ice.

Incidentally, a photo of the incident ended up in *Sports Illustrated.* Not exactly a glorious image like Bobby Orr flying through the air on the Stanley Cup winning goal, but it certainly captured what was happening. At least I wasn't intimidated by the Mariners and I never quit fighting.

Not one of my teammates came to my aid. The most anyone did was pair off and hold onto a Maine player away from the six-on-one.

It was one of the worst nights I had during my entire career. My parents were in the stands that night, traveling from Boston to Portland to see the game. A former girlfriend was also there that night. I hated that they had to witness it.

After the game, I refused to board the team bus with those

cowardly Rockies farmhands. I changed and showered in the officials' dressing room—foreshadowing my future—and flew to the next game at my own expense.

In the aftermath of the incident, I got fined $850 by the AHL. George Piszek refused to pay my fine. That was a first—back then, teams usually paid fighting-related fines for their players. I told him he'd regret it.

I appealed it to league president, Jack Butterfield, who said I would get the money back over his dead body. I went to Jack's funeral a few years ago; no, he did not leave me $850 in his will.

I wanted nothing further to do with the Firebirds.

Ultimately, I landed back on my feet. I also symbolically got back at Piszek for his cheapness. Every time I went to a grocery store, I went to the frozen food section. I'd rip open one box of Mrs. Paul's fishsticks and empty out the contents. Did it for years. I ended up being up about $2,000 on the deal. Do you think I'm joking? Well, maybe I am and maybe I'm not.

Smith eventually recalled me because the Stingers were again getting bullied and Forbes wasn't the answer. Barry Melrose got his head handed to him one night in Hartford and so he called up Smith and told him, "I can't do this anymore. We've had a vote. We want the Cat back." I wanted to tell Smith to go take a hike, but just looking at him with disdain was enough so that he understood what I thought of him.

Finally, one day, I had had enough and met with DeWitt. I asked Bill if he was aware his coach was trying to move me so much in an attempt to get me so frustrated I'd quit. DeWitt asked me what I wanted to do. I told him to send me to Cape Cod, an Eastern League team coached by Johnny Cunniff and owned by Sandy Reiss, a porn video producer. Seemed like a good place to play and, for me, it was all about blades on the ice and playing.

"Let me finish out the year there and then trade me or buy me out," I said. DeWitt was a class act who appreciated what I had done for his team the previous year. Off to the Cape I went, eating fried clams, living in my own house two miles from the rink, and still getting major league money. Smith thought he was punishing me by sending me to the Cape.

"Enjoy those twelve-hour bus rides," was his parting shot.

"They have a US post office on Cape Cod, keep sending those checks!" I replied. I was glad to go because I got the chance for more playing time.

Before leaving for the Cape, there was a bench-clearing brawl in Hartford and I didn't even go over the boards to help right away. I sat on the bench until Smith walked down the bench and told me to get out there. So I walked all the way down to the farthest gate, opened it unenthusiastically, and slowly stepped out onto the ice. I stood there holding onto some Whaler or another who likely thought I was going to kick his ass. I wasn't interested because Smith had made it his goal to take my usual enthusiastic spirit and kill it. He tried to beat me psychologically by moving me around from team to team every few weeks, trying to get me to quit. That night on the ice was my form of protest. What he failed to understand, however, as did many of the other bosses I had after this time, was that my love and loyalty to the game would never allow them to beat me. I was down but not defeated.

At that point, little did anyone know it, I was just one year away from realizing my dream by making it to the NHL. My hockey career was long from being finished. I just didn't yet know how I was going to make that next step.

And then the WHA folded.

## CHAPTER 10: C'est La Guerre

The World Hockey Association had folded after a deal was struck to merge four of the WHA teams and the National Hockey League, making Les Nordiques de Quebec an NHL franchise. The previous season had been a stressful one for me because rumors constantly had swirled about the WHA folding. I had worried quite a bit about where I might end up playing. Talks already had begun during the 1978-1979 season to merge the two leagues. The Houston Aeros, knowing they weren't going to become part of the NHL, folded before the 1978-1979 season had even begun. The Indianapolis Racers also folded just twenty-five games into the season.

That left just six franchises (Edmonton, Quebec, Winnipeg, New England, Cincinnati, and Birmingham) remaining in the WHA at the end of the 1978-79 season. The WHA, indeed, ceased to exist following the 1978-1979 after seven seasons of operation. The Winnipeg Jets won the final WHA championship, their third title in four years. Of the six teams, only four became members of the NHL: Quebec, Edmonton, New England Whalers (later the Hartford Whalers) and Winnipeg. Cincinnati and Birmingham joined the Central Hockey League. It was part of the deal.

The 1979 NHL Expansion Draft happened June 13, 1979. I didn't know it even happened when it did. Soon after, I received a phone call from then-Quebec Nordiques coach Jacques Demers while at Jan's family cottage.

"Cat, you're back with me," Jacques said.

This cat had nine lives! I was told (not by Demers but by others) that I was the final player selected in the dispersal draft. With the last selection, Jacques requested that the Nordiques take me.

I don't know if that is true, but who cares? It's like being the last kid picked for backyard baseball. Once the game starts, no one cares who was picked where because playing is the ultimate reward. Demers had coached me in Cincinnati but was the head coach of Quebec during the Nordiques final season in the WHA in 1978-1979. He retained his position when the Nordiques joined the NHL.

Me—a nice, quiet (well, not so much), Irish Catholic boy with an American passport—was a Nordique in the land of Jean Beliveau and Jacques Plante! *C'est incroyable*!

Standing in an elevator at the Hilton Hotel, the door opened and in walked Quebec Nordique tough guys Curt Brackenbury, Wally Weir, Bob Fitchner, and Steve Sutherland. It was the first day of the now-NHL Quebec Nordiques' training camp in September 1979.

Brackenbury, Weir, Fitchner, and Sutherland had all played with Quebec when it was with the WHA. All four had played extremely hard against me. Weir and I had fought many times before in the WHA when he played for the Nordiques and I played for the Stingers. Back then, we both received treatment in the same training room after fighting each other. Lying on opposite tables, we exchanged some unpleasant words, then fought right there in the training room.

A tiny French doctor unsuccessfully attempted to separate us. I used to call Wally "Meat Head" and "Wally Weird." Seeing the odd way he taped his skates, I also called him "Spats." Now we all were teammates and about to be friends. Well, at least I thought we were supposed to be friends. Being from Groton School, where shaking hands happens routinely, I extended my hand to them. But these four wanted no part in pleasantries. They acted like vampires, wanting my blood.

"You think you're going to make our team?" one sneered. "We're going to kill you at the rink."

"Why wait? I asked. "We can go now. Who's first? Or do ya wanna go all at once?"

Just then, the elevator doors opened to the hotel lobby. No elevator fight happened. I regret not hitting the close-door button, but I also was against the odds at four versus one.

To the Colisée de Québec I drove, headed for the practice rink and what ended up being a long day at the office. Medical trainer, Larry Ashley, and equipment manager, Rene Lacasse, had my locker prepared. The number three sweater hung in the stall. Seeing it, I yelled across to Weir.

"Hey, Wally, after today, we'll see who'll be wearing this Number 3 and who will have your old Number 2." The gauntlet had been thrown down publicly.

In the midst of our team intra-squad scrimmage, Weir, a 6'2", 205-pound bruiser dropped his gloves and flew at me. There, during our scrimmage at the practice rink behind the Colisée de Québec, Weir and I exchanged a few punches and wrestled to the ice. A linesman grabbed him and another linesman grabbed me, pushing me farther back and causing me to lose my balance. While I was on one knee, trying to break loose from the linesman still holding me, Weir escaped from the grasp of his linesman, stood, and kneed me square in the face. He broke my nose. I bled like a stuck pig while Brackenbury stood nearby, laughing.

I grabbed a stick and swatted Brackenbury, then dropped the stick and skated at Weir. We fought again even as I bled profusely and it all dripped onto the ice. Weir and I went at it harder than the first time until the linesmen stepped between us. Weir skated to the penalty bench and I skated in his direction, pointing at him and shouting that he had made a mistake. I stared into the stands at General Manager Maurice Filion, head coach Jacques Demers, and former player-turned Player Personnel Director George "Chief" Armstrong.

"You guys made a mistake!" I yelled to them. "You want to find out who's the toughest? You'll bury the one who isn't." I pointed at Weir and added, "When I come out from the dressing room, we're going to the death. I'm gonna kill ya!"

Hyperbole? Not the way I was feeling at that moment of rage. I changed out of my ripped jersey and bloody equipment into new gear. I also took a moment to straighten my nose as best I could. I returned to the ice, yelling at Weir to fight. He just sat in the penalty box.

All eyes were fixated on me as I raced to the box, reached over the boards, and threw rights at Weir. I lost track of time but didn't tire. It was a fight to the death, or at least that's what I considered it at the time. Demers hustled down and along with some players, including my former Stingers teammate Robbie Ftorek, pulled me off Weir. Defenseman Gerry Hart wasn't practicing that day. I believe he was holding out to negotiate a new contract. But he was there.

As I skated off the ice, Hart said something like, "Holy Jesus."

"You know me from New York," I replied. "You and everyone else better stay out of my way." The madness caused the first day of practice to end early.

While I received treatment from Ashley (better known to us as "Ash"), Demers poked his head into the training room and summoned me to his office where the Nordiques' brass all sat. Weir was sitting in there, too. I took a seat, and Filion got right down to business.

"I've seen enough," he said.

"He kneed me in the face. It's not enough for me," I interrupted. Weir and I were no longer at the Hilton with three of his buddies protecting him. I didn't care how long it took, I planned to pay him back. Him kneeing me and anyone using stick work were two cardinal sins in my mind. Weir stood like he wanted to fight. I hopped to my feet, too. Filion looked horrified and screamed for us to sit.

"Tomorrow we're going to the death," I told Weir, then looked at the brass, I said to them, "Bring a body bag because I am going to kill him and I might do it today. I'll get him. That's not a threat, it's a promise. I'm going to get him."

Filion produced a six-pack of Carling O'Keefe beer from under his feet and placed it on the desk. Carling O'Keefe owned the Nordiques during the 1970s.

"Enough! Shake hands and drink a beer together," said Filion, also threatening to fine us if we fought again.

"I don't care if you fine me," I said. "I'm gonna gouge one of Weir's [bleeping] eyes out, or perhaps even both."

"Shake hands or get your shit and go home," Filion warned us. "Shake hands and go to dinner together tonight."

He was serious. We complied, and then cracked open a beer as Filion watched us.

As Weir and I walked outside, I told him I still had a problem that he kneed me. "But if not fighting you means I get to stay in the NHL, then I'll make peace and go along with Filion."

We patched things up then and there, somewhat. We didn't eat dinner together. The beer and handshake were enough of a backpedal in one day for me. A man can only change or forgive so much.

The following morning, the Quebec newspapers told the story of the horror that took place at the Nordiques' practice the previous day. That afternoon's scrimmage was moved over to Le Colisée, which was open to the public. Little did the packed house know that no rematch was in the cards, although everyone came to see us go. They all wanted a war.

Despite the truce, I remained unsure whether to trust Wally and his buddies so I kept an eye out for them. Somehow, we never seemed to take the ice at the same time that day. Oh, well. As they say in Quebec, "*C'est la guerre*!"

Believe it or not, Weir and I ended up becoming friends. Our fighting wasn't really personal. I know it sounds odd to say that you want to gouge out someone's eyes and literally kill them in the same sentence as saying it isn't personal, but it wasn't. Back then, battles for NHL roster spots were like a war. We were both just trying to establish ourselves on the team, and to cement our spots on the roster. I've said it before—friction is a part of hockey. We weren't fighting for any other reason. I actually came to enjoy most everyone on that team. They were good guys when I got to know them.

I had a sweet deal. I was earning a paycheck from the Quebec Nordiques and received one-way American money. I also earned $2,500 just for reporting to camp. The other guys got multi-colored meal money; mine was in American greenbacks. I had negotiated that as part of my contract. All my monies, expenses included, had to be paid in U.S. dollars. I may appear like a goon sometimes, but I did graduate from Penn. I was earning a decent paycheck and that wiped away any possible shame of being the last pick. Who cared? I was in the NHL.

I also enjoyed playing for Jacques Demers. He's one of the more human and caring men I ever met. I don't necessarily know if he knew more hockey than other head coaches but players often self-coach at the NHL and WHA levels, anyway. In Cincinnati, Demers had veteran players such as Whitey Stapleton, who had played fifteen years in the league and sat on the bench instructing the younger players. Robbie Ftorek, Butch Deadmarsh, Rich LeDuc, and Hugh Harris all had done the same. Demers coached four WHA teams (Chicago, Indianapolis, Cincinnati, Quebec) and then coached in the NHL for Quebec, St. Louis, Detroit, Montreal, and Tampa Bay. The Montreal, Quebec native led the 1992-93 Canadiens to the Stanley Cup with a 4-1 series win over the Los Angeles Kings. His record speaks for itself. He was always kind to me and pulling for me to succeed. I'd have done anything for him.

Quebec had several tough guys, but nobody was in the same class as Weir, Brack, and me. And nobody, not even Weir, was as tough as me. No, I'm not bragging all these years later. Maybe it's untrue, but, back then, that was only the truth and the way I had to think to make the team, any team.

As camp continued, however, I saw the writing on the wall. The Nordiques would not cut veterans such as Weir in favor of me because they had been with the team when it was a WHA organization. They spoke French. Also, unlucky for them but lucky for the Nordiques, they earned Canadian dollars, which were trading at forty percent less than the U.S. Benjamins I received. All of these reasons compelled the ultimate outcome: a return for me to Cincinnati.

Little did I know during training camp, a deal already had been stuck between the Nordiques and Bill DeWitt's Cincinnati Stingers back during the summer. The deal ensured my return to Cincinnati, then of the Central Hockey League, upon the start of the 1979-80 regular season.

Back to Cincinnati I went, where I played under Al Karlander, with all his theories, prejudices and lack of true coaching vision. For a coach, he never took the time to try to coach me. Karlander hardly talked with me except to tell me I wasn't dressing. He'd wait to do it right after I had warmed up.

"Why? Did I have a bad [bleeping] warm-up?" I asked Karlander one night. Our relationship was unpleasant. Karlander, seven years my elder, retired as a player following the 1976-1977 season. He played in 212 NHL games, scoring 36 goals and adding 56 assists (92 points) in 212 games. He also played 269 WHA games, netting 60 goals and adding 111 assists (171 points).

I considered Stingers GM Ron Ryan a fine gentleman, but he never came to my defense for more playing time. Ryan had coached the New England Whalers (1973-75). He and Karlander played who they wanted to play or who Jack Kelley, the Whalers GM, told them to play. I received limited minutes in twenty games, scored one goal, added one assist, and accumulated 79 penalty minutes.

Despite my problems with Karlander, life in Cincinnati was good. Remember, I was on a one-way contract with U.S. currency. I was living the dream. Yes, I was disappointed playing in the Central

Hockey League and not in the NHL but still hopeful of realizing my boyhood goal of playing in the NHL. I lived on Mt. Adams, a beautiful apartment in a grand old home. I went to The Blind Lemon for drinks and The Rookwood Pottery for dinner. The Blind Lemon had an outdoor bonfire in its courtyard, a little touch of Vermont in Ohio. While in Cincy, I even attended the deadly The Who concert when eleven people were trampled and killed as they rushed for the best seats at the then named Riverfront Coliseum. I was there and saw the stampede and left immediately. When I got home, I saw all the ambulances from my apartment's balcony overlooking Riverfront.

During early November, the Stingers embarked on a two-week road trip without me. I was told to stay in Cincinnati. Being left home might sound like a disappointment, but it ended up being a godsend because I went to a boxing gym every day and sparred with several fighters, including Aaron Pryor, who later became the World Junior Welterweight Champion. I also boxed with Eddie Mustafa Muhammad. I became a curiosity to them: a big white kid in an all-black gym, hitting the bag and looking for ring time.

I ran and worked out hard in those days. I had dropped some weight, from 210 down to 195 pounds. I had strength, endurance, and toughness, plus some frustration and fury that I wanted to unleash on someone, anyone. That all factored into making me intriguing to the gym's promoter who wanted me to become a full-time boxer and turn pro. I wanted to do it but couldn't, being under contract with Quebec.

In a twist of fate, when the Stingers returned from their road trip, Quebec got in trouble with the Bruins and needed some extra muscle. There had been a testy game two days before Thanksgiving Day 1979 between Quebec and Boston in which Weir had fought both Terry O'Reilly and Al Secord—all because Nordiques' center Robbie Ftorek had sliced Bruins right winger Bobby Schmautz with a stick while defending himself from this known hatchet man. Boston wanted revenge against Ftorek and they thought they were going to get it on Thanksgiving when the two teams met again for Round Two, this time at the Boston Garden in my hometown of Boston.

I was just the muscle they needed. My promotion to the Nordiques came at the perfect time. I was in excellent shape and had improved as a fighter in the brief time I spent under the watchful eyes of Pryor, Muhammad, and their managers. When promoted to the

Quebec Nordiques to play against Boston in my hometown, I had some business to take care of.

First, I stopped by the hotel where the Nordiques were staying to kiss coach Jacques Demers smack dab on the face. Next, I stopped by the hospital to see Christos Kaldis. Christos was an eight-year-old boy who lived two doors away from the home Jan and I had bought down on Cape Cod. He loved sports, especially hockey, and often stopped by the house during summer of 1979. He'd sit there in my garage, which I had turned into my own mini-gym with my free weights and the heavy bag Coach Crocker had given me at Penn.

I also shot pucks in the driveway and several of the neighborhood kids, including Christos, joined me. We'd all end up playing a street hockey game together. I began to notice Christos often looking fatigued and not acting his normal self as the summer continued. I asked his sister about it.

"He has leukemia," she told me.

It had been a little more than two years since I had said goodbye to my friend Barry Ashbee, who died of leukemia briefly after being diagnosed in May of 1977. It all was difficult to digest. I was a strong, healthy professional hockey player. I didn't truly understand the destruction of cancer, although I learned approximately two decades later when my own colon cancer ate away at my body and muscles.

I knew I had to do something for Christos, even if it was to take him out for pizza. I sat down with him one day and asked a simple question.

"If you had the chance to do anything in the world what would it be?" I asked him.

"I want to play in the National Hockey League," he replied.

I made some calls to friends in the NHL and pro hockey who lived on or near Cape Cod. We scheduled a game at Falmouth Arena. It lasted about an hour. I played. So did New York Rangers enforcer Nick Fotiu, Rangers right wing Anders Hedberg, and goalie Wayne Thomas. Christos Kaldis was an NHLer on the ice that day. We all had fun. We were boys playing the game we loved. Cancer was an afterthought. We enjoyed a clambake at Fotiu's house afterward.

Christos died on December 30, 1979, only five days before what would have been his ninth birthday. I felt horrible at his funeral. His parents buried him at Ancient Cemetery in Yarmouth Port in one of my hockey sweaters. His tombstone has two hockey sticks on it. I still think of Christos occasionally and my eyes fill up with tears. He didn't deserve what he got.

I did get to see Christos a little more than a month before he died, thanks to that promotion to Quebec to play Boston at Boston. "Watch me on the TV when I play the Bruins," I told him. "I'm going to wave to you. I promise."

It was time to live my boyhood dream, with Christos Kaldis deep in my thoughts and in my heart. When I finally got to stand on Boston Garden ice, no one but me would know the many reasons why I would not go down this night.

## CHAPTER 11: The Big Show

"Ya wanna go?"

Those were the three words Boston Bruins enforcer Terry O'Reilly said to me as he stared me down during the second period of a Thanksgiving Day game between the Bruins and my Quebec Nordiques at the Boston Garden on November 22, 1979. Or maybe I said them to Terry first. His version and mine differ. Either which way, we were both willing combatants.

"You're not the only Irishman in the building tonight," I replied, ready to duke it out with the 6'1", 200-pound bruiser. I had finally earned a promotion to the Nordiques, making that contest my first National Hockey League regular season game. The road there had been a lengthy one. Nobody had given me much of a shot to make the NHL. The only reason I still was playing hockey was because I fought. To that date, I had had accumulated 745 penalty minutes in 169 games combined between the NAHL, NEHL and AHL as well 288 penalty minutes in 65 WHA games. I fought opponents and teammates and managers and coaches. I fought against that inner voice that asked whether I really had what it took. I fought all of those battles and had finally won the war—my first NHL regular season game.

I certainly hadn't realized my dream of making the NHL because of a Wayne Gretzky-like scoring ability, but rather, my big boxing hands, innate toughness, extreme determination, love for hockey, and willingness to fight whenever, wherever, and whomever. When someone asked "Ya wanna go?" I never hesitated to reply, "Absolutely." I had proved all the doubters and haters wrong.

That propensity to fight led Nordiques' General Manager Maurice Filion to add me to his roster for that game; he needed an extra enforcer after a testy game between Quebec and Boston two days earlier. Boston wanted revenge against Ftorek, a former star at Needham High in Massachusetts. Ftorek had been a friend of mine from our days playing together the previous season with the Cincinnati Stingers of the WHA. It was my job to protect him.

It was more than professional; it was personal. I refused to let any Bruin put a finger on Ftorek. Then, when O'Reilly stuck his stick into the back of Weir's knee, jabbing him slightly, I took it as an invite—and I stepped between them.

"Are you going to fight him or me?" I asked O'Reilly. O'Reilly and I dropped the gloves and began jockeying for position. I waited for him to get in tight and close to me to prevent him from throwing his devastating overhand lefts. We continued to battle for position, then the two linesmen, Gerry Gauthier and Randy Mitton, jumped between us. Referee Dave Newell sent O'Reilly and me to the box for two minutes each for delay-of-game penalties.

As I sat in the box mentally preparing for the fight that would soon happen with O'Reilly, I asked Boston goalie Gerry Cheevers to pass me a water bottle. Cheevers didn't start that night. Gilles Gilbert was in net for Boston. At the old Boston Garden, the Boston bench and penalty box were "side by each," as they say in Quebec. Cheevers, right beside me, refused to pass the water bottle. He instead squirted it at me.

"Okay, wise guy," I told Cheevers, knowing a lot about my former idol, including that he owned racehorses. "When this game's over, I'm going up to your house in Lynnfield and I'm going to burn it down and shoot your [bleeping] horses." I never let anyone give me crap. The tougher and more chippy a game, the more to my liking.

After our matching penalties expired, O'Reilly and I squared off. That was when he said those three words: "Ya wanna go?"

Absolutely. A lifetime of dreams hinged on that very moment. I wasn't going to let him knock me down—and I didn't. I never looked at hockey fights in terms of wins and losses, but, instead, as rounds as in a boxing match—except, in hockey, the next round happens during a later shift or when our two teams would meet later that season.

"We're going to kick your ass," Gary Doak said, skating at me after I finished fighting O'Reilly.

"Do yourself a favor, go back to the bench because I'm only fighting the heavyweights tonight," I replied to the 5'11", 175-pound

Doak. I not only fought O'Reilly, but also slugged it out with Stan Jonathan and Al Secord during the third period.

I'd developed strategies to fight every opponent. I fought Jonathan the exact opposite way than I did O'Reilly. I didn't want Jonathan to get in tight. I wanted him farther away from me. I let Jonathan throw me against the dasher. When he did, I extended my arms out because of my long reach. Jonathan, one of the toughest men I've ever fought, was 5'8" so his reach was shorter than mine. I needed to keep him away because I had seen the damage he could do inside with uppercuts before, especially when he fought Pierre Bouchard of the Canadiens. Bouchard took a tough loss but I studied that fight and used it as my own lesson plan.

I'm told that during one of the fights that Thanksgiving night, my mother turned to my father and said, "We didn't bring him up to act like that. It must have been something in his food."

By night's end, I had fought the hat trick of Bruins tough guys and earned an ovation from the Garden crowd in the process. Maybe everyone knew that I was a Boston kid even though I donned a Nordiques sweater. Maybe they just liked seeing the fights. Or maybe they all just recognized and respected my determination.

As I left after being assessed an automatic game misconduct by referee Dave Newell, I waved and the cameras caught it. I was waving to my eight-year-old buddy Christos Kaldis who was watching from his hospital room. I hope he enjoyed that night as much as I did. People probably thought I was showboating. I did do some showboating that night and throughout my career. That was just my style. I had waved up to my family and friends in the stands when skating out during warm-ups, but that final wave was for Christos.

The Nordiques lost 7-4 to the Bruins and my family had no big celebration for me after my first NHL game.

The team stayed in Boston before leaving for Hartford the following morning to play a game against the Hartford Whalers on Saturday, November 24. I went home with my parents and stayed in Jamaica Plain for the night, ate some leftover turkey, then went to bed, sleeping in the bed I had throughout my childhood. My father never said a word to me about the game. He just looked at me, winked, nodded, and touched me on my back.

I didn't play against Hartford, a 4-4 tie, that Saturday. After the game against the Whalers, we chartered back to Quebec for a November 25 showdown with the Washington Capitals. I dressed, took the warm-up, and then Demers—about halfway through the first period—sent a line out but recalled one of the wingers back to the bench in favor of me. I got to skate from the bench all the way to the far corner to take my position for the faceoff.

The fans in Quebec gave me a standing ovation. They liked what I had done in Boston and I liked the way they thanked me. I'm an emotional guy. I cry. I've cried often reflecting on my life while working on this book. It's a cheaper form of therapy—maybe one I needed in some regard.

As the Colisée de Québec crowd roared, I raised my stick to show my appreciation. Mike Gartner—who had played with me in Cincinnati the year before—was a member of the Capitals and he laughed. He said something like, "I guess they like you here, Stew."

As I said before, Demers might not have been the best X and O hockey coach ever, but he knew how to treat his players and make them feel valued. He picked the best spot to put me out there. He knew how the crowd would react and he wanted me to have that moment. That was a fantastic moment and I will always be grateful to Jacques, Andre Boudrias, Marcel Aubut, Maurice Filion, and my friend, Robbie Ftorek. A special thanks to Bobby Schmautz. If he wasn't such a stick man, I might not have had this night of nights.

Filion and Demers optioned me back to Cincinnati following the game against Washington and I felt no disappointment when they did. After all, I had achieved my lifelong goal of playing in the National Hockey League and had fought the Bruins hat trick of tough guys in the process. What more could an underdog, a tough boy from Dorchester who bled hockey, have asked for out of life?

Upon my return to the Central Hockey League, Cincinnati coach Al Karlander, who had hardly talked with me during my first stint with the Stingers that year, was effusive and shook my hand. What a fraud, huh? I hate that. Still, he began treating me a little bit better during my second stint and I played a little bit more. But my stay in Cincy lasted briefly.

One December day, I received a call from former Cincy teammate Tim Sheehy who told me the Stingers were about to fold that night because the Hartford Whalers had decided to send their minor league players to the Springfield Indians of the AHL. The Stingers consisted largely of Hartford-controlled players so the organization didn't have enough personnel to continue. As Nordiques property, I had no idea where I would end up playing.

Approximately a week before Sheehy called me, we had played a game in Birmingham against the Bulls. Management there had held a Bulls T-shirt giveaway night and I had taken one of the tees. After Sheehy's call—knowing the Stingers were about to fold and that the Bulls had a player-friendly coach in John Brophy and always were scratching for players—I packed my Bulls T-Shirt and headed to Riverfront Coliseum for that night's home game against the Oklahoma City Stars.

The Stars had 5'10", 186-pound tough guy Ted Olson, a sixth-round Boston Bruins draft pick in 1976 who accumulated 435 minutes in penalties playing for the Edmonton Oil Kings of the Western Hockey League during the 1973-74 season. Olson and I fought during the third period. As I sat in the penalty box, I decided to get tossed from the game early. The only thing that separated me and Olson were the game timers and a small piece of glass.

"Move your seats forward a little bit," I told the timers. They did and I walked right behind them as the play continued down in the far end of the rink. As all eyes remained focused down the other side of the ice, I reached over the glass and grabbed Olson's sweater and smoked him. The fight continued, punches were thrown, and we both received game misconducts. Olson was tough as nails and had a head like concrete.

Central Hockey League President Bud Poile (a Hockey Hall of Fame inductee and the father of current-day Nashville Predators President of Hockey Operations and General Manager—and fellow Class of 2018 U.S. Hockey Hall of Fame inductee—David Poile) attended the game and held a press conference afterward to announce the Stingers were folding. With my hand swelled up and an ice pack wrapped around it because I had missed Olson with one punch and instead hit the glass, I went to the press conference wearing my Birmingham Bulls T-Shirt. A reporter asked me if I already had joined the Bulls. I pointed to the T-shirt and told him I was headed home to Cape Cod for Christmas (it was about three days before Christmas).

"But maybe I'll end up with Birmingham after that," I told him.

I drove from Cincinnati to Pittsburgh and stayed overnight. I then drove home to Cape Cod, assembled a Christmas tree, and spent the holiday relaxing by the fire and not worrying about hockey.

In the meantime, Christos Kaldis died of leukemia. I was sad for all of that sadness, but happy I was there to offer the family my support. Hockey was not even an afterthought.

Fortuitously, on January 3, 1980, the Detroit Red Wings traded Dave Hanson to the Minnesota North Stars and a spot opened in Birmingham. The Bulls literally called me the next day and, just like that, I was a member of Birmingham, which had a roster that included Paul Henderson, Reggie Lemelin, and Jimmy and Harvey Bennett. Birmingham was a hodgepodge team. It consisted of a bunch of different players from different organizations, sort of like the Arizona Fall League in baseball. Henderson was a Christian athlete and gave me a bible when I got there. He gave me a television for my apartment as well as sheets, pillowcases, and towels because I had nothing but a suitcase of clothes and skates when I arrived there. Bennett, a 6'4" monster, had an unfortunate mishap while I was there. He reached over his head one day to retrieve a saline solution for his contacts and he instead ended up putting some other type of cleaning solution in his eyes. I ended up having to hold him down while the trainer flushed his eyes out.

When I arrived in Birmingham, the staff paid for me to live in a hotel and I told the team's public relations rep that I needed to find a car.

"Go over to Bart Starr's Lincoln-Mercury dealership," he told me. He drove me over there, and Starr was there. I got talking with him. Starr, the four-time Pro Bowler and two-time Super Bowl MVP (1966, 1967) with the Green Bay Packers, was a little like me in a way because his ability had been overlooked. A University of Alabama graduate, he wasn't drafted until the 17th round and 200th overall in 1956 NFL draft. We developed a rapport.

"What kind of car do you like?" asked the retired Hall of Fame quarterback and Montgomery, Alabama native.

"I like that red Cougar right there," I replied.

"It's all yours. Just don't whack it," he told me. He gave me the keys and I drove away in a red Lincoln-Mercury Cougar, able to use it courtesy of Starr for the time I was in Birmingham.

Someone must have been jealous because, soon after, I found my oil pan drained outside the rink. I noticed the oil under the car. I went to the store and bought a plug and five quarts of oil and filled up the Cougar. From then forward, I parked the car in the Zamboni pit.

My highlight from my brief ten-game stay with the Bulls came when we rolled into Dallas, Texas to play the Dallas Black Hawks. The Black Hawks had Jeff Bandura, a tough-as-nails 6'1", 195-pound Vancouver Canucks second-round draft pick who was strong and wiry. He ran into one of our smaller players and I didn't appreciate that. I can't remember what he did, but we went at it, swinging our sticks at each other before getting tossed. He walked into the Dallas dressing room. I walked into the visitors' locker room. I quickly removed my skates and went right into the Dallas dressing room, charging at Bandura without saying a word. We fought, throwing a couple punches each before being separated.

The Dallas police considered charging me with assault. While being ushered out the door, I reminded Bandura of the Black Hawks' upcoming game in Birmingham.

Round two came, this time in Birmingham, and it was definitely not pretty. Before the game, I filed the front of my helmet with a rasp, roughing the exterior. Every time Bandura threw a punch, I ducked so his hand hit my helmet. His hands bruised so badly that I felt bad and apologized to him after the game while he underwent treatment in the medical room.

I ran into Bandura during the 1983-1984 season when I reffed in the American Hockey League and he played for the AHL Maine Mariners. I asked him how his hands felt and we shared a friendly laugh. He was a tough kid only trying to make a living, and I respected him for it.

After that game against Dallas in Birmingham, coach John Brophy summoned me into his office, telling me he had good and bad news. The good news: the Nordiques had recalled me. The bad news: I was headed to Quebec where it was 10 degrees Fahrenheit compared to 70 degrees in Birmingham. But everything he said to me was music to my ears. After all, I was headed back to the NHL. I never expected to return to Quebec. I figured the Nordiques weren't going to bring me back. I expected to finish the year in Birmingham and for Quebec to then buy me out at the end of the season. But the

Nordiques lost to the Bruins 7-2 on February 2, 1980—they got the shit kicked out of them—Ftorek and Marc Tardif asked Filion to bring back the Cat.

I remained with Quebec for the rest of the season and did the best job I could. I knew why I was there. I knew my place.

Approximately four months after my first NHL game, the Nordiques played the Kings in Los Angeles during the week of my 27th birthday. Demers walked over to me at the hotel and handed me a room key.

"I want to shake your hand," he told me. "You've done nothing but good stuff since you've been here." The key, Demers' birthday present to me, was for a presidential suite that had everything in it: a fruit basket, bottle of champagne, basically, everything but then-United States president Jimmy Carter.

I think back on that moment in Los Angeles often and remember how, just four years earlier, I had been cut from the varsity hockey team at the University of Pennsylvania. Who laughed the hardest? Who laughed last? Who got the most out of his ability? Nobody can take away that moment in Los Angeles from me. It is one of the best moments in an incredible, humorous, difficult (and often bloody) journey called my life.

As the Nordiques were boarding a plane one day, the customs officer called our names aloud.

"Tardif. LeDuc. Lacroix. Stewart. Wait. What? Stewart? Are you with the Nordiques? I thought all the Nordiques were French?"

"Not the tough ones," I quipped and winked. "They had to go to Boston to find a tough guy."

I had fun in Quebec. I really did. By now, Weir and Brackenbury had become my friends. All of the negative feelings that had existed during training camp disappeared and we became friends as well as teammates. We are still friends to this day. When my dad came with us on a road trip one time, Brackenbury and my dad hit it off immediately. They had so much fun together, talking sports and skating in the morning skates.

Bobby Schmautz, who had been part of the bad blood between Quebec and Boston earlier that year leading to my initial first NHL stint, had since been traded from the Boston Bruins to the Edmonton

Oilers and then to the Colorado Rockies. When our Nordiques rolled into Colorado, Ftorek still felt he had to keep an eye out for Schmautz. My job was to keep Schmautz away from Ftorek at all costs.

"Don't worry, Robbie," I said. "Schmautz won't get anywhere near you." Demers had warned me about the possibility of Schmautz trying to stir more trouble. I surely wasn't afraid of Schmautz or anyone.

Don Cherry coached Colorado and I skated by the Rockies' bench during pregame warm-ups. "Hey, Don, will you do me a little favor?" I said, loud enough for everyone to hear. "Can you put Schmautz out there against me?" Cherry looked at me sort of strangely and then I nodded at the coach.

As Schmautz and I skated in different directions, I pretended not to see him and then ran into him with a forearm shiver to the sternum, driving him back probably ten feet. What I did was not necessarily wrong, but also not necessarily right either. I could have hurt him. If I raised the forearm up another three inches, I could have taken his head off, but I wasn't like that.

In retrospect, I wish I had.

He bounced up quickly and rushed toward me, trying to spear me with his stick. He nearly sliced me in the eye. He did gash me in the face. He and I jousted using our sticks, then both of us were given matching game misconducts. The Rockies bench was on the rink's northeast corner and my team's bench was on the southeast corner. A long corridor stood between leading to both team's dressing rooms.

I ran down the corridor in my skates and got to him before he could get into Colorado's dressing room. I tried to hit him, but he put his stick up and blocked it. Away we went. A photo of him and me standing in the hallway swinging our sticks at each other appeared in *The Denver Post* the next day. I was (and am) against fighting with a stick, but not against him. Not under those circumstances.

I didn't care that I got ejected. My job was to keep Schmautz away from Ftorek and I succeeded in doing so. Ftorek wasn't a fighter, although he could fight. But he was known for being a finesse player and obviously quite a successful one, with 77 goals and 150 assists in 334 games. With Schmautz no longer in the game, Ftorek played his style of hockey and that benefitted us as a team.

A year later, I ran into Schmautz at a charity golf tournament to benefit autistic children in Pawtucket, Rhode Island. He was on the putting green, and we got into it again. I swung my putter right at his head; I'm not proud of that. He put his putter up and blocked it, and Milt Schmidt stepped in between us. My job was to serve as an enforcer. Brackenbury, Weir, and Gilles Bilodeau were tough guys, but it wasn't in their nature to fight night after night. For me, fighting wasn't just part of my resume, it was part of my existence.

I had improved as a skater while with Quebec which later helped me immensely during my reffing career. Demers made me skate twice a day every day for forty to forty-five minutes with Andre Boudrias, who had just retired as a player and was a first-year assistant coach for the Quebec Nordiques in 1979-1980. A Montreal native, Boudrias had played 662 NHL games, scoring 151 goals and adding 340 assists. He also had twenty-two goals and forty-eight assists in 140 WHA games. He and Demers took the time to coach me, unlike some other professional coaches I had, to make me a better player. I appreciated it.

I scored two goals and didn't hurt the Nordiques. The only problem was I lost a couple of fights.

The first loss came against Canucks 6'1", 210-pound left winger Brent Ashton in Vancouver. He scratched the cornea in my eye and that was pretty much the extent of the fight.

Another fight I lost came against Philadelphia Flyers' Al Hill, who ran into me, so I followed him to the bench and swung a punch at him as he took a seat between shifts. Suddenly, there came six-foot Jack McIlhargey, six-foot three John Paddock, and six-foot three Behn Wilson skating directly at me. I began to wear a visor attached to my helmet after Ashton scratched my cornea. McIlhargey yelled to me to take the helmet off and fight him. I removed it. The fight happened at the 11:42 mark of the second period. "Bucky" struck me with a strong left and cut my face. The linesman later told me I had been pushed by either Paddock and Wilson, who had surrounded me, as McIlhargey cut and bloodied my face.

I remember wondering "Where are my teammates?" They were nowhere to be found. We had some great guys on that team, but we didn't possess much grit and toughness. That's probably why the 1979-1980 Nordiques finished 25-44-11 (61 points) and in fifth place in NHL's Adams Division. Ftorek was a terrific team player. He won the Player of the Week award and, with it, came a check for $1,000. He used it to take the team out to dinner. If everyone on the team thought and acted the way Robbie did, we would have won many more than twenty-five games.

The reason I was in the NHL was because of players like Ftorek. Players went after him because he was a bit of an agitator in his style of play. He was a nonstop go-getter, sort of like current-Bruins winger Brad Marchand, but taller and with more skill.

I was with Quebec for about fifty games, even though my stats show only twenty-one games played. I sometimes didn't dress. Other times when I did dress, I didn't receive any ice time. If you didn't touch the ice, they didn't count you as having played a game. I didn't make every road trip with the team. It was a much easier pill to swallow. I was still an NHL player and no one could take that away now. And I was playing in Quebec, a national league town with NHL fans. I loved being there.

During one of those road trips in which I remained in Quebec, a more high-profile teammate asked me to go skiing with him. This teammate had been left behind because of a minor injury. I promised him I would never mention his name when telling this story and so I will keep my word. But this story is too good not to tell.

He went skiing at Mont Sainte-Anne in Beaupré, Québec. He fell and twisted his knee on the slopes. Having difficulty walking, he panicked because he risked his contract being voided if the Nordiques learned he twisted the knee doing something non-hockey related. But I told him not to worry about it despite how our team was scheduled to return to town that very night and practice around 10 a.m. the next morning.

I picked him up about three hours before the practice. We arrived at the rink at about the same time as our trainers. I helped the player inside the side door and to his dressing room stall where he dressed. I then helped him onto the ice.

"Here's what we're going to do," I explained to him. "Stand here and just pass pucks to me. Just pretend you're here early helping me with my shot. Then, when the team skates out for to warm-ups, I'm going to run you over and make it look like an accident. You'll fall down and pretend to hurt your knee. They'll never know." We did just that. I pretended to not see him while skating. We were headed in different directions. I made it look like I plowed into him. All I did was fall on him a bit.

My final game with the Nordiques was uneventful. I actually feigned an injury before that game against Montreal. Teammate Reggie Thomas had played in thirty-nine games. He needed to play in forty games to receive his full pay. Management didn't want to give him the full pay so they had Demers hold him out of the final game in favor of me. I stumbled during warm-ups and pretended to sprain my ankle in an attempt to give Thomas his forty games played.

"No, you're dressing," I was told. I warmed the bench the entire game, going from left to right, right to left. I was asked to play the final six seconds. I said, "Jacques, I really would like to go out there, but I don't have my skates on anymore." I pointed to my feet. Since I hadn't skated a single shift all night, I took my skates off and sat on the bench in my hockey socks.

That game turned out to be my final one in the NHL.

It probably wouldn't have been if I hadn't tried to save my marriage the next year. After that game, I returned home to Cape Cod. In early June, I received a letter from the Nordiques management documenting its decision to release me. Included with the letter was a $33,000 check. I had known the Nordiques planned to release me. I had talked with Filion about returning for the 1980-81 season, but my contract called for me to be paid $70,000 American money. The Nordiques went with Kim Clackson for thousands less in Canadian money. There was a forty-percent difference on the dollar between American and Canadian money. It was a business deal. I understood it.

Quebec holds a special place in my heart. That organization gave me the chance to fulfill a life's goal. During my stay there, I was sitting in a restaurant with some teammates when then-Premier of Quebec, René Lévesque, sitting at a table nearby, recognized us and asked us to come over to drink with him.

"As an Englishman, do you have a problem being here in Quebec?" he asked me.

"Well, I'm not English, I'm American," I told him.

"Well, is being here a problem for you as an American?" he asked.

"No, because I'm in the home of hockey where Jean Beliveau and Guy Lafleur played," I remember telling him. "This, to me, is a great honor being able to participate in hockey in this province. Nobody appreciates the game as much, and the fact remains that I'm in the National Hockey League. But I'm going to tell you another thing. I've got somebody who talks for me up here."

"You have an interpreter?" he asked.

I pulled out an American dollar and put it down on the table.

"Nah, George Washington does all the talking," I said. "If you have enough of those, everyone pays attention."

Lévesque laughed. His English was as good as mine.

To be able to say I had a few drinks and talked politics with Lévesque is one of those milestone moments or Forest Gump moments where I reflect on now and think, "Holy smokes!"

I had been one-hundred percent truthful with Lévesque. I loved playing there because I appreciated hockey and the opportunity. Many years later, I showed my appreciation to Quebec in 2008 when asked to ref an old-timers game between former NHL players to celebrate the fiftieth anniversary of the Quebec Pee-Wee Tournament. Each player was introduced individually and a spotlight followed him on the ice as he skated to his team's blue line. The final three in the runway waiting for introductions were Mark Messier, Mario Lemieux, and me.

I asked Lemieux and Messier which of us three would receive the loudest ovation. Lemieux just smirked slightly. Mess said that Lemieux would receive the most boisterous of cheers because he is a native of Montreal.

I respectfully disagreed.

"I'll bet the two of you dinner at Cafe de la Paix that I receive the loudest ovation and that it will be bigger than both of yours combined," I told them.

They looked at me like I head two heads and we all laughed. Messier received a warm ovation. Lemieux then received an approximately one-minute ovation. Everyone stood and clapped. Quebec residents take a great deal of pride in the sons of their city. The people just didn't stop cheering. They appreciated Lemieux. Then my turn came.

"And now for the referee of tonight's game, a former Nordique,

Number 22, a former NHL referee, Quebec's Paul Stewart," the announcer called out.

I skated out between both teams to center ice and received a weak ovation. When I arrived at center ice I did a little figure skater-style stop with one foot. I looked at Lemieux and Messier. They stood next to each other smirking at me.

Not so fast, boys! I stopped and put my hands up over my head, then unzipped my referee sweater and took it off. Underneath, I wore my old Nordiques jersey.

The place went nuts. I skated around the whole rink and everyone stood and cheered. A picture ran in *Hockey News*. As I skated by Messier and Lemieux, I said, "And I think I'll have some wine with dinner tonight."

Marcel Aubut and other team officials from when I'd played for the Nordiques were sitting in the VIP section and they just really got a kick out of it and appreciated the gesture. Yes, I was having some fun. Yes, I like to ham it up sometimes. But I also wanted the people of Quebec to understand that I was so proud that I had been a Nordique.

I always felt badly that the team was taken from the fans and moved to Colorado. The reasons for the move were obvious. The arena was small and didn't include all of the amenities of a modern arena. But it also was because of the political climate and the decreasing economy. The Nordiques had trouble signing players and the city refused to pay for a new arena. I felt like players' refusal or reluctance to play for Quebec showed disrespect. For me, I was grateful for the opportunity and always appreciated playing there. Quebec always will hold an important place in my heart.

## CHAPTER 12: Dark Times

My life spiraled out of control after my NHL playing career ended, a descent so great I contemplated taking my service revolver, sticking it in my mouth, and pulling the trigger. At the time, I had been working several jobs, including serving as a reserve police officer down on Cape Cod. I was trying to find my niche outside of hockey.

The pistol sat there on my lap. I glanced in the mirror and felt disgusted with myself and my life. But I also realized if I quit—in other words, if I killed myself—the people who always doubted me would win. I put the gun down and stood up. I ended up giving the pistol to my brother to hold because I just didn't trust myself with it at that time.

My descent to rock bottom began when Jan and I returned to our Cape Cod home after the Quebec Nordiques' final game of the 1979-80 season. I began searching for a new organization in early June after the letter arrived from the Nordiques documenting their decision to release me and buy out my contract. The Buffalo Sabres and Chicago Blackhawks quickly became the two front-runners. Chicago head coach Keith Magnuson expressed interest in signing me. Magnuson, a Saskatchewan native, served as a Blackhawks enforcer from 1969-80. He played just three games during the 1979-80 season and then served as a Blackhawks assistant coach before being promoted to head coach the next season. Magnuson was in search of some muscle to add to his team. I respected him greatly, but I, instead, accepted an invitation to Sabres' training camp.

Buffalo's roster included 6'4" defenseman/tough guy Larry Playfair. The Sabres had selected Playfair thirteenth overall in the 1978 draft, but they also were looking to add some additional muscle. That's where I entered the picture.

Training camp went well. Then-Buffalo General Manager Scotty

Bowman invited me to the chalet that he used as his office with then-head coach Roger Neilson and assistant Jim Roberts. The three offered me a two-year, two-way contract with the potential to earn $60,000 with Buffalo or $25,000 if optioned to the Sabres' American Hockey League affiliate, Rochester. The deal included a bonus if I played a certain number of games with Buffalo. Bowman planned to option me to Rochester to begin the 1980-1981 regular season because he didn't need me in Buffalo immediately. Never before had I been offered a two-way contract. I mulled over the contract offer and knew it was a great opportunity. I called my wife at our home in Cape Cod.

"No, I won't go," she said. Jan was tired of bouncing from one city to another. She wanted us to settle down, stay in one place, and raise children. She disliked frequently packing our bags and changing organizations. She delivered a straightforward ultimatum: Quit hockey or end the marriage.

I made my decision. I had worked at a radio station on the Cape during the summer of 1980 and management there offered me a permanent gig before I left for training camp with the Sabres. With the radio station offer still on the table, I decided to return home to my wife to save our marriage. The decision eventually backfired, leaving me not only without hockey, but also without a wife—but with plenty of resentment.

I ceded to my wife's wishes. During the entire drive to Saranac Lake Airport (now the Adirondack Regional Airport) I knew I was making a mistake. I wanted to return to Bowman and ink the deal he'd offered me. After all, I was a hockey player. I always had been a hockey player since my days as the Boston Arena rink gofer. Any wife who couldn't accept that fact probably shouldn't have been my wife in the first place. I understood she had her own goals for our relationship, but marriage involves compromise and sacrifice both ways. She knew what hockey meant to me. I think she should have given me more time to pursue my dream.

A young adult only has so many years to chase his or her personal goals and dreams. That's something both people in a relationship must realize. Each partner needs to sacrifice for each other. But, ultimately, the decision was mine.

My clock for playing pro-hockey was ticking, and, apparently, her biological clock was ticking equally loudly for her. To me, we could have started a family in Rochester or Buffalo, if not right away, then soon after. Maybe I should have tried harder or communicated my message in a better way. I'm not perfect. I'm at fault for what happened. As I mentioned before, I was in love with Jan, but I'd felt lonely at Penn and was in need of acceptance. She made me feel less lonely. That's one of the reasons I married her. Loneliness is not a reason to marry someone.

I boarded the plane and my downward spiral began. My wife wanted kids. I wanted hockey. I thirsted for it. That thirst only intensified being separated from the game at the professional level.

Back on Cape Cod as a radio host, I conducted several prominent on-air interviews with legends such as New York Yankees owner George Steinbrenner, long-distance runner Johnny Kelley (who ran the Boston Marathon a record sixty-one times and won twice), heavyweight boxing champ Joe Frazier, middleweight boxing champ "Marvelous" Marvin Hagler, boxing trainer/manager Goody Petronelli, and baseball stars Joe Cronin and Pete Rose. Rose, whom I befriended in Cincinnati, appeared on my show just days after he and the 1980 Philadelphia Phillies beat the Kansas City Royals for Philadelphia's first World Series championship in franchise history.

I had a Rolodex filled with contacts from having been a professional hockey player. I used those contacts to my advantage in the radio business. I enjoyed hosting the show, but it aired for only one hour a day and just three days a week, meaning I wasn't earning much money. I was forced to find additional work.

From 1980 to 1983, I worked more odd jobs than most others probably do in a lifetime. I served as a year-round reserve police officer in Yarmouth, a car salesman at Mid-Cape Ford, and an evening manager at a Laundromat a friend owned near the Ford dealership. I also found work scrubbing bathrooms, cleaning rugs, and selling advertising. From my perspective, Jan was never satisfied with the combined income I was earning from these several jobs. I remember her commenting that she could not run the house on the money I earned. Those comments angered me, especially because I turned down fairly good money from the Sabres in favor of the "normal" life she felt we needed in order to stay together.

I grew tired physically from juggling all of my jobs simultaneously.

Even with tons of coffee, I occasionally nodded off when my partner drove during those dark winter nights on patrol. It was difficult not to nod off. I even napped on the couch at the car dealership, trying to maintain the pace.

I lost the radio gig during summer 1981. I wanted to perform color commentator duties for Cape Cod League baseball games alongside then-Boston Bruins announcer Fred Cusick doing play-by-play. I thought it would be nice for fans to have games to listen to during the 1981 Major League Baseball strike, baseball's fifth work stoppage in the span of a decade. The program manager's decision to include me in the Cape League broadcasts was an unwavering "No."

The station also had difficulty selling enough advertisement spots to support my sports talk show, and the program manager wasn't keen on doing more sports. Out the door I went with the dirty carpet.

I attempted to fulfill my craving for hockey by coaching the varsity team at Dennis-Yarmouth Regional High from 1981 to 1983. But fighting Terry O'Reilly, Stan Jonathan, and Al Secord in the same game wasn't as tough as sparring with parents who think their kids all are future NHLers. We did help a few players into college and that certainly was a positive take-away from my time coaching there. I also learned about coaching first-hand, which eventually helped me when I became an NHL referee.

Needing more money in 1981 and regretting my decision to quit hockey, I attempted a comeback as a professional player. My wife didn't appear too upset about the comeback attempt because we needed the money. Bob Crocker, my former Penn coach, secured me a tryout with the AHL Binghamton Whalers. I made the team but played sparingly under my former Binghamton Dusters coach and then-Whalers coach, Larry Kish. I appeared in fifteen games, scored two goals, recorded one assist and accumulated fifty-nine minutes in penalties. While playing for the Binghamton Whalers briefly, I again crossed paths with NHL referee John McCauley. This chance encounter wound up transforming in my life.

In my very first encounter with John McCauley, he tossed me for accidentally pulling Philadelphia Flyers left wing Steve Short's hair during the exhibition game I played at Madison Square Garden for the New York Rangers on September 27, 1976. This time, John was reffing in the minors while working his way back to the NHL after suffering a severe eye injury. Following the final game of the 1979 Challenge Cup Series between the Soviet Union and the NHL All-Stars at Madison Square Garden, a crazed fan punched McCauley in the eye while he ate dinner across the street from the Garden. The assault caused nerve and muscle damage and resulted in McCauley suffering from double-vision and a loss of depth perception. After five surgeries, McCauley returned to the NHL as a referee on February 15, 1981.

But before his return to the NHL, he booted me from yet another game in Binghamton. As I skated off the ice, he told me to see him after the game. I did as he requested.

"You should think about coming over to our side when you're done playing," he told me after the game in the officials' dressing room. "You have the bloodlines."

I told him I'd think about it.

After fifteen games in Binghamton, I returned to Cape Cod. For a brief time, I latched on with the Cape Cod Buccaneers of the ACHL. I wasn't there very long, but it was an interesting experience as well as a painful reminder of just how far I'd fallen from the NHL.

In an odd twist of fate, while trying to make the best of my situation, I crossed paths with Vince McMahon Jr., the famous (some would say *in*famous) chairman of what is now called World Wrestling Entertainment. At the time, Vince Jr. was dabbling in the hockey business, having promoted games at the Cape Cod Coliseum (where he'd purchased an ownership interest) and then owning the short-lived Cape Cod Buccaneers of the Atlantic Coast Hockey League (1981—82). McMahon's interest in hockey was more financial than personal, having seen the sport's rabid and loyal following that was somewhat akin to the cult following that the pro wrestling business had at the time.

McMahon's vision for how to promote hockey was steeped in what he was familiar with from pro wrestling. He had been around hockey and its people just enough to know it was filled with some rather colorful characters, myself included. McMahon wanted us to magnify those natural personalities into something he could market. It was partially the same blueprint he also later unsuccessfully tried in football with the ill-fated XFL.

At any rate, Vince invited me to play for the Buccaneers and I did for five games. The team did not even last the full season, as McMahon decided to fold it early.

From the opening night of the season, McMahon was not happy with how the league was run. It was his belief that hockey could use more non-stop action and less structure. He liked the collisions and fighting, and wanted even more of those things (mind you, this was during the early 1980s, not all that long after the Broad Street Bullies and *Slap Shot*). Basically, McMahon dreamed of a league-developing hockey product that also had elements of roller derby and pro wrestling thrown in, minus the choreography and pre-determined outcomes.

Although never confirmed, it was rumored at the time that McMahon proposed the ACHL adopt some rather unconventional rules to make it stand out from other hockey leagues. Not a single one of his suggestions was approved. I don't know all the specifics, but one of his more well-known offbeat ideas that immediately got shot down was to eliminate things like offsides and icings from the rulebook so that the puck could be played anywhere by either team.

To McMahon's dismay, the ACHL turned out to be just another nondescript hockey bush league, just as its predecessor the Eastern League had been. There was plenty of fighting (and I knew Vince didn't want me for my dazzling hockey skills), but that really wasn't much different from most of the minor circuits of the time or even the NHL.

Furthermore, McMahon could not get along with any of the five other club owners in the seven-team league. Just about the only thing that that constantly bickering lot of men could agree on was that they all thought Vince McMahon, Jr. was a kook.

No, there was not a typo in the previous paragraph. There were seven teams in the league, but only six different team owners, because Schenectady and Fitchburg were both owned by Robert Critelli. McMahon was livid when he found that out. Fitchburg was placed under a league suspension and folded just six games into the season. The Schenectady team folded after nine games.

And then there were five...

McMahon's Cape Cod team, like all the others, hemorrhaged red ink. In January, 1982, McMahon requested a $15,000 loan from the league to keep the franchise afloat. The request was considered for about two-tenths of a second before it was denied. McMahon then folded the Buccaneers.

And then there were four...

With just four teams left in the league, everyone was now guaranteed of a playoff spot. So the format was changed to minimize travel and to have the two geographically closest teams play each other in the playoffs. As a matter of fact, the rest of the regular season was scrapped and the playoffs began shortly after the Bucs folded. Bill Horton's Mohawk Valley Stars won the championship.

So much for my short career as a Buccaneer. However, I was once recognized as a member of the team.

I was asked, "Hey, don't you play for the Cape Cod Buccaneers?"

I said, "Buckin' A right!"

Both McMahon and I moved on to much bigger and better things than the ACHL. I haven't spoken with him in over thirty years, but when his name pops up in the news, I sometimes glance at what's going on with him and his family.

With another failed foray back into hockey and now alone in Cape Cod, I drank more than I ever had. This behavior should have frightened me because my mother was a closet alcoholic. But it didn't because I lacked self-respect at that time. I wasn't happy. I didn't feel much hope. Drinking was just something to do. I hated the direction my life had taken. I began to get out of shape physically. I soon became everything I wanted never to be, and, to top it all off, I was earning less money than I would have with the Buffalo Sabres or their AHL affiliate, Rochester.

In addition to that, Jan and I had begun trying to have a child during the 1979-1980 hockey season. After a lengthy, unsuccessful stretch, our doctor suggested my sperm count be tested. I underwent the first test at Hôpital de l'Enfant-Jésus in Quebec where a nurse provided me with a cup, magazine, and private room. I leaned my back against the wall in this room and accidentally set off the help button. The nurse used an intercom to ask me, in French, if everything was okay.

"Do you need any help?" she asked in French.

"Sure, come on in," I told her. I've always had a quick wit. It runs in the Stewart family. Later, after yet another test at Cape Cod Hospital, it was diagnosed that I had little to no sperm count.

I was diagnosed with varicocele, which is an enlargement of the veins within the scrotum. This condition possibly resulted from Paul Baxter spearing me in the testicles during a World Hockey Association game when I played for Cincinnati and Baxter played for Quebec. Baxter stuck me so hard he broke my protective cup. The head of his stick injured my testicles. Later that game, Baxter skated around the net with the puck and I came off the wing, dropped my glove, and belted him as hard as I could, square in the face. A picture of Baxter with his head turned sideways appeared in a WHA publication. The bloodied Baxter needed to be helped off the ice. He struck me in the testicles and I punched him in the face. No love lost between us.

Baxter and I played together with the Nordiques in 1979-1980. We acted polite toward each other, but courtesy is not respect. I had little, if any, respect for the way Baxter played. He was a stickman like Bobby Schmautz. I never liked that. I didn't appreciate when Baxter stuck Bob Nystrom of the New York Islanders on February 27, 1980. Apparently, Nystrom did not appreciate it either because he turned around and beat the hell out of Baxter. I sat on the Nordiques bench silently pulling for Nystrom—and not my own teammate Baxter—because I can't fathom any reason to stick someone.

There's no actual way to tell whether Baxter's hit resulted in my condition. It's just a theory of mine. I underwent surgery to repair my testicles, but Jan and I never did have children together, thankfully. A litter of Airedale terrier puppies is all we ever raised. Our relationship grew quite distant and stale in our final months together. I attended my tenth Groton reunion alone. She didn't join me.

The straw that broke the camel's back came in 1982. Jan, yet again, told me over Saturday morning breakfast, before another grueling day at the dealership, that I wasn't making enough money. That's all I needed before a ten-hour shift drumming my fingers on the hood of some used car that I was trying to sell.

"You need to make more money," she reinforced. She had forced me to turn down a deal with the Buffalo Sabres that would have had us making plenty of dough!

*Snap*! I furiously pounded my hand on the table and almost entirely cut off my finger on a glass dish. I underwent multi-hour microsurgery and wore a cast for nearly four months because of my injury. Consider that the death knell of the marriage. Not long after, we sat at the dinner table together. After a long silence, she asked me if I wanted potatoes.

"No," I replied. "I want a divorce."

The happiness and love I'd felt when we first got together in 1973 was gone forever. I was confident it was done. I packed my belongings that evening and didn't look back. We proceeded with the divorce and sold the house. Everything about our marriage felt and appeared fine while I played hockey, although it probably wasn't as perfect as I imagined it to be. But when I quit, I stopped making money and things went south. All of the other issues we'd face became magnified.

Jan moved west. She packed her bags and made a new life in Denver, eventually marrying her brother's roommate. That and everything about it has passed. No hard feelings exist. It was so long ago, now. I think money, or a lack thereof, was the main issue. She maybe felt pressure from her parents, who were well-off and wanted the same for us. Ending the relationship wasn't as easy as I might have made it sound. It's not easy to break things apart after all those years together.

I don't blame her. I was the one who made the decision not to sign the Sabres' offer. I accept that now. But I had trouble accepting it then. I felt resentment toward her for not letting me pursue my hockey career.

A lot of people don't like me for leaving her, but I didn't want to remain in an unhappy and loveless relationship any longer. I am like my father in many ways, but he never left my mother despite her alcoholism and the destructive behavior that resulted from her excessive drinking. Maybe Dad should have left Mom, or maybe he shouldn't have. He made his own decision and I made my own decision. I couldn't continue on with Jan.

I dated another woman during the separation. Some friends and family thought I ended my marriage because of this other woman. I didn't leave my first wife for someone else. I left Jan because of who I had become. I couldn't get along with Jan anymore, mainly because I was filled with self-loathing and had no self-respect during that time. During our final few months together, I often thought about the relentless go-getter I had once been and the person I had become, spiraling out of control. I looked at the new me with disgust. You can't be good for another person when you aren't even good on your own.

Those underlying feelings were probably why my life hardly improved after we separated. I continued to experience regret and hostility. I felt like I had taken my life—everything I had worked so hard to achieve—and destroyed it. I didn't like selling cars. I didn't like working at a Laundromat. This is when I thought about killing myself. I stayed out drinking until the wee hours several mornings. My depression manifested from a hopeless feeling that I'd never be able to rectify my mistakes. I knew I'd never make it back to the NHL as a player.

With no hockey, no wife, no children, no house, I began to wither to nothing; I lost my will to fight. As then-*Sports Illustrated* writer Morin Bishop wrote about me in 1987, I lacked the urgent motivation that always before existed in me and made me tick. For the first time in my life, I had no goals. More than anything else, this scared the hell out of me because I flourish with challenge.

Coach Junie O'Brien from Groton confronted me. We had stayed close over the years. He knew I was depressed. He invited me to Boston to attend to a Bruins game. We went to the game together, then drank at a bar on Boylston Street. It was quite a night and a worse morning. I welcomed the sun as it rose over the curbstone. I was completely wrecked and Coach O'Brien sat with me. He stayed there as I hit rock bottom that very night. I wasn't a pretty sight. Junie told me I was thinking too much and drinking too much. I needed to get right with myself. I needed to talk to someone who could steer me back toward who I was or who I was capable of becoming. It was Coach O'Brien who suggested I see someone and talk about my problems.

"Paul, you have a lot more to give," he said. "There are people who have believed in you. Don't let them down by letting yourself down. You are tougher than that. Go see someone and talk it out." Back to the Cape I drove, knowing I needed to battle the demons head-on. My old coach from Groton, looking back, was a guardian angel sent to save me from myself.

I didn't feel like a weakling by scheduling an appointment with a psychologist because I knew I needed help. People bring cars to mechanics to be fixed. People hire plumbers to fix their sinks. I felt the same way about this. I was hiring a psychologist to help me fix my mind. People sometimes need to clear their cobwebs, and I had lots of thoughts dashing around my head making me confused. The psychologist and I met three, four, maybe five times. That's all. I wasn't in therapy long because the solution to my problem was rather simple except I was so wrapped up in my own self-pity I couldn't see what was patently obvious.

"If I had to put you any place in the world right now, where would you be the happiest?" the psychologist asked me.

"Drive me over to the rink," I replied. "I love being in the rink. I love being around the game and doing the things I did."

"I don't need to see you anymore then," the psychologist replied. "Go get yourself a job back in hockey. Become a scout. Run a skate shop. Sell hockey equipment. Just do something that involves hockey. Be where you're happiest."

And, just like that, my life started to get better again. I realized I could be Paul Stewart again. I just needed to figure what part of hockey I was best fit to have success.

I recalled John McCauley's advice and thought about reffing. After all, he was right: refereeing is in my bloodlines.

# CHAPTER 13: Donning the Stripes

I passed the AHAUS and National Ice Hockey Officials Association tests, becoming certified to officiate games. I started at the youth level and spent most games hoisting players over the boards. I reffed my first game along with a friend, Pat Twohig, at the Falmouth Youth Hockey Arena. I wore a pair of black pants I'd purchased the night before and a referee sweater borrowed from my dad. I earned five bucks for my first game.

Five dollars. Yes, just five hundred pennies. It wasn't much, but reffing felt right.

I officiated high school games on Cape Cod along with the usual youth hockey assignments. I received some prep school reffing assignments from local Massachusetts legend, Jack Etter, the athletic director at Browne & Nichols from 1956-1994. Jack coached football, basketball, and baseball, taught algebra and health science at the private institution in Cambridge. Etter, who died in March 2011, assigned officials for the private school league games. I knew him pretty well because he had played football and baseball for my dad at Boston English. He served as a Marine during a leave of absence from high school and then returned to finish his schooling.

Another friend, Anne Glover, with the ECAC, assigned me Division III college games as a fill-in referee. My assignments included Mass Maritime club team games and Bridgewater State varsity games. It wasn't anything major, but it was a start.

The divorce proceedings began in June, 1982 and took approximately six months to complete. When everything was signed and finished, I continued to sell cars and I stayed at my friends', George and Pam Kaplan's house. George Kaplan had graduated from Boston Latin and I recently had sold him and his wife, Pam, a car. He had worked for the State Department as an intelligence analyst, and he offered me the chance to stay at his home and live there while he and his wife were out of town on business, rent free.

His house was in New Seabury and I stayed there for six months. I kept it clean and did the yard work. I stayed there because, I promise you, I didn't have two dimes to rub together. I obviously wasn't making enough money from reffing so I continued to work several odd jobs.

I began working out again. I got back in terrific shape with the help of friend and former Cincinnati Stingers teammate, Tim Sheehy. Tim, a former Boston College and WHA star who played twenty-seven NHL games, was tough and a better fighter than most people will ever know. Nobody wanted to mess with him. He captained Team USA to the Silver Medal in the 1972 Olympics. Sheehy and I made a bet with each other on who could drop to under 190 pounds and finish the Falmouth Road Race in the fastest time. We both trained relentlessly for the race. I finished the seven-mile race in forty-two minutes, not bad at all, but not quite as good as Sheehy's time. I remember running up the final hill to Falmouth Heights and Sheehy booting it ahead of me because of our bet. Friends like the Tim Sheehy helped me realize I could and should do something to better my life.

Sheehy now works as a certified NHLPA agent at ICE Hockey Agency with his brother, Neil Sheehy, who also played in the NHL. Neil, a defenseman, starred at Harvard and played in 379 NHL games with Calgary, Hartford, and Washington. I once fought an exhibition three-round boxing match against Neil at On The Rocks, a bar on the Cape. Neil was captain of the Harvard Boxing Club at Harvard University. President Theodore Roosevelt and President John F. Kennedy also were once members of the boxing club. How could I pass up a chance to thump a Harvard guy? It also benefited the Jimmy Fund so it was all in good fun.

While moonlighting as a referee whenever I could find game assignments, I also continued with my full-time reserve police officer gig in Yarmouth. I started to gain back some of my urgency. I was making money, but also had aspirations of working my way up to becoming a Division I college hockey referee. My police officer duties included dispatch, booking, details at places such as Rascals and the Mill Hill Club, sitting in front of motels, and patrolling up and down the beach. I took the job seriously and considered making it a full-time vocation if the reffing didn't pan out as I had hoped.

I worked a detail almost every Friday and Saturday night at Rascals, which no longer exists. It was on Route 28 in West Yarmouth. When the small parking lot filled behind the bar, as it always did, patrons parked in a larger lot across Route 28. None of the other police officers enjoyed this detail, probably because it mainly consisted of crossing-guard duties, dealing with drunk college students who occasionally called the officers derogatory names such as "Summer Cop," "Asshole," and "Rent-A-Cop." This detail didn't bother me, though. I accepted every detail my superiors offered me.

One summer night working at Rascals, I recognized one of the college students, Kevin Mutch, a Boston University hockey player from 1981-1985. I had told his group to stand on the curb while I stopped traffic. Mutch didn't listen. He stepped out to the edge of the street and started to cross. I grabbed him and told him to stay on the sidewalk. He became a bit testy, mouthing some gibberish about kicking my ass and he resisted me. I grabbed his arm and then flipped his hand Aikido-style, turned his thumb down, putting him down on one knee. I cuffed one of his hands, walked him to the split-rail fence nearby and cuffed him to the post. I told the young woman with him to go home.

"He's coming with me," I told her. A few minutes later, when the bar cleared, I put Mutch in the backseat of a cruiser and we drove him home. He lived with two other hockey players that summer. I walked the partially-passed out Mutch into the house, uncuffed him, and dropped him into his bed. I left a note on his table.

It read, "I have your driver's license. Come see me at the station." The next day Mutch visited the station. "You never know who you're dealing with, do you?" I asked him. He didn't quite understand so I helped him: "I played in the NHL," I told him. "I know all about college hockey and I know those two chumps you're living with. If you ever do anything again to cause me a problem, I'll beat you to a pulp. By the way, I know your mother and father and they would agree."

Both ironically and sadly, Mutch was struck and killed by an automobile September 7, 1992. I attended his funeral where his mother told me her son would still be alive if I had been on the detail at Rascal's. I often think about that. Funny how life takes people in different directions. Kevin Mutch had a big smile; he was a nice kid. It was a waste that he died so young.

Police work helped prepare me for reffing. My neighbor back

then, Sergeant Harry Craig, worked as a Massachusetts State Trooper. His first advice to me was to keep my pistol in its holster unless I was prepared to fire. The two times I unholstered, I was prepared to fire, to do what I had to do. This concept of being judicious in doling out punishments was certainly analogous to refereeing. During my reffing career, I tended not to give many misconduct penalties, especially to coaches, because it's almost like firing a bullet: you can't take it back. Police can manage people without using or threatening lethal force; Referees can manage players and coaches without removing them from the game completely.

I went out to eat one night with some referee friends, Ed Buckler, Harry Craig, and Pat Twohig after we had attended a National Ice Hockey Officials Association meeting at Barnstable High on Cape Cod. Their message was straight to the point: they said I was wasting my time down on the Cape reffing games, selling cars, and working as a reserve officer. They thought I had enough talent to be reffing professional hockey and I should make it happen. But the idea of being an NHL ref seemed as improbable as a flight to Mars. All the same, I was intrigued.

I phoned Brian Petrovek, now the president of the AHL Adirondack Flames. At the time, he served as assistant commissioner of the ECAC. I inquired about reffing collegiate hockey. But Petrovek refused to help, citing the league never would want someone with my reputation working their college games. He said the type of player I had been would not best represent the good aspects of hockey.

"You'll pay to get in the next time you see me ref," I told Petrovek and then I hung up the phone. My family's officiating roots run way deeper than Petrovek's. College coaches in the northeast region used to send my dad their schedules. He assigned referees to all those games. I sat in the den with my dad, watching him rotary-dial every referee and go over their schedules one-by-one. And my grandfather, of course, was the first American-born NHL referee. I felt I deserved a little more respect from Petrovek. But now I had something to prove; I was determined to back up the statement I had made to him.

I have seen Petrovek since and have told him he's the one responsible for getting me to the NHL as a ref. It's partially true because, literally within one minute of hanging up the phone with Petrovek, I called my friend, Dale Hamilton, who served as then-Bruins

General Manager Harry Sinden's assistant. I asked her whom I should contact to inquire about reffing professionally in the NHL. She gave me Referee-In-Chief Scotty Morrison's phone number. Ironically, Harry Sinden's assistant, Dale, aided my return to the NHL as a ref. How did I repay the favor? I disallowed a Bruins winning goal during my first NHL game as a referee. We'll get to that.

I actually had chatted with Morrison in Philadelphia when I played for the AHL Philadelphia Firebirds in 1978-1979. I had been tossed from a game for fighting. I saw Morrison after showering and had walked upstairs to watch the rest of the game. Morrison was sitting by himself when I approached him. Not one to be shy, I introduced myself. We talked about the game. He told me he had known of my grandfather.

"If you think about it, maybe someday you can umpire or referee like him," Scotty said back then.

Approximately five years later on the phone with him, Morrison wanted to know if I truly was serious about reffing. I promised him I was and I'd do whatever it took. Morrison told me he and others would give me a look at Bruce Hood's officiating school if I could pay my own way to Milton, Ontario later that month.

I hardly ever asked my father for a dime, but I did this time, and, of course, he lent me the money for the trip to Ontario. A couple of days before I left, my father fell ill. He was diagnosed with prostatitis. His prostate was so enlarged that the doctors had to operate. My father's health had been deteriorating for years. He also suffered from Paget's disease, a thickening of the spine and the rib cage. The spongy bones compressed his lungs to the point where he had great trouble breathing. I felt terrible. My dad couldn't talk and had a tube in his throat. The doctors said he might die. He had such issues in the final years of his life but never complained.

I told my sister Pat about my hesitation to attend the Bruce Hood School in light of our dad's illness. Dad was about to undergo emergency surgery.

"You know better than me that, if he could talk, he'd tell you to go," my sister told me. "He'd say you have to go. You must be about your father's business." Funny, I think I also read that in the New Testament.

I left for the camp. My dad survived the surgery. He lived for another four years, in time to see me referee in the NHL.

Thanksgiving Night, 1979: Dorchester Hat Trick in my NHL debut. Did Terry O'Reilly say "Ya wanna go?" to me first or did I say it to him first? Either way, I am forever grateful to Terry for giving me a chance to prove myself. I told Terry, "You're not the only Irishman here tonight." He said, "I'm gonna kick your ass!" I responded, "Really? What part of Dorchester are you from?" *(Boston Globe photo)*

Sports have always been not just a passion but also a profession for the Stewart family, whether in hockey, baseball or football. Umpiring third base here, my grandfather Bill Stewart Sr. is in perfect position as the Dodgers' Jackie Robinson slides to the bag safely. My grandfather had been the first pro baseball player to enlist to serve in World War I. Robinson, apart from breaking the baseball color barrier, was a World War II veteran. My grandfather umpired four World Series and four Major League Baseball All-Star Games. *(Paul Stewart photo collection)*

My "Grampy," Bill Stewart Sr., was the first American-born coach to steer an NHL team – the 1937-38 Chicago Black Hawks, to the Stanley Cup championship. The team also featured eight American players. *(Paul Stewart photo collection)*

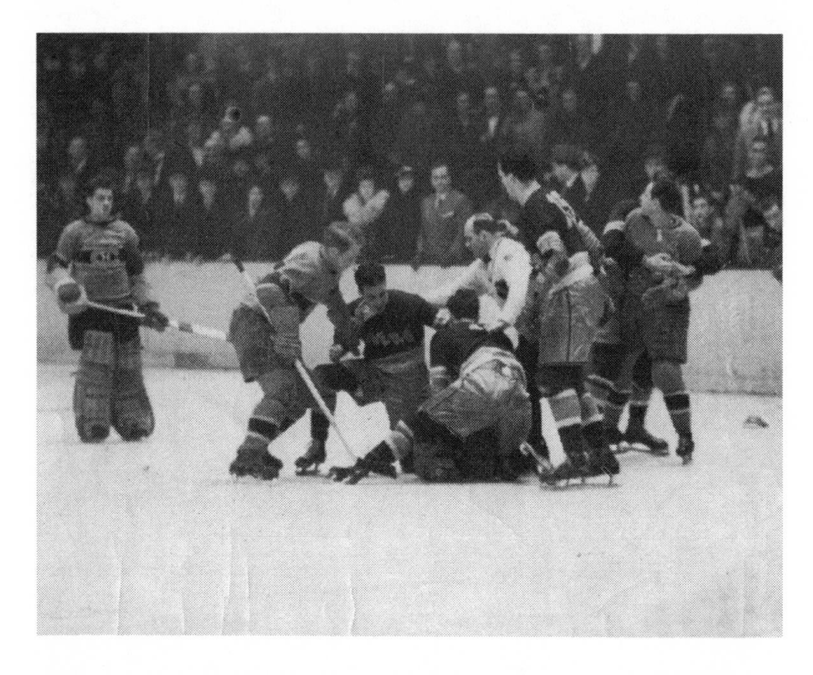

Before and after his Stanley Cup-winning coaching stint with the Chicago Black Hawks, my grandfather was an NHL referee. He refereed in five Stanley Cup Finals. In the late 1950s, he was the de facto general manager of the U.S. national hockey team. Grampy was posthumously elected to the U.S. Hockey Hall of Fame. If you ask me, he belongs in the Toronto Hall, too, in the Builder Category as well as the Baseball Hall of Fame for his prolific umpiring career. In this photo, Bill Stewart Sr. breaks up a fight in a game at the old Madison Square Garden. *(Paul Stewart photo collection)*

My two greatest role models and personal heroes: My dad, Bill Stewart Jr., is on the right, with my grandfather to the left. My dad was the apple of my grandfather's eye. *(Paul Stewart photo collection)*

Thanksgiving Day 1960: With my dad at Harvard Stadium after the English vs. Latin game. The team had just thrown us in the shower. I am at right in the photo. Wherever my dad was is where I wanted to be. When he asked me, "you wanna go?" whenever he was officiating, coaching or doing most anything, my answer was always, "Yes!" *(Paul Stewart photo collection)*

In this photo taken during my Groton days, I'm the catcher and my dad is the home plate umpire. He also refereed some of my hockey games. He called me for more than one penalty and rang me up on strikes a few times when I was at bat. That's as it should be. They were the right calls. *(Paul Stewart photo collection)*

The next Jean Beliveau? I wish. Here I am as a senior at Groton in 1972. *(Paul Stewart photo collection)*

University of Pennsylvania, 1975. Nice buckets, eh? Notice the neck brace I'm wearing. The Flyers' Barry Ashbee gave it to me. I had injured my neck after getting clubbed with a stick. *(Paul Stewart photo collection)*

Taking the ice before my first pro game with the NAHL's Binghamton/ Broome Dusters. No black eyes.... yet. *(Paul Stewart photo collection)*

Binghamton Dusters: From left to right: goalie Kenny "Dutch" Holland (my first pro hockey roommate, poor guy), Pierre Laganier, Randy MacGregor, and yours truly. *(Paul Stewart photo collection)*

Quebec Nordiques, 1979-80. Playing in the NHL and loving every day of it. *Je me souviens! (Paul Stewart photo collection)*

Wind Beneath My Wings: Signing an autograph with my dad right behind me. The two boys in front of me are my nephews, Scott and Chip McDonald. *(Paul Stewart photo collection)*

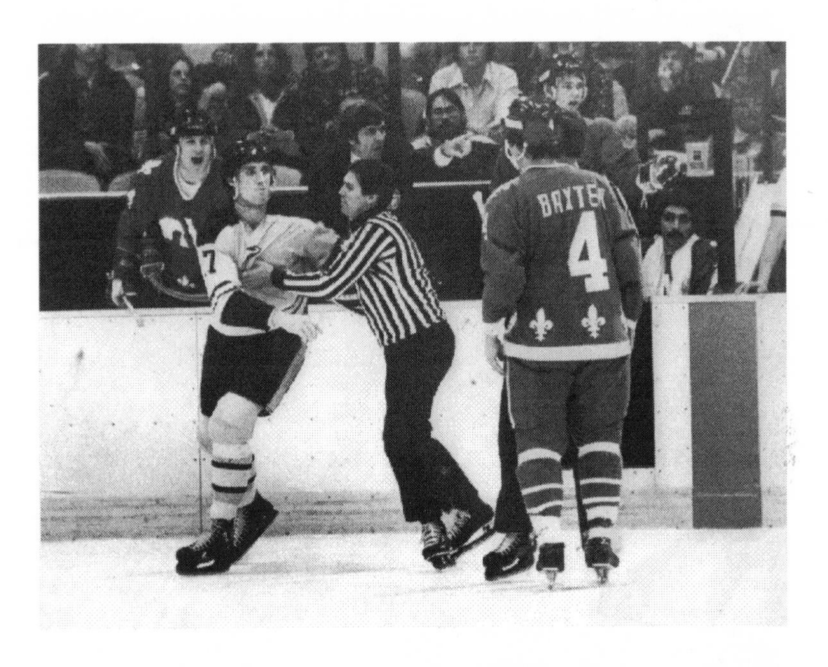


Paul Baxter speared me, and I'm being restrained from trying to deliver some fistic retribution. We later became teammates in Quebec. In hockey, you forgive but you don't forget. *(Paul Stewart photo collection)*

School picture at St. Gregory's, Dorchester 1963. I look angelic, don't I? Looks can be deceiving. *(Paul Stewart photo collection)*

Fishing with my dear friends, Billy and Michael Carroll, at Island Pond, Vermont. I am at right. Michael was my best friend. He died at age 18 in an accident on a rainy Sept. 18, 1971. The grief was, and still is, overwhelming. I still visit his grave, and miss him terribly. He and his family are wonderful people. *(Paul Stewart photo collection)*

Packing my reffing gear just like Grampy and my dad used to. In this photo, I am packing for my comeback game in the NHL after beating colon cancer. The laces on my skates are brand new. *(Paul Stewart photo collection)*

Here is Bill Stewart Sr. packing his trunk with his umpiring gear. *(Paul Stewart photo collection)*

My boys, McCauley, Max, and me. *(Paul Stewart photo collection)*

Wedding photo with Lori, Oct. 9,1997. *(Paul Stewart photo collection)*

This is one of my favorite family photos. *(Paul Stewart photo collection)*

An officiating "Chorus Line." I am very proud of my crews. This photo was taken at the ECAC championships. *(Paul Stewart photo collection)*

My officiating mentor and boss, the late John McCauley, was always in my corner. We named our first son McCauley John Stewart in tribute to him. *(Hockey Hall of Fame photo)*

Several times, I finished in the top two of the NHLPA Players' Poll for "best referee." My league bosses didn't necessarily agree. However, players often cited my feel for the game and communication ability as two of my biggest strengths. I earned acceptability, and the respect factor was mutual. That did not, of course, mean there was never any friction. Friction is part of the game. *(Paul Stewart photo collection)*

From left to right: Gene Binda, Don Garcia, myself, Marty Demers, and Derek Sanderson at Hartford Whalers Alumni vs. Bruins Alumni. *(Paul Stewart photo collection)*

Then, now and always: Positioning sells calls. Benoit Hogue of the New York Islanders is the shooter. *(Paul Stewart photo collection)*

Sporting a black eye, ready for action. *(Paul Stewart photo collection)*

1,000th regular season game as an NHL referee. I appreciated the sentiment of the sign. I would work an additional 10 games after this one before retirement. *(AP Photo)*

A very happy, young Binghamton Duster, starting to live out my dream. In old-time hockey, "stretching" meant reaching for a cup of coffee, a cigarette or the newspaper. *(Paul Stewart photo collection)*

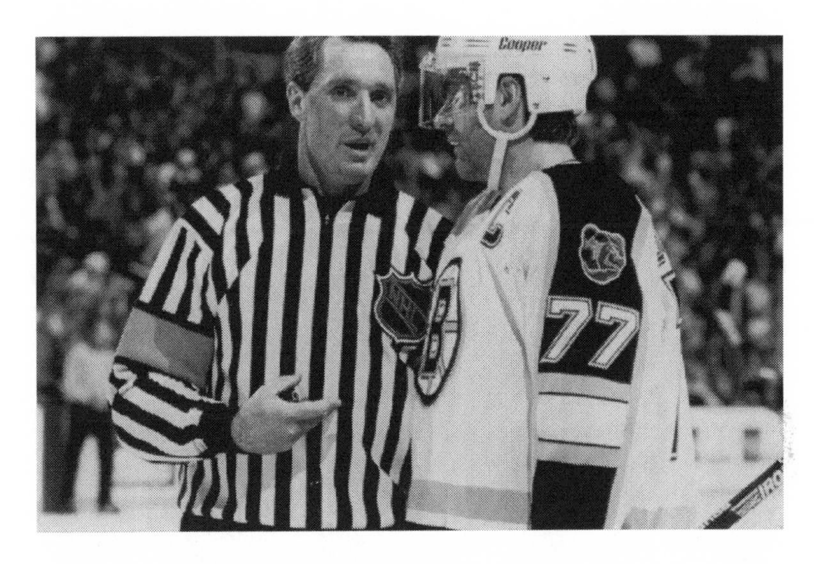


I always had immense respect for Raymond Bourque. He was not just a great player, but an outstanding captain for his team and a quality person. It was an honor to be on the ice with the likes of Ray, Wayne Gretzky, Mark Messier (my old Cincinnati Stingers teammate), Jaromir Jagr and many others. *(Paul Stewart photo collection)*

Confronting Stan Jonathan during my NHL regular season debut, Thanksgiving 1979. When they closed down the old Boston Garden, Jonathan told me I was the toughest guy he ever fought. He honored me. *(Paul Stewart photo collection)*

In addition to my cameo in "Slap Shot," I had small roles in two other movies: "Letters from the Dead" (I played a serviceman killed on World War II's final day of combat) and "Kennedy" (as a Secret Service agent). This photo was taken during a break on the set of "Letters from the Dead." *(Paul Stewart photo collection)*

2000 NHL All-Star Game: McCauley, bottle in hand, walks to center ice with me for the Hockey Fights Cancer presentation. *(Paul Stewart photo collection)*

1987 Canada Cup photo: The defining moment of my playing career, in my eyes, was my fight withTerry O'Reilly at the Boston Garden during my three-fight NHL debut. However, the single most special moment of my hockey career was refereeing the championship round of the 1987 Canada Cup before I had even yet worked an entire NHL regular season game. In this iconic photo, I am signalizing a good goal for Team Canada as Mario Lemieux and Wayne Gretzky celebrate. It still gives me goose bumps to have been part of the greatest game ever played. From a personal standpoint, it also marked the takeoff point of my 17-season NHL refereeing career. *(Getty Images)*

## CHAPTER 14: Hairspray Can & Winter Tan

One off-ice activity required of me and the other prospect referees at the Bruce Hood Referee School was to perform a skit at the camp talent show. I wrote a parody of the Irish ballad “The Wild Colonial Boy.” I titled it “The Wild Old Boston Boy.” Here are my lyrics:

There was a wild old Boston boy,
Paul Stewart was his name.
He was born and bred in old Beantown,
To play this hockey game.
He was his mother’s middle son,
His father’s pride and joy.
He played it rough.
He played it tough.
This wild old Boston Boy.

And then one day a thought came,
To my battered brain.
There must be another way,
To stay in this hockey game.
Perhaps I should be a referee,
A shirt of black and white.
A hairspray can,
A winter’s tan,
That comes from neon light.

Well, it really is amazing,
It’s almost out of sight.
I’ll tell you what’s amazing,
As it’s near the end of the night.

If you ask me what's amazing,
And you ask me what's outta sight,
Next time you see me on TV,
I'll be stopping, instead of starting, the fight.

We also were required to introduce ourselves on camera; I did my intro in English, then French.

"Why did you just do that in French?" one instructor asked.

"Because this is Canada," I replied. Everyone laughed.

"I see you took my advice," said John McCauley, who was there at the school evaluating us trainees.

"Yeah, I made my way over to the enemy," I joked.

For me, life isn't just about persistence. It wasn't a matter of sticking around; it was also about making the most of every chance I received. It is the difference between being alive and truly living. I wasn't given many chances as a player, but I was given a fantastic opportunity to succeed as a referee thanks to Scotty Morrison and John McCauley. They saw something in me, something others didn't. I made the NHL as a player mainly because of persistence. I made it back to the NHL as a referee thanks to skill and taking advantage of every opportunity given to me.

When the opportunity to attend the Bruce Hood Referee School presented itself, I knew I needed to make the most of the chance. I took the cheapest way possible to the school; I flew from Boston to Buffalo, rented a car in Buffalo, and drove the rest of the way to Milton, Ontario. As I mentioned before, I had to pay my own way, so I did my homework and found the most affordable route.

The school was operated by the late Bruce Hood, an Ontario native who reffed 1,033 regular season NHL games from 1963-1984. Hood also worked four NHL Stanley Cup Finals, including the 1970 Final when Boston Bruins star defenseman Bobby Orr scored the series-winning goal in overtime of Game Four against the St. Louis Blues. Hood wrote in his nhlofficials.com bio: "The picture of him flying through the air after scoring is still one of the most famous sports shots of all time… if you look down in the bottom corner of the picture you will see my arm and hand—my claim to fame!"

He has many more claims to fame than just that. I had seen Bruce ref and knew about his accomplishments because I grew up watching and studying hockey. I love the game's history and have always loved it since hearing stories about Art Ross from my dad when I was five years old.

Our officiating coaches there included past and present NHL officials and supervisors, including McCauley, Lou Maschio, Wally Harris, Frank Udvari, Leon Stickle, and John D'Amico. They watched us referee games and participate in skating drills.

I felt that I was the strongest skater at Hood's School. This was with many thanks to my former Quebec coaches, Jacques Demers and Andre Boudrias, who worked with me tirelessly after morning practices during the 1979-1980 season. Andre was the rabbit and I chased him all over the rink for forty-five minutes after every practice. I was in great shape now, having run the Falmouth Road Race with ex-teammate Tim Sheehy. I weighed 190 pounds, was ripped, and wanted desperately to return to the NHL in a new role.

I minded my business there and listened attentively to every suggestion and instruction. I also had fun. I used my quick-witted personality to my advantage. I went there with the reputation for being crazy from my playing days, but I worked to diminish this perception. I wrote/performed that song for the talent show and also introduced myself in English and French because I wanted people to realize—even though they don't always believe it—there's more depth to me than they know. Some people assume I am stupid just because of my past as a fighter, a hockey goon or "just a jock." That's as foolish as assuming someone is intelligent because of their position in life. Each person should be judged on his own merits, not on preconceptions about them based on where they come from or what their job is. That is one of the fundamental lessons my father taught me.

Some people have taken the time to really get to know me and my personality. I like to think I got to where I have in life largely because of great family and friends. In the end, all my family and true friends came to help me like George Bailey's friends did in the classic film *It's a Wonderful Life*. My friends were the ones who picked me up when I felt life was anything but wonderful after my divorce. Even my mother, although she had her own flaws with alcoholism, came to my rescue when I hit rock bottom. She approached me after Coach O'Brien did, around the time I visited a psychologist. Mom gave me tremendous advice; it was one of best pieces of advice I've ever received. She mailed me father's resume. She wrote on the top of it, "A busy man is a happy man. Get busy."

Getting busy, for me at least, didn't mean juggling five or so jobs at once like I had already been doing. It meant finding what I truly loved to do the most and doing that. My father wore so many hats: schoolteacher, coach, referee, mentor, tremendous dad, etc. He loved wearing all his hats. He felt a true appreciation for life. But for me, the secret wasn't in shuffling different roles but in throwing myself, one hundred percent, into my passion. What my mom meant by "getting busy" also was working my butt off to make my new life and career goals come true.

No stranger to challenges, though, I recognized the same pattern emerging when I became a referee that had happened before in my life. I had several friends/mentors, such as McCauley, Morrison, Harris, and Udvari, who stood by me. They came to my help. They did everything to help me succeed because they believed in me.

Approximately a week after returning home from the Bruce Hood Referee School, Morrison phoned me. He told me McCauley intended to call me the next day to arrange my travel to the annual NHL Officials Association training camp. I felt absolutely thrilled. And, fortunately, the NHL paid for my travel there. McCauley sent me an airline ticket. Off I went to Toronto, ignorant about what was expected of me but excited about a new challenge. My urgency had returned. I felt like Paul Stewart again.

I underwent a physical test, a psychological test, and a written NHL rules test. I passed the physical, and I apparently scored high on the physiological test. One question asked was whether I'd rather attend a party or throw a party. Just ask anyone who knows me; they'll tell you I'm a terrific party host. I failed the written examination but that came as no surprise. I never had previously studied the NHL Rule Book or reffed higher than Division III college hockey. I broke all the hockey rules for a living. What could you expect?

The training complex in Toronto included two rinks. As I walked down the hallway separating them , I asked McCauley and Morrison which direction they wanted me to go. They pointed left. I didn't realize at the time that the two rinks were separated into referees and linesmen. Someone told me later that night that I had trained with the refs. That came as a pleasant surprise.

Stepping onto the ice, I saw different officials, including Bill McCreary, Bob Myers, Kerry Fraser, and Andy Van Hellemond, as well as Dave Newell, who soon became one of my closest friends. Many of the established officials were friendly and gave me pointers. Some weren't as kind. "Cold" and "distant" are two adjectives that come to mind when I reflect on a few of them. My own training camp roommate, Tom Monahan, a former Merrimack College hockey player, never talked with me the entire camp. He stood and walked out of the room whenever I tried to talk to him or asked him a question. I was his competition. Monahan, of course, never worked in the NHL until being a replacement official during the NHL referee strike in 1993. He never reffed in NHL again after the National Hockey League Officials' Association and the NHL reached a new collective bargaining agreement seventeen days into the strike.

Before the first day of training camp ended, all the referees and linesmen joined together for a game of shinny hockey using a tennis ball instead of a puck. As I skated up the ice controlling the tennis ball, linesman John D'Amico came testing me. D'Amico, who died in 2005, is one of sixteen officials in the Hall of Fame. After his retirement in 1987, he worked on the NHL Officiating Supervisory staff. He came out of retirement for one night in March, 1988. Sitting at home in Toronto watching a Toronto Maple Leafs game, one of the linesmen left because of an injury. D'Amico drove to the Maple Leaf Gardens and worked his 1,689th and final NHL game.

As I controlled the tennis ball with my stick, D'Amico "accidentally"—read: deliberately—drilled me in the face with his stick, causing a gash. Everyone stopped playing. The NHL officiating brass looked down from the stands, wondering if I'd strike back like I always had done as a player when opponents ran at me or my teammates. I removed one of my gloves, felt the cut with my hand, and then stared down, seeing a great deal of blood dripping from my nose. My natural instinct throughout my career had been to throw down both gloves and bloody the face of anyone who had victimized me.

I felt a sense of rage building inside of me. My heart beat faster. But I did something I never knew I was capable of doing: I took a deep breath and restrained myself for the first time in my hockey career. I looked over at Newell, my team's captain. He nodded to tell me to skate over to the bench. I did.

"I was sort of figuring that, if I hit him, then today would be my first and last day at NHL training camp," I told Newell.

"You think?" Newell replied. "You think it didn't happen on purpose?"

I opened the door, took a seat on the bench, grabbed a towel, wiped the blood off my face, placed a strip of white tape on my forehead and nose, then returned to the ice. That was all. It was over. I didn't retaliate. D'Amico either was testing my restraint or trying to get me thrown out of camp. Either way, I passed the test with flying colors.

It didn't surprise me that some officials didn't want me there. First of all, I was a minority in a Canadian-dominated league. Approximately eighty-seven percent of NHL officials in today's game are Canadian. The rest are United States natives. The percentage of US-born officials was even more minuscule in 1983. At the time, the league had only one U.S.-born referee, Mike Noeth (Ayer, Massachuetts) and just three U.S.-born linesmen: Kevin Collins (Springfield, Massachusetts), Gord Broseker (Baltimore, Maryland native), and Dan Schachte (Madison, Wisconsin).

The main reason the NHL hired me? Supposedly, it was because the U.S. State Department had pressured the NHL, telling the league it had to exercise more diverse hiring practices. Thus, I arrived just in time, an ex-player with American blood. I was better than forced bussing. I'm not anti-Canadian. I've never been and never will be. My grandmother was born in Halifax, Nova Scotia. I played for two Canadian teams. My good friend, linesman Brian Murphy, recently called me a legend in Quebec. My greatest officiating mentors, such as John McCauley, Scotty Morrison, Frank Udvari, and John Ashley, all were Canadian. I wouldn't have had nearly as successful an officiating career if it had not been for these Canadians and other Canadians who took the time to work with me.

But I do have one issue: Still, to this day, officiating jobs in the NHL seem to go primarily to Canadians, especially Canadians who speak English. This baffles me because the NHL is not just a North American league; it's a world league. Some of the better players are European. It makes no sense that the NHL failed for so long to employ any European officials. Even to date, the number of European officials to work in the NHL can be counted on three fingers: Marcus Vinnerborg of Sweden, Evgeny Romasko of Russia, and Libor

Suchanek of the Czech Republic. Of the three, only Suchnacek remains. In 2018, he became the first non-North American official promoted to full-time NHL status.

If my nationality was one strike against me, my reputation and personality were strike two. I take some fault. I say and do things I regret. I have a tremendous memory; one that still allows me to remember every line from "The Wild Old Boston Boy," and also able to recite all my lines from *The Taming of the Shrew*, learned in 1968 at Groton School. But there are some nights when I wish my memory wasn't so vivid. They say when a person dies and arrives at the Pearly Gates, his or her whole life is recounted. But I recount my life every day. I remember things that make me shudder. I think, "Why did I do that?" I ask myself, "Why did I say that? I didn't mean that."

I also had flair as a player and some of my excitement as a ref might have been mistaken for showboating. That might have turned off some people who worked with me or for whom I had to work. In reality, I used to get so psyched up before reffing a game that I actually had to try to calm myself down. I just loved being out there.

One example comes to mind: I reffed Game Two of the 1987 Canada Cup Final between Russia and Canada. Canada won 6-5 in double overtime. The game is considered one of the best hockey games ever played. You should have seen me before that game. About ten minutes before game time, I looked at the two linesmen—D'Amico being one.

"Let's go," I said. "I can't sit in here anymore."

"There's still seven minutes to go before the anthems," D'Amico replied.

"I don't care," I said. "Let's go take a skate." I couldn't just sit in the dressing room. I needed to get out there. It was the biggest game I had worked to date. It was the largest crowd I had ever worked in front of as a ref. People misinterpreted it for showboating. I just needed to get out there so I could get myself past being worked up. I needed to stop being so itchy. I needed to get comfortable. It's like hitting a bucket of golf balls at the practice range before playing eighteen holes.

Many people thought it rather inappropriate and or strange that a fighter—who compiled 273 penalty minutes in 46 games for the Binghamton Dusters in 1975-1976 and 288 penalty minutes in 65

World Hockey Association games—was attempting a comeback as a ref, a job centered on keeping the peace.

But it was the best decision I made in my hockey career. I ended up enjoying reffing more than I did playing because I was on the ice the entire game and I just loved being out there. I loved to skate and it was where I really found my natural freedom, my niche. Playing depended so much on my teammates, and, many times, my teammates had not come to play all-out. Reffing, on the other hand, was all up to me and I have always been able to rely and depend on myself to give my usual one-hundred percent effort. I learned quickly that I could impact the whole game and make it so it was fair.

The final night at my first NHL officiating training camp, I almost used my fists, but not on a fellow official. We all went to drink at a bar. I sat there talking with William "Dutch" Van Deelan, a referee supervisor who lived in Western Canada. He was an older gentleman who had reffed in the Western Pro Hockey league. He had played some pro hockey himself. Dutch played in the Western Canada Hockey League for the Regina Kings during the 1940s. He wasn't very big, about 5'7", maybe 5'8". This was the first of many times Dutch and I smoked cigars and told hockey stories together. He and his wife never had children. Every time I was with him, I felt as if he treated me like a son and not just a green official trying to break into the ranks. While there, referee Don Koharski, who had officiated in the NHL since 1977 and had worked in the WHA before that, got into a verbal argument with a young man who'd purposely bumped into Koharski. That bump led to a heated exchange.

It was not surprising that someone tried to get under Koharski's skin. He had a recognizable face long before his most defining career moment, which came during the 1988 Stanley Cup playoffs. After a game between the Bruins and Devils in the 1988 playoffs, furious Devils coach, Jim Schoenfeld, was caught on tape shouting at Koharski, who thought Schoenfeld shoved him. Schoenfeld replied, "You fell, you fat pig. Have another doughnut!"

"Just a second," I told Dutch when I saw Koharski going at it with this drunk man. As I walked over with a beer bottle in my hand, Koharski got pushed. He looked ready to fight. I stepped between the two. Nobody knew Paul Stewart, but they all knew Don Koharski, so I thought it best for me to take care of the situation. I grabbed the man's shirt.

"You want to fight? Then fight me." I told him.

"Who the hell are you?" the fellow asked.

"I'm the guy who's going to kick your ass," I said, making direct eye contact.

The bar became quiet.

"Make a move, and I'm going to shove this beer bottle down your throat."

He hesitated. The bouncers broke it up and escorted the hostile man out of the bar.

"That was pretty good," Dutch told me when I returned.

"Koharski doesn't need any shit," I said. "I fight for a living."

"Well, you can't do that anymore," Dutch said. "You're a referee now. But you fit here like a glove. You're going to be all right." The next morning when camp broke, McCauley and Morrison gave me the number for the man who ran the New England Junior League, my next step on the ladder.

I headed home to Roslindale, Massachusetts. Not long before, I had moved from Cape Cod to Roslindale, a neighborhood in Boston. I had moved to Roslindale with a friend who I had known from the radio station. She had accepted a job at WBZ radio in Boston and we shared an apartment together. I began reffing Junior games and dabbled in many other occupations to pay the rent.

Just down the street, I found work as the permanent building substitute teacher at the Washington Irving Middle School in Roslindale. The school had been Roslindale High many years back and my parents met there in the gym at a dance. I enjoyed the teaching job. I became known there for lugging two hockey bags full of dictionaries, one bag in each hand, around the hallways and teaching the kids vocabulary words. "Stump the Teacher" was the game.

No matter what class I substituted for—math, science, English—I handed out the dictionaries and asked the kids to find words that they thought I didn't know. I'd write the word on the blackboard and tell them the meaning. "Sphygmomanometer" and "Zoroastrianism," those were the words they picked. If they stumped me, they got a free ice cream at lunch. We made it a game and an event. The kids were learning, having fun, and I was using my seven years of Latin and all the reading that I had done at Groton, Penn, and those long bus rides in the minors to help kids expand their vocabulary.

I also worked as a greens-keeper at the George Wright Golf Club in Hyde Park and as a furniture mover for Casey & Hayes Movers in South Boston. Neil Sheehy knew the Casey family and helped me get hired. I still have my Teamsters Union Card, local 82 (now 25). My first job there was to remove all the furniture out of a Harvard dorm so the dorm could be renovated. I finally made it to Harvard! I also continued to drive back to Yarmouth each week to work twenty-plus hours as a reserve police officer. I still worked the Happy Hour details, club details, night patrols, booking, and dispatch.

Unlike before, I was not bothered by the many hats I needed to wear to make ends meet. I knew all these jobs meant something new. They all were a means to an end, a way to earn a living until I learned and perfected my trade as a referee. My focus was to become a full-time referee in the NHL. Everything was suddenly okay.

Morrison and McCauley helped me receive assignments in the New England Junior League, where I began to refine my game. Commissioner Mike Carroll send good reports to Toronto. McCauley called me in October. He told me to call Ray Miron, the commissioner of the Atlantic Coast Hockey League who'd also once served as the NHL Colorado Rockies General Manager.

"I've been waiting for your call," Miron said. "Can you drive to Utica tomorrow night?" I asked the principal the next morning, a Friday, to leave school early to make it to Utica on time. He was fine with me doing it.

It was time.

Off to Utica for my first ACHL game as a minor league professional referee. The Mohawk Valley Stars of the ACHL played in Utica. I loaded up the gas tank of my 1972 AMC Gremlin—then a $1 per gallon—and headed to Utica that Friday afternoon. My car looked like a big white sneaker. I went from owning a Chrysler Cordoba with "fine Corinthian leather," as a professional player to driving a shitbox three-speed. That Gremlin was a real chick magnet, I assure you.

I arrived in Utica a few hours before game time and stretched out on the trainer's table, catching a short nap for approximately an hour. I was familiar with the rink. I had played a couple of games for the Stars when they were short during a playoff run in 1983. I knew their coach, Billy Horton. The Mohawk Valley Stars were playing the

Roanoke Valley Rebels, a team that included the son of a former NHL scout. I knew of the son, a Massachusetts boy, because I had watched him and his brother play in summer leagues during my playing career.

That night in Utica, I called a penalty against him. Instead of heading to the penalty box, he skated at me, pointing with his stick. I asked him what he planned to do with the stick. He told me was going to shove it down my throat.

"You better not miss," I said. "And by the way, you're all done."

I ejected him and gave him a three-game suspension for abuse of the official. Later in the hallway, he walked by me still flapping his gums.

"Don't ever threaten a referee again," I said, taking the stick away from him and snapping it in half over my thigh.

Commissioner Miron upheld the three-game suspension and I was off to the races. Almost every weekend that hockey season I reffed games in the Atlantic Coast Hockey League. I even was selected to work the league's playoff finals.

It was a long way from Falmouth and the five dollars for the first game I ever reffed. I worked prep school games at home during the weekdays and attended games at the Boston Garden to observe NHL referees. I had become about my father's business.

## CHAPTER 15: The Greatest of Mentors

I continued to hone my craft. During the 1983-84 hockey season, I refereed in the Atlantic Coast Hockey League each weekend and continued my several jobs at home near Boston. I also reffed prep games around Boston during the week days.

Invited again to the NHL Officials Association training camp before the 1984-1985 NHL season, John McCauley had written me a letter a month earlier with a demand. He reminded me that I had failed my first NHL rulebook test in 1983. He told me to submit to him a hundred questions, one question for each category in the rulebook. This exercise forced me to learn the NHL rulebook from cover to cover. I ended up acing the test my second NHL officiating camp.

When the NHL finally signed me to a contract before the 1985-86 season, McCauley had another important demand: be younger.

I brought him my birth certificate when I was about to be hired and he looked at my date of birth: March 21, 1953. He later called me. "Oh, there's a mistake on this," he said. "That date of birth is supposed to say 1955. We don't hire anybody over thirty. If anyone asks, you were born in 1955."

McCauley mailed me the birth certificate not long after with the three in the 1953 changed to a five. It was impossible to tell it had been fudged. I never asked McCauley about it and he never told me how he did it.

Soon after, I had my driver's license changed to 1955, too. I was friends with a World War I fighter pilot named Eddie and helped take care of him after I got divorced. I used to go by his place, take care of him at night, shave him, and take him to the grocery store or wherever he needed to go. He had been my next-door neighbor when

I was a kid growing up. One day, I was telling him how McCauley had changed the date of birth on my birth certificate. He told me that his wife had worked at the registry of motor vehicles. She had served as the registrar's assistant.

"I'll have her fix your date of birth on your license, too," said Eddie, who died at the age of one-hundred three, but at the time had a license showing him to be ninety years of age with no restrictions on his license. His wife made a call for me to a friend at the registry in Roslindale. The friend asked me what was wrong with the license.

"My date of birth is wrong," I told him. "It's supposed to be 1955." With one click, the DOB on my license changed from 1953 to 1955. That helped. Whenever I rented a car and submitted receipts for reimbursement, my date of birth read as 1955.

After McCauley died, I think management caught on somehow because I received an inquiry about it. I sent the league a copy of the birth certificate that McCauley had fudged, a copy of my driver's license, and some other documentation. I never heard another word about it.

Nobody bothered me about it for decades. I certainly am not the first person to change his birth year. Just look at Major League Baseball. Until recent years, nobody was quite certain of the exact age of many of the Latino baseball players. What's the difference anyway? At the time I looked twenty-six, not thirty-two. It wasn't until after the terrorist attacks of September 11, 2001 that my actual age became discovered when I applied for a new license. I went to renew my license and my date of birth got flagged by the computer under heightened security measures under the Patriot Act. I played dumb, returned home, got a real birth certificate and a passport, brought it back to the DMV and with one click, I was back to 1953.

With the matter of my age resolved, my assignments increased. When 1984-85 training camp ended, I received assignments to work games in the International Hockey League, the Western Hockey League, and the Ontario Hockey League. NHL referee supervisors often watched me ref these contests. Matt Pavelich, Sam Sisco, Lou Maschio, Dutch van Deelan, and Hall of Famers John Ashley and Frank Udvari all supervised my games.

Each one of these men spent entire days with me. They'd ride in the car with me, take me to lunch, tell me hockey stories, and teach me aspects about the game I never knew. All these men were extremely valuable in helping me make it to the NHL. Just by refereeing more and more and observing other referees, I learned so much more about hockey that I'd never known. Players don't know the rules too well. I obviously didn't know them well during my first NHL officiating camp in 1983.

Ashley once told McCauley right in front of me that he was unsure if he could make me a referee.

"He's pretty raw," Ashley told McCauley. McCauley took his glasses off and pointed at Ashley.

"You're a Hall of Famer," McCauley told Ashley. "It's your job to teach him to be a ref."

Ashley and I ended up spending a great deal of time together and became close friends.

Frank Udvari was also a terrific mentor. Remember the story about how John D'Amico came out of retirement for one night, one year after retiring? D'Amico drove to Maple Leaf Gardens to work as a linesman after watching a Toronto game on television at his home and seeing a linesman suffer an injury. That story pales in comparison to what Udvari once did.

Udvari came out of retirement an amazing twelve years later. He officially retired in 1966 and soon after became a supervisor of NHL officials and the referee-in-chief for the AHL. But on December 30, 1978 Udvari replaced an injured Dave Newell during a game he was supervising between the New York Islanders and Atlanta Flames. Udvari's bio on nhlofficials.com tells the story of how he borrowed skates from Bryan Trottier of the Islanders, and how, ironically, Udvari disallowed a Trottier goal that night.

Udvari once pinned me against a wall after an AHL game in Springfield. He pressed his finger into my chest. "If you don't have the guts to make that call in the AHL, you certainly won't have the guts to make it in the NHL," Udvari yelled.

The best advice I ever received about reffing came from Udvari: He told me not just to read the rulebook and referee by the book. He told me to referee by the feel of the game. "Remember yourself as a player, and how you felt during a game," he once told me. "If an opponent does something to you that you would get ticked off at, then that is a penalty. Forget all the other things about trying to read the play because you will end up over-officiating. Just feel the play." As a referee, I applied the "Udvari Rule" and looked at the time on the clock, the score of the game and the significance of the game.

Kerry Clark, the brother of Wendel Clark, was a minor league enforcer who routinely racked up more than two hundred penalty minutes per season, and even had 372 PIMs in 1990-1991 with the Salt Lake Golden Eagles. He wasn't much of a scorer and when he did score goals, he showboated. He planned out his goal celebrations like some NFL players plan out their touchdown celebrations. After scoring a completely meaningless goal in a meaningless AHL game I was reffing, he moonwalked the distance of the ice. I stood there pissed and would have fought him had I been an opposing player. As a ref, I watched, then gave him a misconduct. I applied the Udvari Rule.

John McCauley occasionally visited to watch and so did Morrison. I constantly was monitored and coached. Every supervisor discussed positioning, thinking through the game, acceptability, and picking the right battle to fight because I did do some crazy stuff out there.

Like that one night in Salt Lake City…

Between periods at a Salt Lake Golden Eagles game, a fifteen-year-old male contestant received a chance to shoot a puck at a hole in a sheet of plywood that hung from the net for a chance to win a one-year free lease on a car if successful. The opening was barely large enough for the puck to fit through. The puck ended up stopping 99.6 percent past the goal line, but not entirely through the hole.

"What should we do?" asked Golden Eagles PR executive Doug Palazzari, a former pro-hockey player who had played 108 games for the St. Louis Blues.

"We need to get the period started," I replied. "I'll take care of it." I skated by the net and nudged the board with my foot and pointed: GOAL! The puck went into the net and the crowd roared. But the Golden Eagles general manager accosted me after the period, staring and screaming at me furiously.

"You don't have the right do that," he yelled. "Who do you think you are?"

"Maybe a referee out of work?" I answered. "Maybe I can get Doug's job?"

My hotel phone rang the next day at 7 a.m. Salt Lake City-time. It was 9 a.m. Toronto time. It was Scotty Morrison and he was furious. I tried to explain myself, but he shut me up immediately and told me just to listen. I listened to him for about ten minutes, although it seemed much longer. The phone was a good foot from my ear. I thought he was about to fire me. In fact, he ordered me to go to the Salt Palace to see Golden Eagles owner, Mr. Arthur Teece, and apologize.

That morning, I sat in the Salt Palace office lobby waiting when Mr. Teece appeared, looking extremely joyful. He clapped me on the back.

"Paul Stewart!!" he said upon seeing me. "I want to shake your hand!"

"I came over to apologize," I told him.

"Apologize? What for? What you did was fantastic! You helped my team. Look at the front page of the paper today. Look at all the publicity we're getting. What a story! I'm mad at my team for not making the decision to do the same thing you did. That boy's dad is the vice president of our biggest season ticket and advertising client, Coca-Cola. What a great night. Thank you!"

I told Mr. Teece that I came over because Morrison was pretty upset with me; the Golden Eagles' GM had called him and wanted me fired. Mr. Teece was incredulous.

"Well, that isn't going to happen," he said, reaching for the phone. "By the way, I'm originally from Springfield. I knew your grandfather. Quite a guy he was. The apple didn't fall far from the tree."

Mr. Teece called Morrison and urged him not to fire me.

As I reflect back on the Salt Lake incident, I know what I did wasn't smart. But it wasn't bad either because hockey is show business. Mr. Teece—who also owned the Triple-A baseball Salt Lake Gulls from 1969 to 1983—was kind and Morrison was even kinder. And the boy should not have been allowed to be a contestant anyway. It was a lottery and he was only fifteen. He wasn't even old enough to drive the car.

Mr. Teece was right about the apple not falling far from the tree, too.

I was green as grass in the ranks of officiating. I had grown up listening to stories about my grandfather and father who never took shit when they reffed or umpired. As mentioned before, my grandfather told MLB Hall of Fame manager Leo Durocher to meet him at his hotel to fight. "When the game's over, I'll meet you there in my hotel room. Whoever leaves first, wins.'" I heard other similar stories about my granddad's response to Chicago Black Hawks owner James Norris, Sr., also a league governor, when Norris was upset about a call and told my granddad it would be the last time he'd referee a game in the league. "Well, if this is the last game, I'll finish it, and if you can get my job, it's not worth having anyhow. What a great league governor you are, abusing an official!" my granddad told Norris. Former Boston University coach Jack Kelley once told my father that dad had ruined his reputation after calling a bench minor for too many men in a game at UNH. "BU, right? You guys have reputations?" my dad responded. I grew up listening to those stories. That was my basis as a new referee.

The Western League Portland Winterhawks owner Brian Shaw—who had coached the WHA Edmonton Oilers for two seasons—confronted me one night with three of his players (Scott McMichael, John Kordic, and I think Glen Wesley, who later played for the Bruins) by his side after a game. He came right into the officiating dressing room in Kamloops, British Columbia.

"You have to have ten guys behind you," I said. "If I decide I'm going to kill you, I will."

"You'll never referee in this league again," he told me.

"One-hundred bucks, Canadian. You're doing me a favor. Get out of my room." I returned to the hotel and Morrison called me.

"Did you threaten Shaw?" Morrison asked. "What happened?"

"No, he brought three players. They came into my dressing room and, in front of the linesmen, and challenged me to a fight."

"Did you hit him?" Morrison asked.

"No. I took my sweater off, flexed, and told him I was going back to my hotel. That's where I am right now having pizza with all the scouts."

"So you didn't hit him?"

"No."

"Okay, no problem," Morrison said, hanging up the phone.

What I told him was true. I had taken my sweater off and told them to come try me. Sometimes I acted like I was a cowboy from the Wild West, but I didn't know any other way. I was flying by the seat of my pants. Shaw was quite feisty himself. During the 1971-1972 season, while coaching the Edmonton Oil Kings of the Western Hockey League, Shaw was suspended for two games and assessed a

$150 fine for trying to get into the stands to go after a fan who hit him with a program after he had been ejected for arguing a penalty call. It was pretty clear that everyone was waiting for me to go flying off the handle, and give somebody the beating they probably deserved. That wasn't going to happen, but I still sometimes got myself into trouble.

My conversations with Morrison about conduct becoming a professional referee remained ongoing. On a separate occasion at the Salt Palace in Salt Lake City, a puck struck me in the head and I fell to the ice along the sideboards. As a trainer and doctor helped me to my feet, a fan reached over the low glass and poked my shoulder.

"I hope you die," he told me.

"Go [bleep] yourself!" I shouted out, as any kid from Dorchester would reply.

That fan reported me to the league. He wrote a letter and the league made me call the man to apologize. Morrison used the situation as a lesson.

"You have to be above that," Morrison told me.

After the trainer and doctor helped me to my feet, I continued to referee that game in Salt Lake. I was concussed although didn't know it at the time. I don't remember much about the rest of the contest, only that the fan had poked me. I don't think Morrison necessarily was mad at me, but he and McCauley were forced to deal with some situations they weren't accustomed to dealing with when I arrived on the scene. I received calls from Toronto frequently.

The most difficult part of transitioning from a player to ref was I sometimes wanted to act too much like a player. I'd skate by a player who did something wrong and I'd tell him the way I saw it. If I thought it was a chicken move, I told him as much.

For example, then-Regina GM/Coach Bob Strumm said something to me one night that I didn't like.

"Why don't you get back behind the bench and coach? Besides, your power play sucks, anyway," I retorted.

Strumm and I laugh about it now, but at the time, he was furious. In hindsight, I can't blame him. It was not the way a ref should respond.

Despite my occasional antics, Morrison and McCauley saw the potential in me. The NHL signed me to a contract before the 1985-1986 season. I ended up refereeing 144 games that year between exhibitions, regular season games, and playoff games. I officiated in the International Hockey League, the AHL, the OHL and the Western Hockey League.

I went on one road trip for thirty-nine straight days with thirty-seven games in thirty-nine nights. I came home for four days and then went back out for twenty-five games in thirty nights.

Some of those road trips were doozies; off the ice as well as on. One stop that remains etched in my memory is what I like to call my "Blizzard Bingo" experience (or, if you prefer, the Regina Monologues).

I've seen so much snow, ice and snow drifts in my hockey travels and New England upbringing that maybe I should be sponsored by the Weather Channel. Without exaggeration, I could rattle off a chapter's worth of on weather-related stories. That would probably get monotonous pretty quickly, though. So let's cut to the tale of my most memorable blizzard-related experience.

One night, I found myself in Regina, Saskatchewan, during one of the worst blizzards I have ever seen. I barely made it to my hotel. Shortly thereafter, I contacted the Calgary-based league office and found out the Pats game had been canceled (that tells you something right there). Not even trucks could get through.

With virtually nothing to do—the TV wasn't working in the hotel—I went down to the front desk and asked if there were any restaurants nearby.

"Your best bet is to stay here at the bar," I was told.

That didn't particularly interest me.

"Is there anything to do downtown?" I asked.

"Well, most things you might want to do are down at the mall but it's closed."

"OK," I said. "Are there any activities at all around here today I can get myself to?"

"Actually, there's a bingo night going on just down the road. It'll be packed tonight."

Under the circumstances, that sounded good to me. I'd never played bingo before—really had no idea what went on in a bingo hall—and figured at least it might be some interesting people watching and a different sort of life experience.

Was it ever!

I get to the bingo parlor and, as described, the place is mobbed. Almost everyone there was from a First Nation community. The cigarette smoke was so thick and the air in the place so stale that I could hardly breathe. When I walked up to the desk, I was handed a bingo dauber.

"How much do I owe you for it?" I asked, not even sure yet what it was or how it was used.

The woman laughed. "It's free. Have you ever played bingo before?"

"Umm, no," I admitted.

She gave me a quick crash course. I thanked her and settled in. Didn't win a thing but came close a few times.

Two other players, both female, sat next to me. I made some casual small talk with the two women and tried to go on about my night of losing repeatedly at bingo.

"You ain't from around here, are you?" asked one of the women.

"No, I'm not," I said. "I'm traveling."

"What brought you here?" asked the other.

"Hockey," I said.

"Hockey?" they said in unison. "We love hockey! Do you play?"

"I used to," I said. "Played in the NHL for Quebec. Now I'm a referee. I was supposed to ref the Pats game tonight but it got canceled."

In the meantime, I felt my already cramped personal space getting less and less. I tried to be polite but it was starting to make me uncomfortable.

"So where are you staying?" one asked.

I told her.

"Oh," she cooed. "That's a nice hotel."

Now, let's stop the story for a second. These two women had maybe six teeth between them and weighed approximately a deuce and three quarters apiece. One of them kept pouring mystery contents from a metal flask to give her beer more alcohol kick. Both reeked of cigarettes and body odor.

Praying that they didn't have in mind what I increasingly suspected they did, I made one final attempt at polite small talk.

"Yeah, the hotel is alright," I said. "The damn TV isn't working, though."

"Oh, that's OK," woman number two said. "I'll keep you entertained."

"Excuse me just for a moment please," I said. "I have to go to the bathroom."

"Hurry back," she said.

That I did. I walked away in increasingly fast steps and then broke into a full sprint through the snow back to the hotel, leaving the dauber behind. I'd already had quite enough entertainment for one evening, thanks.

During my apprenticeship as a young referee, I met some people within the game who became lifelong friends. There were also some experiences from which I learned hard lessons.

Some of the folks who are the most special to me are the linemen I worked with in the junior leagues and the American Hockey League. Hockey people who've never been an official cannot relate to the life of a referee, nor can the vast majority of fans.

To put things simply, when you are a referee, your only real friends are your officiating teammates on the ice. No one else is glad to see you from the time you don your striped sweater until you're ready to leave the building. They are your only comrades, and you are outnumbered on all sides on hostile turf. Everyone else has an agenda to win. As officials, your only agenda is call the game right and fairly.

It is from this shared experience that many of my closest friendships have been developed. Some of the linesmen from my AHL days later joined me in the NHL -- for instance, my dear friend Pat Dapuzzo, whom I first got to know in New Haven -- while many others did not. Back then, the linemen usually worked close to where they lived, so when I see an old photo of myself with a linesman, I can usually tell where and roughly when the photo was taken.

I'd be remiss here if I did not also make mention of the late Romeo LeBlanc.

Romeo was the godfather of officiating to an entire generation of officials and remained a close friend throughout the years. Pretty much every official who made the NHL in my era owes a debt of gratitude to Romeo for the way he cared for us and nurtured us as young officials, whether it is myself, Dan Marouelli, Bill McCreary or a host of others. He helped break in many future NHL linesmen, too, including Bernie DeGrace. On the ice and especially off the ice, Romeo was a treasure.

Romeo was an official for 35 years, including 20 in the AHL. He got a late start in professional officiating, but always had an unbridled passion for the game and for the officiating craft. At age 31, he was working as a machinist in New Brunswick and officiating local games as an avocation. In 1978, he finally got his chance to become an AHL lineseman.

No one ever pulled on the striped shirt with more pride than Romeo LeBlanc. Having broken into the professional ranks so late, however, he knew from day one that he had no shot at ever making the NHL. Instead, he dedicated himself to helping other, younger officials get to the top level.

Romeo never officiated a game in the NHL. However, he once had an opportunity when the league approached him during the official's strike of 1993 to be a replacement linesman. He refused.

"That's scab work," Romeo explained, simply.

Now you have to understand something: Hockey was LeBlanc's life and passion. His fondest dream was to work in the NHL. But he was a working man at heart and far too loyal to his friends to even entertain the idea of accepting such an offer under those circumstances.

In so doing, he passed up his chance to officiate in the NHL. The league should have done the right thing and let him work just one NHL game before he retired -- something that every official in the NHL would have applauded, as would all the players and coaches who knew him from the AHL -- but the powers-that-be wouldn't hear of it. That was wrong.

Ultimately, though, Romeo was a man true to his friends and his principles. Just like my own father, he had no regrets and owed no one a thing. When I think of Romeo, I can't help but smile. He was a delightful man with a great sense of humor.

One time -- this was long before the introduction of replay -- I disallowed a home team goal over the judgment of the goal judge behind the net (remember those?). We really couldn't trust a lot of those guys, because they tended to be a bit too hasty on the trigger finger in turning on the goal light.

"No goal! Didn't cross the line," I said to the home team bench in a quick fly-by, going right past Romeo, too, as I took a skate.

"Stewy, where are you going?" he said.

"If they can't catch me, they can't argue," I explained.

Romeo laughed heartily.

Apart from being a great teammate on the ice, Romeo's friendship, wisdom, support and guidance off the ice were invaluable. Romeo would often pick up fellow officials at the airport and drive them to his family's home. He also drove us to games in Fredricton. It's just the type of human being he was.

Many a time, Romeo and Sylvia had me over as a guest as their home in Dieppe, where we would share one of Sylvia's excellent home-cooked meals and hours of conversation. His daughters Monique and Carole are also wonderful and caring people, and Carole in particular knows as much hockey as anyone I've ever met. The LeBlancs were always the most gracious of hosts, and Romeo even helped me work on my French (when I was accused on being anti-French).

I always looked forward to going to Moncton and seeing Romeo. His garage was like a hockey museum. His most prized possession, apart from the most extensive puck collection I've ever seen was a picture of him doing a very special faceoff drop. It's special because Wayne Gretzky is in the picture. It was taken on the night Edmonton played a game in Halifax.

It was also Romeo who introduced me to the joys of "lobster hot dogs." On many other occasions, we'd get together in Moncton for a bowl of seafood chowder -- some of the best I've ever had in my life -- and then retire to his garage to share a few beers and hours of laughter and conversation. Those were some of the happiest times of my life.

On off-nights, I attended NHL games in order to observe. I went to the Boston Garden a lot, when I was home, to observe there.

After one Bruins game I watched from the press box, I took then-NHL referee Rob Shick out for a few beers at a local bar. As Shick and I walked down State Street en route to my Gremlin after the bar closed, we heard a woman screaming for help. We walked closer, then saw two men holding a woman by a white van. One man had the woman by her feet, the other held her up by her shoulders. They were trying to pitch her into the side of the van. I also noticed another man in the driver's seat.

"It doesn't look like she's having a lot of fun," I shouted.

The man holding the woman's feet let go of her and reached into the van. He grabbed a tire iron.

"Mind your own goddamn business!" he yelled. He stepped

toward me. I pulled out my pistol and police badge. The man with the tire iron threw it at us. The other man dropped the woman on the ground and hopped into the van. The driver peeled off straight across State Street and smashed into a parked car. All three men hopped out of the van and sprinted down State Street.

I didn't run after them. I helped the woman to make sure she was okay. Shick and I helped her stand up. She was in her early twenties and worked as a waitress down the street. She did not know the men. Shick and I brought the woman back to where she worked and I phoned the police. "Where did you get the gun!?" Shick asked me.

I told him, "I'm a reserve police offer. You didn't know that?"

I didn't have many nights off at all between reffing and observing. After observing a game in Vancouver one night, referee Dave Newell, who had worked that night, asked how everything was going. I felt a little frustrated, to be honest, because I wasn't making enough money. I vented to Newell.

"They send me out to places like Calgary, Edmonton, Lethbridge, Swift Current, and Moose Jaw and they're only paying me one-hundred bucks a game. And the Canadian dollar is only worth sixty-five cents. So, I'm only getting sixty-five bucks a game, before taxes. If I work five games in a week, that's only $325. I can make one hundred bucks a day teaching school, and do two games at home and make three hundred bucks. I am not making enough money."

"Let me talk to McCauley," Newell said.

McCauley boarded a plane and flew from Toronto to Calgary where I was staying at a hotel and reffing games around there in the Western Hockey League. He met me at the Delta Bow Valley Hotel.

"Newey tells me you're having a hard time," he said.

"John, I'm just not making enough money," I said. "Even though I'm on the road, I have an apartment at home and I have rent to pay. And I haven't been home. Not that I *want* to go home."

"I'm going to give you so many games, it's either going to kill you or make you a referee," McCauley replied.

I don't know how I came up with the number but I told McCauley if he gave me $5,000 between then and the end of the year, I'd survive because my rent was $700 a month.

"You've got it," he said.

The next day, he gave me a $5,000 check. I always appreciated that Scotty and John and the others showed me understanding, loyalty, encouragement, support, and real human kindness. I also appreciated their patience.

Up until being signed by the NHL, I still was working as a reserve police officer in Yarmouth. I also was coaching Babe Ruth baseball down the Cape. I coached Neal McDonough, who played Buck Compton in the TV mini-series *Band of Brothers*. The person in charge of the Babe Ruth baseball program down there was a field officer for the FBI. He asked me one day how I liked police work.

"Would you be interested in the FBI?" he asked. "I think you might make a good FBI agent."

I submitted an application, had a couple of interviews in Boston, underwent a physical, and did a firearms test. It wasn't long before I received a letter inviting me to the FBI training school in Quantico, Virginia. Ironically, right around the same time, Chief Chapman from the police department in Yarmouth offered me a full-time position with his police department. It was at that same time that Scotty Morrison sent me a letter telling me the NHL was ready to hire me.

Unsure of what to do, I went to see Chief Chapman. "You should go to the NHL," Chapman said. I visited with the FBI one final time. "Have a good career in the NHL," they told me.

And so I went.

I continued to hit a few speed bumps. I refereed an AHL game during the 1986-1987 season in New Haven one night, between the Maine Mariners and New Haven Nighthawks, coached by ex-teammate and friend Robbie Ftorek. New Haven trailed by a few goals at home to the Maine Mariners, a squad that included right wing Doug Brown and coach Tom McVie, a longtime dominant Western Hockey League goal-scorer. About five seconds remained in the contest when a fight broke out. The two teams separated and skated to their benches. A rule back then required teams to return to their benches and remain there during fights. When the scuffle ended, Ftorek refused to put his team back out on the ice. He wanted me to call a match penalty on a Maine player for kneeing.

I told Ftorek the Maine player didn't commit the infraction, but Robbie still refused to return his team to the ice. I told linesman Marty Demers to drop the puck and resume play without New Haven. Demers wanted no part in that.

"Give the puck to me," I told Demers. Standing at center ice, I asked Doug Brown if he was ready. I then gently laid down the puck. Brown banged it into the open net as the clock ticked down to 0.00. I skated off the ice and Ftorek stood there with his arms crossed like Pee-Wee Herman.

"Stew! We've got to talk," Ftorek insisted.

"I'm not talking to you," I replied. "You just embarrassed me."

One of my NHL bosses was infuriated when he learned of the incident. He called me and told me I had embarrassed the game and he wanted my resignation. I faxed it over.

Within an hour, John McCauley called me.

"I have your resignation in my hand," he said. "What's this about?" McCauley told me to meet him at the Boston Marriot the next day. He picked me up there and we drove to the Boston Garden together with linesman Gord Broseker. McCauley didn't say a word to me the entire drive. When we arrived at the Garden and parked the car, he told Broseker to go inside. He then pushed me against a concrete wall on the Southeast Expressway down ramp. He poked me in the chest with his finger, then waved his finger in my face.

"Everyone wants you to quit and so you quit?" he yelled. "You take this resignation back. I'll tell you when to quit. Scotty and I were the ones to hire you. We'll be the ones to fire you. Don't do that again. I won't let you quit or fail, but don't give these people any ammunition to use against you."

A couple days later, I reffed in Montreal and Jim Gregory, the Vice President of Hockey Operations for the NHL and a long-time league executive, was there to watch. He told me to meet him the next morning and so I did. Gregory drove around Montreal to a seminary where Gregory visited one of his friends or a relative. He went inside alone. I waited outside. When he returned, we continued to drive up and down the streets of Montreal.

Finally, Gregory spoke. "I like the way you referee and I like what you did in New Haven," he said. "But you can't be giving points to a player for nothing. That wasn't smart. You could have just taken the puck, thrown it into the corner and counted the five seconds off the clock. That is the only thing that's sort of bothersome. Other than that, everybody got a big chuckle out of it."

Lesson learned.

# CHAPTER 16: Debut at the Garden

I sat in the press box at the old Boston Garden, watching the Boston Bruins play the Montreal Canadiens game on March 27, 1986, absentmindedly picking away at a tub of popcorn. John McCauley, then the NHL Director of Officiating, sat right beside me. We sat there chatting about everything hockey: style, positioning, and philosophy. The Dean of the Boston Bruins, Nate Greenberg, sat safely two seats away.

Early in the second period, Canadiens' left wing Mats Naslund turned quickly in a fit of speed and collided with nearly-stationary referee Dave Newell, who hit the dasher and bent around the stanchion, breaking his ribs. Newell fell to the ice and didn't rise. The Garden crowd grew dead silent. Linesmen Leon Stickle and Ron Asselstine, as well as the medical trainers, checked on Newell. Stickle and Asselstine bent over Newell, then Stickle stared straight up to the press box at McCauley and pointed to his own ribs. He made the broken sign with his hands and then shook his head.

McCauley leaned over and touched my hand, and calmly said two words I'll never forget:

"Get dressed."

My time had arrived. I was back in the NHL.

I never had refereed an NHL game before. Here I was, in my hometown and about to make my NHL officiating debut. I had debuted in this very same historic arena.

I put down the tub of popcorn and stood without saying a word to McCauley or anybody else. I stooped under the small doorway at the rear of the press box, sprinted down the stairs two at a time in my FootJoy black tassel loafers (my father and grandfather always told me to dress to the nines), then hustled down the hall to the referees' room. I always brought my equipment bag and a pair of clean underwear in case one of the officials got injured and I was needed. I would place my equipment bag under the bench in the officials' dressing room, then watch from the press box. I don't think some referees liked when I brought my equipment. They probably thought I was going after their jobs. But my grandfather and father had always taught me to be prepared. "Preparation is the key to victory," taught General Douglas MacArthur.

When I arrived there, I flung the door open. It banged into Newell hard while he was bent over trying to catch his breath. If he hadn't broken his ribs on the ice, surely I finished the job. Ironically, Newell had refereed during my first NHL game as a player and was the reason for this game becoming my first as a ref. I undressed out of my navy blue three-piece suit and striped club tie. McCauley entered the room and spoke with Newell, then turned to me. He asked the question he should have directed at Newell.

"You okay?"

"Sure," I replied.

"Well then, have a good game and don't forget to have some fun out there."

The Boston Bruins had just five games remaining in the regular season and entered with 34-30-10 record. The Canadiens had four games remaining and entered at 37-32-6. The Bruins, therefore, trailed the Canadiens for second in the Adams Division standings by just two points. The Canadiens entered with a 4-3 edge in the season series.

Boston and Montreal were fighting for second place (behind the Quebec Nordiques) and home ice advantage during the first round of the Stanley Cup playoffs. Montreal, at the time, had lost six straight, and nine of twelve games that March, to date.

I finished putting on my shin and elbow pads and changed into my tight polyester striped shirt. I felt sweaty but happy and extremely exuberant and hyper. I left the room, crossed the small hallway, and climbed up four stairs before walking to the threshold. I stopped there to take a quick look. I had seen that same view in 1979 before making my NHL playing debut for Quebec.

I quickly skated two laps around the ice, but something didn't feel quite right. My shin pads were askew. I skated to the Bruins bench where defenseman Ray Bourque handed me black tape. Defensema commented, "It took you long enough to get out here."

"Yeah, about six years," I joked.

I taped my shin pads, then skated back out. I blew my whistle, pointed to Asselstine, telling him to drop the puck. He did and my newest NHL career began. I felt confident, but my debut went up in the flames within thirty seconds.

Bruins center Steve Kasper captured a puck along the sideboards and quickly turned to shoot on net. Canadiens goalie Patrick Roy butterflied and clamped his hand on his chest while a steaming Geoff Courtnall drove toward the net. I had turned low in the corner and was skating exactly where I should have been, on the goal line ten feet from the net. I felt certain Roy had the puck clamped under his armpit as his Montreal cardinal red sweater had turned dark from his sweat. I tried but I couldn't see the puck. I blew the whistle, and the puck slowly and magically appeared between Roy's pad sitting on the goal line so still and untouched that I could read the Bruins logo on it. Courtnall nudged it into the open goal and the crowd went wild. Courtnall celebrated and so did his teammates.

Roy immediately glanced and shouted, "You blew the whistle. No goal!"

Roy knew it. I knew it. Courtnall even knew it. And in just a few seconds, the other 14,448-plus inside the Boston Garden plus thousands more watching on TV would know it, too. Standing tall, I pointed to my whistle and waved my arms across my chest. Bruins co-captain Ray Bourque skated over, stood squarely in front of me and calmly said, "I know you blew the whistle. I know it's no goal, and I know that you know it's a mistake. Are you going over to talk to my coach?" I looked around Bourque, seeing the Boston head coach Butch Goring, who stood in the open door with his hands outstretched like the praying evangelist Billy Graham. Goring's neck veins bulged out like two red Maine boiled lobsters.

"Nah, I'll explain it to him later." I said. "Let's drop the puck."

Almost sixteen minutes still remained in the second period and then a whole third period loomed. The last time I had been on the ice at the Boston Garden, Newell had asked me to leave after earning a minor for roughing, three majors for fighting, and a game misconduct. Here, a little more than six years later, a bunch of disgusted Bruins fans and employees wanted to tell me to get the hell out this game.

Taking deep breaths to try to calm my racing heart, I stared down at the ice and picked up a small piece of paper. Surprisingly, the fans threw nothing onto the ice. Perhaps they were all too stunned to react as this rookie referee had just disallowed a Bruins' goal that would have turned out to be the game-winner.

The game ended in a 3-3 tie. I officiated the best I could and put the no-goal call out of my mind the rest of the way. I was right when I blew the whistle because I had lost sight of the puck. So sad, too bad; on with the game!

Bruins General Manager Harry Sinden described me as a $20,000 referee who just cost the Bruins home ice and a $1 million game. I either read his comment in the newspaper or heard him say it on the radio. I can't remember exactly. But I do remember thinking to myself, "The league could pay me more if it would make Sinden feel better." Ironically, it was Sinden's assistant, Dale Hamilton, who had aided my return to the NHL as a referee. How did I repay the favor? I disallowed a Bruins' winning goal during my first NHL game as a referee. As it turned out, Montreal won three of its final four games, and finished one point ahead of Boston in the Adams Division standings. The Canadiens used home-ice advantage to their favor. They swept the Bruins in the first round and won that year's Stanley Cup. Perron earned a new contract and never sent me a dime—that's gratitude for you.

I went out to the Marriott Copley and drank a few beers with McCauley after the game. He told me that he was proud that I didn't wilt on him after disallowing the goal. He sent me back to the AHL and Baltimore the next day. His parting words, "Tomorrow is your next big game. Don't let me down."

Who woulda thunk that people in Baltimore would have watched the Bruins/Montreal game? It was on ESPN with Sam Rosen calling the game. I heard from nearly everyone about that no-goal call. "You remind me of the first day of hunting season!" one fan yelled. The punchline was something about Buck Fever and pulling the trigger too quickly. Yuk, yuk.

As a young, emerging ref, I learned the best lesson that stood well with me for the next seventeen seasons and more than 1,000 NHL games: Get to the net, get to where you can see the puck, and take an extra second before blowing the whistle. You can't get back the sound of the whistle. Also, when you screw up, you should have the guts to admit the mistake. Try not to make too many mistakes. They can be your ticket out of a job, no matter how many times you apologize.

When I blew that whistle, I was too hasty, even if I was technically correct as I had lost sight of the puck. As a hockey guy, though, I knew I could do better than hiding behind a technicality.

For the record, I didn't feel that I owed anyone. I gave everyone on that ice one hundred percent. I didn't owe them any more than that. I only owed hockey. My one true loyalty is to the game.

The two most renowned disallowed goals during my career came during Game Two of the 1987 Canada Cup Finals on September 13, 1987, a 6-5 double overtime victory for Canada over the Soviet Union at Copps Coliseum in Hamilton, Ontario. Many consider that game the greatest hockey game ever played. Mario Lemieux scored the winner, assisted by Wayne Gretzky at the 10:06 mark of the second overtime.

When the tournament was announced during the 1986-87 NHL season, I asked how the referees were selected. McCauley told me the selection process was done by nationality, and that he expected Mike Noeth and me to represent the United States.

"I don't control the selection process, though," he added. "I just submit a list of names to the International Ice Hockey Federation which has the final say."

Toward the end of the 1986-1987 NHL season, McCauley called me and told me I was in. I could hardly believe it.

I recently had been diagnosed with chondromalacia patellae, an inflammation of the underside of the kneecap and a softening of the surrounding cartilage. I wasn't about to tell McCauley right then that I was about to undergo knee surgery for fear I would be replaced in the tournament; I did tell him after the fact, though, later on during the tournament. The surgery was performed in early July, and my surgeon, Dr. Diane English (a "10" as a doctor and as a person) told me to stay off the skates for a couple weeks. I took the downtime as an opportunity to study the International Ice Hockey Federation rulebook.

I contacted former referee, James Cerbo, who had a working knowledge of all the rulebooks. Cerbo helped me learn the international rules. We spent time down at my new summer house in Hyannis Port, sitting on the deck studying, page-by-page, the differences between the NHL and International Ice Hockey Federation rulebooks.

My first assignment was a round-robin game in Regina, Saskatchewan between Czechoslovakia and Sweden, in front of a crowd of 5,126. Sweden prevailed 4-0 against the Czechs and then twenty-two-year-old Czech goalie, Dominik Hašek. I don't have any vivid memories about Hašek during that contest. He didn't debut in the NHL until four years later, in 1990, as a twenty-five-year-old with the Chicago Blackhawks. Hašek didn't really rise to prominence in the NHL until the 1993-1994 season with the Buffalo Sabres, when he won his first of six Vezina Trophies during his Hall of Fame career. I do remember Sweden looked strong. Its roster included right wing Bengt-Åke Gustafsson, who played nine seasons with the Washington Capitals, and Mats Näslund (a.k.a. *Le Petit Viking*) who played eight seasons with the Montreal Canadiens and one season with the Boston Bruins.

The Regina Agridome, eventually renamed the Brandt Centre, was packed and I simply was just in awe that I was there. All the Western Hockey League officials who used to ignore me when I refereed WHL games in Regina came by to say hello. What a difference a sweater and a contract make! It wasn't too exciting a game as reflected by the score, but it was a good game for me to get my feet wet.

My next round-robin game featured Sweden vs. Finland at Centre 200 in Sydney, Nova Scotia. It was a more bitter rivalry and a rocking crowd of 4,500. I called my game. I let the players play, and I set the pace. I called fourteen minutes of total penalties combined between the two teams. I kept the game under control. The players challenged me a bit. Many of them knew me.

Finland's Esa Tikkanen, who played in the NHL from 1985-1999 with seven different organizations (the Edmonton Oilers, New York Rangers, St. Louis Blues, New Jersey Devils, Vancouver Canucks, Florida Panthers, and Washington Nationals), ran into me in the corner and I leveled him. I knocked him flat out and cold.

All I could hear was him screaming, "Fuffjsisrjisfjgjddc!" I don't speak Finnish but I understood the meaning.

The game ended, I boarded a plane home to Boston, and I thought my work in the Canada Cup was finished. I watched the Canada Cup semifinals at a bar inside Quincy Market in Boston. American Mike Noeth refereed the game between Canada and

Czechoslovakia. Team Canada head coach Mike Keenan and the television announcers got on Noeth when he disallowed a Glenn Anderson goal. Noeth seemed to lose sight of the puck. I didn't think anything about it at the time.

NHL officials training camp was about to begin the morning of Game Two of the finals on September 13. I arrived in Toronto for training camp September 12, the day after the Soviets beat Canada in Game One of the best-of-three final. I checked into the Holiday lnn, settled into my room, and then walked downstairs for an officiating meeting. McCauley and Morrison were sitting at the head table with a couple other supervisors. I sat in the back, between Dave Newell and Andy Van Hellemond, both of whom I admired and loved.

John stood and pointed at me. He motioned with his finger for me to walk outside. We met out in the hallway and I followed him down the hallway to a stairwell. He walked down about five stairs and turned.

"What are you doing tomorrow night?" he asked.

"Probably go to The Keg, have something to eat, drink a couple of beers, and watch Game Two," I replied.

"You'll be watching the game but you won't be watching it from The Keg. You're working."

He shook my hand.

"Go out and do the job I know you can do."

McCauley never said much more than he had to say. He could motivate me and get me to do anything just with a look and simple comment, like my father had done when I was young.

We returned to the meeting and McCauley welcomed everyone. He congratulated all the referees and linesmen who had participated in the Canada Cup. He mentioned all our names one-by-one. He then announced John D'Amico and Sven-Olof Lundstrom would be one of the linesman for Game Two and Don Koharski would be the standby referee. Everyone applauded. D'Amico basked, and rightly so, in his glory.

"Paul Stewart is going to be the referee," McCauley added.

You could have heard a pin drop. There was such a deafening silence. Then, Van Hellemond and Newell each gave me a little whack on the arm and shook my hand. Others turned around and gave me the thumbs-up signal.

"I don't think I'll go out tonight," I told Newell and Van Hellemond after the meeting.

Newell laughed. "I think that's a good idea. Stay in, get room service, drink a couple beers, watch TV, and put your feet up."

I had packed a three-piece suit and my grandfather's 1938 Stanley Cup pocket watch. I wore both the suit and the watch to Game Two. John D'Amico drove me there.

When we arrived, I walked around the entire rink to take it all in because I had never been in Copp's before. It helped calm me, as usual, just being in a rink; that was where I was meant to be.

As I stood on one of the team's benches in an empty arena, hours before the game, Hockey Hall of Fame writer Francis Rosa from *The Boston Globe* approached me and congratulated me for being selected to referee. I had known Rosa since I was a little boy because he was friends with my dad. Rosa, when starting out as a hockey writer, would ask my father to sit with him in the Boston Arena press box (with the broken windows behind them and the wind whipping through) and explain hockey and the rules to him.

I showed Rosa my grandfather's watch. "I feel as if destiny took a hand," I told him. "I was meant to be here. I feel a little bit like George Patton because I'm the right man at the right place with the right equipment. I have the temperament to handle this game. I was born to work this game." I don't know if Rosa ever wrote what I had told him, but I'll always remember saying it.

Nervous excitement got the best of me. I couldn't sit there and talk with D'Amico and Lundstrom, so I took my clothes off and showered for fifteen minutes. I always felt better and relaxed when I took a shower. I remember D'Amico rubbing something all over his body in the dressing room before the game. He always rubbed stuff on himself. Some thought it was horse ointment.

Hyped, I went out to skate early after Canada and the USSR teams both took their warm-ups. It was seven minutes before they were to play the national anthems. Team Canada's Mike Gartner, an ex-teammate of mine with the Cincinnati Stingers, bumped into me.

"Nobody would believe this," Gartner said.

"What? That I'm here? Or that you're here?" I replied.

"Stew, you've come a long way from playing," he said.

D'Amico received a nice ovation when he was introduced, but I received a heavy dose of boos. It made me laugh and feel comfortable. I got a kick out of it. I had such a fierce concentration during games that I always used the time during the national anthems to say a brief prayer and blank my mind. The New York Rockettes could have marched out during the anthems and I wouldn't have noticed. Everyone in the front row could have been sitting there naked and I wouldn't have noticed. Well, except maybe Christie Brinkley and Carol Alt.

I replayed in my mind a conversation with my dad. Before I boarded the plane for training camp days before, the last thing my dad told me was, "No matter where you referee this year, think of yourself as only being at The Quincy Youth Arena and it's a youth hockey game between the Mite whites and the Mite blues. It's just a hockey game between two teams. Let them play until they show you they don't want to. That's when you start to referee."

All three games in that 1987 Canada Cup Final ended in a 6-5 score. Game Two deserved all the praise it received. It was a fast-paced and brilliant game between two high-powered teams. Team Russia's Valeri Kamensky took the puck more than half the length of the ice and broke through the defense for the tying goal with 1:04 remaining. That made it 5-5 and sent the game into overtime. Lemieux's double OT winner gave him a hat trick, and Gretzky earned his fifth assist of the contest on the final score.

It not only was a fast-paced game, but also physical. Mark Messier, another ex-Stingers teammate, slapped Vladimir Krutov in the face with the blade of his stick near the red line between the two benches, and I penalized him for high-sticking. I also penalized Gartner when he ran into USSR goalie Yevgeny Belosheikin and banged him into the boards. I called Gartner for charging. He argued with me all the way from the corner to the penalty box, telling me I didn't know the rules. I kept my cool.

The NHL rules allowed for bumping goalies back then, saying they were fair game. But the International Ice Hockey Federation rulebook prohibited it. When Gartner's penalty expired, he continued to flap his gums at me.

"I'll bet you my paycheck tonight against your paycheck tonight that I know this rule," I told him. "You send the stick boy down to my dressing room between periods and we'll figure it out."

"I'm not betting you," he fired back.

"Fine, but send the stick boy down," I reminded him. When I arrived back in the dressing room, I took out the rulebook, folded the page that discussed making contact with goalies, put two stars next to the rule, and circled it. I told the stick boy to give it to Gartner.

"Tell him he can write the check out to the Christian Children's Fund," I added. Gartner didn't say anything the rest of the game. Working in that type of hockey environment, all referees must show that same type of confidence. The only way to gain that level of confidence is by preparing. I was well-prepared.

While leaving the ice following the first period, Alan Eagleson, then the executive director of the NHL Players' Association and one of the founders of the first Canada Cup, confronted me. "You've got to give us a chance, Paul," he said. "You're taking us out of the game."

I turned to D'Amico and asked, "Who is this guy?"

My comment dropped Eagleson's ego down a few notches. I should have asked him if he was the director of the entire tournament or just the Canadian team. Eagleson should have been thanking me after the first period because I had rightfully waved off a Russian goal. I'd started to raise my hand to call the penalty when Sergei Nemchinov took his skate and slid it into Team Canada goalie Grant Fuhr's pad, pulling at Fuhr. Fuhr did a quick little butterfly and then Team Canada defenseman Doug Crossman reached around, grabbed Nemchinov, and threw him down. So I blew the whistle for two penalties, one on Nemchinov and the other on Crossman.

I wasn't watching the puck any longer and it went in the net. I immediately waved it off because I had blown the whistle beforehand. I didn't blow the whistle because Nemchinov had been in the crease during the time of the goal. I immediately waved off another goal when a Soviet player reached up with his stick above his shoulder and knocked the puck past Fuhr.

At center ice for the faceoff following the second disallowed goal, Viacheslav Fetisov skated over to me and said, "My coach wants you to know that he thinks you stink."

I looked up. USSR head coach Viktor Tikhonov, a legend in Russia who died at 84 years old in November 2014, had his index finger and thumb on his nose, waving at me like "You stink!" I looked back at Fetisov and joked, "I think he's talking about you."

Fetisov said, "Ah, don't listen to him. He's a pain in the ass anyway. It was a high stick. Don't worry about it."

I assured him I was not worried.

Watching the game film later, I actually could have disallowed another Russian goal during the first period. Fuhr was out of the crease with Valeri Kamensky standing there in front of him. When Fuhr went to move, he and Kamensky collided. Kamensky might have intentionally bumped him, but I viewed it as a pure hockey play that created an open net. Instead of regaining his position, Fuhr moved toward his right and threw a punch in Kamensky's direction. Fuhr then scrambled back to the left, but the puck sailed past him into the net. If Fuhr had returned to position earlier instead of going after Kamensky, he likely would have made the save, and so I don't feel too bad about making that no-goal call.

The knee I had surgically repaired the preceding July began to cramp during the second overtime. As an unbiased ref, I obviously didn't care who won. But I was so glad when Gretzky fed Lemieux for the game-winner because I was experiencing such severe cramps.

I didn't keep many sweaters from my officiating career, but I kept that one. It was special to me.

While bent over untying my skates afterward in my stall, I saw a foot come into my view and kick the toe of one of my skates. I looked up and there was McCauley. He nodded just like my father used to. John wasn't effusive. He didn't pat me on the back or shake my hand. He just looked at me and nodded. He started to walk away, then he looked back and said one word. "Superb." I get emotional when I reflect back on that moment.

Not long after, he summoned me into the shower room. "The committee's coming in here in five minutes to tell you they want you to work Game Three," he said.

I was overjoyed, and could use the money. It was an extra $1,500 in my wallet.

He was washing his hands, and he looked over at me said, "But you're not going to work."

"I'm not?" I asked.

"The way you performed tonight proved what Scotty and I have been telling people all along," McCauley said. "You're going to be a great referee in the NHL, and your next eighty games are coming from me. If you go out Tuesday night and make any mistakes, whatsoever, it gives them ammunition. So you need to trust me. Put your knee brace on the ground, put an ice pack on your knee. When the committee comes in, try to stand up and be honored, but you tell them that you have to get back to them about it but you don't think so because you just had a knee operation." He dried his hands, took his paper towel, flipped it into the trash barrel, then punched me in the arm. "You should go have a couple beers." Out he walked.

I don't know if people quite understand the reason I loved John McCauley so much that we named our first son after him. He was such a great boss and terrific man. The last thing any of his officials wanted to do was disappoint him. He motivated everyone to perform in a way where the last thing they want to do was let him down. Anyone able to do that is a great boss. And he was.

McCauley informed me one day that I soon would be reffing primarily in the NHL and he asked me to move to Chicago, Illinois to put me in a location where I could go east and west easily to lessen my travel.

"John, I'll move to Chicago tomorrow morning. But have you ever met my dad?"

"No, but I'm looking forward it."

The next day, I introduced McCauley to my father, who by then had become so crippled and in such tough physical shape that John looked absolutely stunned upon meeting him. Dad looked like Yoda from Star Wars. He was bent over with a humped back and his fingers gnarled. His head also had grown larger than normal because of his Paget's Disease. I had moved back into my parents' Jamaican Plain home to help them.

Later that day, McCauley and I sat in a coffee shop at the US Airways terminal inside Boston's Logan Airport.

"Your dad seems like a very nice guy," McCauley said.

"Yeah, he's the greatest. Sad, he's in tough shape. He's at the clubhouse turn."

"Maybe you don't have to move to Chicago. I think maybe you should stay here."

That was John McCauley. That was the reason that I never wanted to fail him. It was the secret to this great coach's success. The last thing I ever wanted to do was to let him down by not trying and not working to improve.

I think about McCauley and my dad every day. I miss those two men so much. Years later, current-day NHL referee Wes McCauley

(John's son) and I shared a big laugh thinking about how our dads are still watching us together; sometimes with pride and sometimes with mouths agape and elbowing each other to silently say, "Look at those two! What are they DOING?!"

All joking aside, in tough times, I can still quite literally hear the voices of my father and of John McCauley speaking to me. I am a Catholic but I find a piece of Jewish liturgy called "We Remember Them" by Rabbis Sylvan Kamens and Jack Riemer to be one of the most eloquent reflections I have ever seen. It brings a tear to my eye, in fact, because it expresses my ongoing relationship with those close to me who have left this earth.

*In the rising of the sun and in its going down, we remember them.*
*In the blowing of the wind and in the chill of winter, we remember them.*
*In the opening of buds and in the rebirth of spring, we remember them.*
*In the blueness of the sky and in the warmth of summer, we remember them.*
*In the rustling of leaves and in the beauty of autumn, we remember them.*
*In the beginning of the year and when it ends, we remember them.*
*When we are weary and in need of strength, we remember them.*
*When we are lost and sick at heart, we remember them.*
*When we have joys we yearn to share, we remember them.*
*So long as we live, they too shall live, for they are now a part of us, as we remember them.*

## CHAPTER 17: Fighting Back the Tears

Back on December 6, 1987, Wayne "The Great One" Gretzky, then a twenty-six-year-old Edmonton Oilers superstar, potted his sixth goal in one game against the Minnesota North Stars in Edmonton. With that goal, Gretzky would have tied Red Berenson for the post-World War II record for the most goals in a single NHL game.

But not so fast. A rookie referee, yours truly, disallowed it. The Edmonton fans were not pleased with me. It was the right call, though. I couldn't be intimidated by the prospect of being unpopular with the home crowd or be swept up in the excitement of the moment as Gretzky stood to make history that night. It couldn't be personal; it had to be business.

Wayne didn't utter a word of protest, not even a disapproving shake of his head. He simply skated away. I found that a tad surprising in the moment. Although Gretz and I go way back with each other to my own playing days and I am proud to consider him a friend off the ice, he was never shy about telling officials what he thought about calls with which he disagreed.

Back in the locker room after the game, my fellow officials were subdued. Officiating supervisor Wally Harris was on hand, too. I vaguely noticed that he was staying a little closer by me than he ordinarily would.

During the car ride back to the hotel, we had the car radio on a news station. The broadcaster said, "Referee Paul Stewart, who tonight..." Wally abruptly shut off the radio.

"You don't need to listen to that crap," he said by way of explanation.

Back at the hotel, Harris said to me, "Paul, when we get inside, we need to talk."

He came up with me, with an ashen look on his face.

"Wally, what's wrong?" I said. "Am I being fired?"

"No, no, you aren't being fired," he said, still frowning.

After the slightest pause, he explained.

"Paul," he said, "your dad died today."

I was the last to know. My father hadn't been well, but it's still news you're never fully prepared to hear. My fellow officials knew before game time, as did the players who knew of my dad. This was the era before most of us had cell phones and were plugged in to information 24/7. I went through my normal game-day prep, totally focused on the job I had to do that night.

That was how my father taught me to be. If you were truly serious about being a player, your focus had to be on practicing and playing. As a student, if you were serious about learning, you had to buckle down even in subjects you found difficult. As an official, the most important game in the world was the one who were reffing that night, followed by the next and the next.

My dad also taught me what I call the "Eleventh Commandment:" If you are in position to help another human being in need and do not make a genuine effort to do so, it reflects poorly on you. My father's caring and humanity was not just for family members but for everyone regardless of race, color, creed or economic status. On many, many occasions, my dad went the extra mile for his students, neighbors and even strangers. I have to be honest. At times in my youth, I didn't understand it. I even may have resented it on occasion. Now, I feel nothing but gratitude. What a role model he was!

I remember the long, long flight back from Edmonton to Boston. I sat in the back row of the plane, deep in reflection and emotion. I've always had a sharp long-term memory but, at this stage of my life, was driven to constantly press forward. No one told me about my dad's passing until after the game because that's 100 percent how he would have wanted it.

"Are you a referee? Are they paying you to officiate?" he'd have asked.

"Yes," I'd say.

"Then go out and be a referee," he'd have replied.

We had the same conversation in other contexts. I'd watch him officiate and I'd watch him coach and his level of focus and attention to detail amazed me, and this was back when I was playing sports rather than being on the other side. The same principles applied. Earn respect and give respect to the game. Be in the right position. Have conviction in your judgment. Be tough but be fair.

I never really realized the full scope of my dad's legacy outside of my own eyes until I arrived back in Boston after his death. I remember landing at Boston's Logan Airport and receiving a handshake and heartfelt condolences from then-Adirondack Red Wings tough guy Steve Martinson. I was surprised, but appreciative.

Martinson and I had almost gotten in a fight a year earlier after I refereed a game between Adirondack and the Nova Scotia Oilers in Halifax. The game had been on a Sunday. I went to a bar called The Palace after the game. Martinson came over, tapped me on the shoulder, and challenged me to a fight. He had gotten his butt kicked during the game and had been yapping at me after his fight. I had told him during the contest that if he wanted his butt kicked again to keep yapping. Everyone followed us outside. Darren Pang, a member of the Nova Scotia Oilers, warned me not to fight Martinson because I would lose my job.

"But he's challenging me, Panger," I told Darren.

Pang stepped in front of Martinson. "If you fight him, he might hurt you because he's good," he told Martinson.

Martinson backed off.

I walked down the street and bumped into Adirondack coach Bill "Foxy" Dineen who had played 323 NHL games. The Red Wings had gotten routed and Dineen did not want any of his players out drinking that night. He had given them a curfew.

I knew the players weren't supposed to be there so I decided to divert Bill and invited him to my hotel room. We sat, drank beer, and told stories until four a.m. there in my room. The next morning, Foxy phoned my hotel room and told me he had heard one of his players had almost fought me.

"You intercepted me," he said.

"Nothing happened," I replied.

"Who was it?"

"Nobody important. Let it go."

About a week later, he called me again and told me found out it'd been Martinson. "He's a kid," I said. "Let it go. Give him a few extra wind sprints, but let it go."

The issue was put to rest once and for all on December 7th, after I had taken the red eye home from Edmonton. There was a lengthy memorial article about my father, written by Willy McDonough, on the front page of the sports section.

Martinson had read the article in the paper. Now he walked up to me, looked me in the eyes and shook my hand, expressing his regrets. It's what's best about hockey players. Though the friction of the game sometimes ratchets up so high that the fight comes off the ice, it truly isn't personal most of the time. I'll always remember that and him for that moment.

That's precisely what I mean about leaving the friction on the ice. Unlike players, referees must do their best to get beyond the friction immediately on the ice to ref the fairest game possible. I always tried my best to do just that. As I said, I never wanted to let down McCauley, so I had begun to curb my tongue and curtail some of my antics and theatrics. I am glad I wasn't timid to make the right call that night in Edmonton. That's the reason McCauley and Morrison believed in me.

They believed in me, yes, but that's not to say that they were always pleased with me.

I specifically recall a lecture over the telephone from Morrison after I told two players during an AHL game in Springfield, "If you don't start fighting, I'm going to kick the shit out of both of you because I'm tired of watching you dance around me." Then-AHL president Jack Butterfield and Al Arbour, a longtime NHL coach and executive, were in attendance and heard me say it.

Still, McCauley and Morrison let things slide with a phone lecture or something similar because they understood what I could do as a referee for sixty minutes each game. I worked fairly and passionately. They never had to worry about me not calling certain penalties for fear of someone's reaction. McCauley told me one night in Buffalo, "You got the whole building rocking and angry, but you didn't fail me when the tough call needed to be made at the end of the game." Same thing with the Gretzky disallowed goal. I didn't consider the crowd's disappointment or how "The Great One" was chasing NHL history.

My relationship with John McCauley transcended that of an employer and an employee. I found a second father and tremendous mentor in him. I know I used his lessons when dealing with referees and others in my own work in the KHL in Russia. McCauley helped me to help myself to learn my trade. He was my favorite professor and a remarkable role model. John's son, Wes, went on to become a fine NHL referee in his own right and a friend of mine.

I had been with John in Philadelphia during the 1989 NHL playoffs. I ran to get him milk several times because he almost constantly complained of heartburn. McCauley had gallstones, but he never visited the doctor. He was afraid of doctors. He called me on the phone the day before he finally checked into the hospital to undergo a procedure. He asked me for a pair of walking shoes. I had a deal with FootJoy and promised to get him a pair.

The next day, my cell phone rang while I was on the golf course. I owned one of the primitive cell phones. It weighed about fifty pounds and I carried it in a bag. I answered. NHL linesman Pat Dapuzzo was the one calling.

"Where are you?" Dapper asked.

"I just finished playing golf and I'm going to have a beer," I told him.

"I have some bad news. We lost our friend." A gallstone had lodged in McCauley's common bile duct and he died of peritonitis. I couldn't speak.

I can't ever get over walking into the funeral home and seeing Ron Finn, a NHL linesman who also was McCauley's brother-in-law. Finn put his arm around me and we walked inside. I felt inconsolable, then I saw McCauley's three children and his wife. I couldn't hold it together anymore. I broke down crying.

About a decade later, I named my first son after John McCauley. I am not ashamed to say that I loved the man. John McCauley, together with Scotty Morrison, gave me my life back.

I am forever indebted to them for the gift of the opportunity to prove myself. I am a better person for having known both of them. I knew how unique McCauley was, both as a human being and a boss, but I failed to anticipate how much things would change after he passed away.

I had always mentally prepared for each game, sizing up my opponents and strategizing before each game to figure out a plan of attack, yet I was blindsided by how my working conditions deteriorated after McCauley was gone. I often find myself still wondering what could have been had McCauley not died so suddenly at age forty-four. How would my life have been different? Would it have been different at all? I think so.

I believe that my reffing career was derailed by some very personal issues between myself and McCauley's successors. My critics didn't evaluate me based on the work I did on the ice, but on their own dislike of me as a person. After McCauley died, I was in the crosshairs of the league. For one thing, they weren't too enamored of American officials in general. For another, our personalities mixed like oil and water.

I also assume my share of the blame. Maybe I rub some people the wrong way. Maybe I showboated too much during my playing career. Maybe my ADHD sometimes makes me do things without thinking first. Maybe my exuberance, flair, style, confidence, and tongue-in-cheek sense of humor have rubbed certain people the wrong way. After John's death and for the rest of my active officiating career, I always got the impression that my performance for sixty minutes each night became secondary to my personality in how the league regarded me.

After McCauley passed, I reffed my contracted seventy-two-game season only once. I typically refereed sixty-something games. My additional contests were given to other referees who received thousands of dollars in extra money to work them. They were essentially paying other people extra just to avoid having me work. How about that for a strong officials' union?

I never worked a Stanley Cup Final despite my reputation as one of the best referees in the game. Multiple times, I finished second—behind only Kerry Fraser—in the NHL Player Association's internal poll of the best referees in the league. I had their respect because I understood their mindset, valued the flow of the game, always hustled into position, and could usually separate the wheat from the chaff on borderline calls. They could talk to me, but I was in control and I knew when the time for talking was done. Those were the keys to me gaining acceptability.

Nevertheless, I never refereed beyond the second round (conference semifinals) of the NHL Stanley Cup playoffs. Like every player, every referee aspires to make the Stanley Cup Final. It felt terrible boarding a plane to training camp year after year, in terrific physical shape, being ready to give one hundred percent every game, knowing I had such strong rapports with teams and having tremendous passion for my work, but also knowing I never had a chance to referee in the Stanley Cup Finals. I would have needed eleven heart attacks to happen to the other referees to have been selected to work a Stanley Cup Final, plain and simple.

People wonder about the reason I occasionally acted out, even as a ref. Hadn't I matured since my days as a player? While I had begun to curtail my tongue before John McCauley died, I acted out after he was gone. I should have handled it better as a professional but I felt like my fate had already been sealed as someone who would never break through the glass ceiling.

I felt an overwhelming sense of frustration and disillusionment. In my formative years of 1983 to 1989, I had a succession of tremendous instructors and mentors. Sometimes I received tough love, but it was deserved and I benefited as a pro. Later, the rank-and-file officials came off to me as bigoted, biased, and purely terrible coaches. Some colleagues may disagree, even vehemently, but that was how I experienced it.

Whereas my father, Junie O'Brien and my early refereeing teachers had led by example and commanded respect, I later encountered league bosses who tried to rule with an iron fist and demanded compliance simply by virtue of their position. The NHL commissioner was sharp and had some good people under him but there was too much of a patronage system. There were folks in authority positions who were petulant and petty, and some who weren't very bright in book-, people- or hockey-smarts. Not a good combination.

As a player, I built a reputation as an over-the-top, exuberant brawler; a showboater without much apparent intelligence. In my defense, I will say the diplomas from Groton School and the University of Pennsylvania, an Ivy League school, that hang over my desk at home show a different side of who I am. I may have earned those degrees with some struggle but I'm only as stupid as the others who graduated. I even know a few multi-syllable words and can use them correctly in a sentence (if I put my mind to it). For many of my doubters, their initial skepticism ceded once they witnessed my ability as a referee and judged my body of work.

One night, Bob Hodges and I worked together in Buffalo. Bob Hodges served as an NHL linesman from 1972 -1997. He worked 1,701 regular season games, 147 playoff games, and 3 Stanley Cup Finals. Hodges was an 11-year veteran during my first NHL training camp in 1983. Anyway, that night, Hodges got knocked off the blue line because the Buffalo Memorial Auditorium was a tight rink.

A player jumped over the boards, ran into Hodges, and accidentally knocked him down, flat on the ice. The play went offside and led to a goal that I waved off. I blew the whistle, disallowed it, skated to Hodgy, and helped him up from the ice. The players asked the reason I disallowed the goal. I told them, plain and simple, the play went offsides. I didn't say anymore; I was a rookie ref, but I wasn't afraid to make the call. I pointed to the dot. Play resumed.

Hodges found a respect for me because of that play. If he had judged me prematurely based on my reputation, after that night he judged me solely on my ability as a referee. He got to know me and learned I wasn't some fool. As an aside, Hodges was a nice man. He worked as a machinist before being an NHL linesman, and part of one of his fingers was missing. I remember him shaking my hand and how strong his hand was despite missing part of a finger.

But for every Bob Hodges I encountered—people willing to keep an open mind and judge me on my merits as a referee—there were others who remained unconvinced that I deserved to be where I was. They never tried—or wanted—to get to know me as a person and primarily judged me based on preconceptions of my personality. That filtered into judgments of my on-ice work, too. One thing was for sure: the league never considered even my most harmless of antics the least bit humorous.

I, on the other hand, find humor in almost everything. I enjoyed the frequent travel and the friendships developed with so many other referees and linesman and the many laughs we shared over the years. Some of my favorite memories were made during those years.

I remember one night when NHL linesmen Mike Cvik and Brad Lazarowich ate nearly three hundred chicken wings between them. We were at an all-you-can-eat Chinese food buffet for $9.50 (the soda wasn't included) right behind the Sheraton Hotel and near the Cabaret Les Amazones, a strip club, in Quebec. The three of us were there on an off-day and Cvik and Lazarowich ate so much to the point where the owner came out and said, "Here's your money! Go! Don't come back!" I think Cvik and Lazarowich's pictures might still be posted there so they'll never be allowed to eat at that joint again.

Cvik and I were two peas in a pod, although from very different backgrounds. He, Pat Dapuzzo and Brian Murphy are people to whom I'd have trusted my life, on or off the ice. We also had a lot of fun.

Cvik used to wrestle under the ring name "Tony Cross" before starting an officiating career, and he certainly was built for it. On skates, Mike stood damn close to seven feet tall. On his bare feet, Mike stood a little over 6-foot-9 and he weighed about 265 well-hewn pounds.

I can still close my eyes and remember games that Mike and I work in Calgary, with our partner official, who was diminutive linesman of Asian descent. We made quite the sight together, the three of us!

I can picture the T-Bird that Mike drove, with the seat pushed all the way back -- and still lacking leg room for him. One day he was driving me around the Alberta countryside.

"What are those things running around?" I asked, pointing.

"They're antelopes," Cvik said.

"I thought those were supposed to be orange, not brown," I replied.

"Antelopes, Stew! Not cantaloupes!" Mike responded.

In the NHL, I returned the favor. When he came to the eastern U.S. for the first time, I thought it was only right if I took him around New York City. I told him we'd go all around the city -- a bit by public transit to cover long distances but mostly by walking around the city.

The weather was a bit chilly, and I was wearing a trench coat as we walked down 42nd Street. Now, this was back before 42nd Street was revitalized. These were the days when the locale was truly something like what was depicted in Taxi Driver: seedy as hell, with all sorts of shady people walking around. Mike had never seen anything quite like it.

As we walk down the street, one of the street characters says hello to me. From the way he was dressed and the jewelry he sported, he was likely a dope dealer and pimping as well.

"Hey! How ya been, my man?" he says.

"Not too bad," I said. "How's business?"

"Aw, real good, real good," he said.

"Well, you have a good night," I replied.

"You too, brother. You, too!"

As we walked on, Mike turned to me with a disbelieving look on his face.

"Do you really know that guy?" he asked.

"Nah," I said. "Never seen him before in my life. He thinks we're cops."

We did look like plain clothes cops, actually. No one else disturbed us as we walked.

Another time, linesman Brian Murphy and I had heard that Peter Luger Steakhouse was the best restaurant in Brooklyn, but it was booked solid and not taking reservations for a week or more. If you don't succeed at first, try, try again. After being refused a reservation the first time, I decided to call back. I phoned the restaurant back with a new plan in mind. This second time was the charm.

"Hi, this is NHL commissioner, Gary Bettman," I said, launching into my best impression of Gary's distinctive voice. "I need a table tonight for me, my best referee, Paul Stewart, and two of our linesmen."

I didn't know beforehand if they even knew Gary there, but it worked. We were seated at Peter Luger Steakhouse forty minutes later. Recently, I reminisced about that story with Murph, and he added some other tales about our times together.

Murphy recalled, "We were in Quebec City for a couple days and we always stayed at the Château Frontenac. By the Château was this famous restaurant called Cafe de la Paix. Everyone went to Cafe de la Paix. Paul just loved to go there because the owners knew him. We went there for dinner on Friday night, lunch on Saturday, and we went there after the game on Saturday night. We ate there three times and there was never a bill.

"But the funny thing is that we were there on Friday night and Pittsburgh was in town. The owner comes to tell Paul that Mario Lemieux was with his family upstairs in a private room. So Paul puts on a waiter's outfit and hat and goes upstairs and goes over to Lemieux and asks him if he wanted some more wine or dessert. So Paul was 'waitering' for Mario Lemieux one night."

Of course, even my sense of humor had its limits, at least on the ice. Lemieux and I had a couple of run-ins along the way. During the late 1980s, I had heard stories about the Penguins' superstar flexing his muscles, so to speak, and berating young officials. He had called himself "The Show" to another referee, at least so I had been told.

"When we go to Pittsburgh, we'll see just how big of a 'show' he is," I told linesmen/friends Gerry Gauthier and Mark Pare. When we visited Pittsburgh for a game between the Flyers and Penguins, Lemieux bumped me at center ice during a stoppage after I disallowed a Pittsburgh goal in the third period with the game tied. I moved him back slightly, putting my hands on his chest. He yelled at me to remove my hands. I told him never to bump me again.

"You bump me and we're going to find out what's what," I told him.

He replied by telling me that he was The Show and that the people there had come to see him.

"Really?" I asked, then did a little spin around center ice glancing up into the crowd. "So all these people came to see you? Well, they can watch you sit over there. Bam, here's a two-minute penalty for The Show." I sent Lemieux to the penalty box.

Rick Tocchet, then a Flyers player, told me, "You have a lot of jam," to which I replied that I wasn't going to take any of Lemieux's abuse or any from the Flyers, either.

Lemieux skated over to me after his penalty expired and asked me if I had played in the NHL.

"You know I played in this league," I replied.

He yapped, "Yeah, and you were a horseshit player."

"Okay, but I was there and in Quebec, too. Now I'm reffing this game."

"Yeah, and you're a worse referee," he said.

"Let me ask you a question now," I said. "Are all these people still here to see you?"

I immediately did another little spin, glancing up at the crowd. I then looked over at Tocchet and commented, "I wonder how we're going to get all these fans who are here to see The Show into the shower room." I dumped Lemieux. Off he went. Hopefully, he didn't use all the hot water. It took a while for the ice crew to scrape all the popcorn and pizza off the ice thrown in my direction.

But like Clemenza's famous line in *The Godfather*, that decision wasn't personal, it was just business. My business was maintaining the order and dignity of the game, which meant not taking shit from anyone, not even The Show. That wasn't the only time I tossed Super Mario, either. I tossed him from another game later in his career after he returned from cancer. Lemieux's back was hurting him. He had trouble bending over to tie his skates. I knew he felt great pain and he mentioned it to me during the game.

"I should dump you," I said.

He told me it wouldn't bother him.

"Just slam that stick on the ice and I can handle it," I told him. I still laugh as I reflect on it.

He slammed it on the boards and waved his arms at me. I gave him the boot. I took the hit for him. Maybe he'll never admit it and maybe he shouldn't, but someone there that day remembers what happened very well. I got the sense he didn't want fans or anyone to know he was hurting so bad. I read between the lines. Maybe I took a little bit of liberty, but I don't think he was upset when I dumped him.

Even superstars aren't above the rules. I ditched Gretzky once, too, after he handed me his stick and bowed to me! I already had taken some verbal abuse from him during the game but had overlooked it up to a point.

"What's this for?" I asked.

He told me the way I was reffing had taken the stick out of his hands so I might as well keep it. That was near the end of the game so I tossed him. I didn't run him earlier for abuse of official because the fans had paid good money to see him there in Hartford, not me.

Next time I saw Gretz I told him never to put me in that position again because I reminded him that people came to watch him play. I told him that Walter and Phyllis, his mom and dad whom I knew, would be disappointed in him when he talked like that. In one week, my *first* week in the National Hockey League, I threw out Steve Yzerman, Gretzky, and Lemieux.

John Zeigler, the league president from the New York NHL office called me and asked, "Are we having a problem getting along with the superstars?" Not me—it wasn't personal, it was just business. Part of reffing is maintaining on-ice a respect for the game and that means respecting the other people on the ice with you.

Lemieux and Gretzky, both of whom I got to know well, were great men off the ice as well as otherworldly on-ice talents. I was lucky to have shared the ice with them and Gordie Howe. Mario, in particular, possessed everything: size, strength, speed, toughness. He could carry a team on his back.

Lemieux was one hundred percent correct about being The Show. He was the reason people came. Hockey fans don't pay to root for the refs or linesmen. I knew my place, despite what others might have thought about me. For example, I called only four bench minor penalties during my entire reffing career.

Lemieux, who returned to the NHL after his own courageous battle with Hodgkin's lymphoma, was extremely kind to me after I was diagnosed with colon cancer. He visited with me the first time I worked in Pittsburgh after I returned to the NHL. I always considered Lemieux the best player I ever saw live, besides Bobby Orr. I'd put him on a hockey Mount Rushmore with Orr, Gordie Howe, Jean Beliveau, and Wayne Gretzky. Yes, my Mount Rushmore has five players, not four.

I credit the Pittsburgh team doctor and a mutual friend, Dr. Chip Burke, for thawing the ice between Lemieux and me. I am not exactly certain what they talked about, but Mario and I got to share a round of golf and a cigar at a Tournament that JR's dad, Wally Roenick, held for Mobil Oil. After that, we kind of backed off each other. Mutual respect can go a very long way.

So even if I wasn't well-liked on the ice, at least I was well-respected by most. Boston Bruins defenseman Zdeno Chara, the 2008-2009 James Norris Memorial Trophy winner, said about me, "He just let players police themselves in games. As far as Paul, he was unbelievable to me and helped me so much on the ice. He absolutely was one of the best referees I've had a chance to play [alongside]. He let things sort out on the ice. Guys wanted to fight—he had no problem to let the guys fight when there was a commercial break. He said, 'Okay, you guys want to go? Go at it.' And that was good. He didn't interfere with what guys wanted to do on the ice."

"He was very fair," Chara added. "He was very human and open to talk to. He explained things. I loved the way he reffed a game. He got emotional at times. I knew he did. But that's just because he cared about the game so much. A lot of the times I'd play the puck and he'd say, 'It was a great play. I know it was icing, but it was not your fault. The forward should have been there.' A lot of times he was almost like a coach on the ice."

I respected those players such as Chara, Lemieux, Gretzky, and Ray Bourque who played the right way. I didn't even like giving great players penalties because they played the game so well, so beautifully. But, sometimes, it was necessary. For example, I always trailed Bourque when he had the puck after staying on the ice for a second straight shift because, if he made a mistake, he only made mistakes when he was tired. He very rarely made mistakes, but, when tired, he tried to do the things he was capable of when he was fresh off the bench. He couldn't always do it and he'd lose the puck at times.

I trailed him because I always wanted to be in the correct position when it happened. One night in Buffalo, Bruins coach Pat Burns triple-shifted Bourque. The Hall of Fame defenseman committed a tripping penalty and I called it.

"I hate to give you the tripping penalty," I told him.

"I'm tired. I need two minutes off," he replied.

Bourque came around the net one night at the old Boston Garden. The ice crew hadn't squeegeed the water near the Zamboni door. The puck skidded and stopped, and an opposing player collected it and fired it into the net. I looked at Bourque and he sort of just shrugged and hung his head.

The period continued and Bourque came around the net exactly as he'd done earlier. He collected the puck in that same Zamboni wet area. I was behind him and saw him glance up quickly at the clock. About six seconds remained in the period. He took a slap shot at the dot from the far end of the ice, just a few feet away from the Zamboni pit where he had lost the puck earlier in the game. The puck sailed at the goalie nearly 190 feet and then it dipped into the net, knuckling to the right. Ray put his arms in the air. The crowd went absolutely nuts. He turned, winked at me, and said, "There is a God!"

On-ice repartee was part of what made reffing so much fun—even when I was on the receiving end. Brian Murphy recalled a little bit of humor that occurred at my expense.

"Paul was famous for coloring his hair after he had done chemo," Murphy said. "He had just colored his hair before a game in Carolina. We got to replay and, usually when you go to replay, the captains come over, so Ronnie Francis was there… and all I can remember is they started chirping at Stewy. They started calling him 'Chestnut.' So Stewy's on the phone and we were calling him 'Chestnut.' Stewy hangs up the phone, and I don't think anyone really cared how the review turned out. We were all just standing around talking about Stewy's hair color. Players always had fun with that."

Speaking of hair, one of my favorite human beings in the game was the late Peter Zezel. He was one of the funniest and kindest people one could encounter in any walk of life; not just among athletes. During his playing days, Pete had matinee-idol good looks and absolutely perfect hair. He also enjoyed teasing me about my haircuts.

During the spring of 1995, I was on the road and decided to get a haircut. I asked for a trim and the barber went a bit overboard with the shears. The next game I refereed was in Dallas. Zezel was the first one who saw me.

"What's the name of that barber you went to?" he said.

I asked why he wanted to know.

"No one should be allowed to do that to one of our guys!" Zezel said with a mock horrified look on face.

Said another player, "Geez, Stewy! Are you auditioning for Forrest Gump?!"

I couldn't help but laugh. Until my hair grew out, whenever someone would call me Paul, I'd say "That's Forrest to you."

Relationship-building doesn't happen overnight. It takes time. But once the relationship is established and a rapport of mutual acceptability is built, there is leeway to short-circuit would-be confrontations through humor. You also learn which people you can joke around with and which ones you can't.

Perfect case in point: Mark Messier and I are old friends and former teammates.

We go all the way back together to the late 1970s when I was playing for the Cincinnati Stingers and Mark was a teenage rookie in his first pre-NHL year of pro hockey. We hit it off right away and the friendship has lasted through the years, even when we switched uniforms and I became an official.

That did not mean, of course, that Messier and I never had a disagreement over a call.

Messier was as intense of a competitor as I have ever seen and I had my own job to do. We weren't always going to see eye to eye. But because we had established a rapport and had a history together, we could say things to each other that might not be appropriate in interactions with others.

One time during Mark's days with the New York Rangers, I refereed a game in Montreal. Several calls went against the Rangers. The New York bench was barking at me, with Messier being the most vocal and insistent. At one point he stood up, hollering.

Finally, I skated over to the Rangers bench.

"Hey, you!" I said, looking Messier in the eyes. "Sit down and shut up!"

Mark knew what I was doing, and that the message was directed at the entire team. He sat down.

Colin Campbell, at the time the Rangers coach, squeaked at me. "Hey! You can't say that to him!"

I smirked. "Why not? I was the one who bought him his first beer."

I didn't hear another peep from the Rangers' bench the rest of the night.

Relationships with players were, unfortunately, not always so easy. For example, my on-ice relationship with Hall of Famer Steve Yzerman was strained from the beginning. It was a shame that we never hit it off, but, back in my reffing days, Yzerman was my least favorite hockey player to deal with on the ice. Everyone raves about Yzerman's intelligence and how he has become a talented GM. He undoubtedly was a Hall of Fame player, captain, and winner. He won three Stanley Cup titles with the Detroit Red Wings. I am not contesting his ability or intelligence.

But we didn't have the best on-ice relationship; I never appreciated how he treated my fellow officials. I made it my business to step up and defend the linesmen whom he treated the most poorly, in my opinion. I had refereed a Detroit game against the North Stars in Minnesota and he was upset I disallowed a goal. But I was in perfect position to make the correct and fair call. Not too long after, I worked a game in Detroit. He berated a linesman to the point where I felt awful for this guy. I stepped in and dumped Yzerman from the game. He was likely still upset with me from the game in Minnesota.

It finally reached the point where I asked to meet with Detroit head coach Scotty Bowman. He and I came to an agreement without Yzerman involved in the meeting. Bowman told me Yzerman had been difficult to get under control. I told Bowman that was hard to believe, coming from a coach who'd won so many Stanley Cups with different teams. I asked Scotty to strike a compromise. Bowman had other players, such as Doug Brown, Viacheslav Fetisov, Igor Larionov, and Chris Chelios, who didn't berate officials and could discuss penalties and calls with me without going over-the-top in a disrespectful manner.

"Pick any one of them to make the point," I said. "Just tell Yzerman not to come near me because the minute he opens his mouth, I'm dumping him."

As with other players, I understood the fans were there to see Yzerman, not me. I really didn't want to keep ditching him, but I had to do what I had to do when a player lost control because it was my job not to lose control of the game. There were thirty-nine other guys taking their cue from a superstar.

Many bad relationships can be repaired just by simply talking things out. If not, as in the Yzerman situation, other means can be taken to settle it. Devils General Manager Lou Lamoriello and I now laugh at an exchange we had following a Devils/Bruins game.

I never favored any teams or never had any bias because of my great respect for the game and my job. I certainly wasn't biased when I reffed a game in my hometown of Boston. That didn't stop Lamoriello from lobbing the accusation, however.

I called an elbowing penalty late in a game against Devils' Ken Daneyko. Boston scored on the ensuing power play to tie the score and the Bruins then won in overtime. When I came down the stairs to the referees' room at the old Boston Garden, there stood Lamoriello.

"You should be ashamed of yourself," he told me. "That was a horrible call and a pro-Boston call. You really showed you're a guy from Boston."

"I don't feel ashamed at all," I replied. "I feel sort of proud."

"Why's that?" he asked.

"Because I remember being in the Providence Arena, the old Rhode Island Auditorium, and you were coaching the Providence College Friars and you said the same thing to my dad. That he should be ashamed of himself. So I guess history repeats itself."

He probably didn't see the humor in it then, but I told that story at a banquet Lamoriello attended in recent years. We howled and laughed about it, and so I try to explain to people that friction is part of hockey. The friction should never be taken personally. Regardless, some guys *do* take it personally.

In twenty years of reffing at all levels, I only ever assessed four bench minors to a coach at any level in hockey. Two went to Ron Wilson because he should have known better that to challenge my "balls." Robbie Ftorek, one of my oldest and dearest friends, got his because he knew the wrong button and he pushed it.

The last one went to the late Bryan Murray. I have had an interesting relationship over the years with Bryan Murray. Many officials considered him a pain in the neck when he was coaching. When Bryan got on your case, he was relentless. I never had too much of a problem with him, however, until one night in Winnipeg when he coached what proved to be his final game behind the bench of the Washington Capitals.

Oddly enough before the game, I had a conversation with Washington Capitals general manager David Poile that foreshadowed what was to come.

"Stewy, I know Bryan has issues with a lot of officials," said Poile. "We track these things and you are the only current referee in the NHL who has never given him a bench minor."

"It's easy, David," I said. "I understand he's doing what he has to do. I do what I have to do, too. I don't engage with Bryan when he starts on me. I just skate to the other side of the rink and ignore him. He'll stop before too long. He knows I can hear him. But if he ever pushes it over the line, I wouldn't hesitate to bag him."

Apart from relentlessly pushing his case, Bryan also had a tendency to refuse to send his players out on the ice until the referee skated over to the bench. That angers many officials. As for myself, I refused to play that game. If I chose to come over to the bench to explain a call, I'd do it willingly. If I chose not to come over to bench, it was because there was no reason to talk.

If the coach persisted, I would tell the team captain to inform his coach that if I did skate over, it would be to issue a bench minor. That put an end to it, usually.

Bryan never pushed that particular issue over the line with me.

But later the same night after I had my conversation with Poile about having never penalized Bryan, I got into it with him at the bench.

The fuse was lit when Washington enforcer Nick Kypreos knocked Winnipeg's Brent Ashton out cold with what was a clean hit by the standards of the time but today would be considered a head shot. With his left leg airborne, Kypreos pivoted his right foot and put all his weight on that side. He tucked in his elbow as he blasted into Ashton. The Jets player went down hard, blood streaming from his nose.

It was a tough hit, but a clean one as I saw it. I told an unhappy Jets coach Bob Murdoch as much. As soon as play resumed, Winnipeg's Shawn Cronin made a beeline for Kypreos off the faceoff. They fought, of course. Next shift, Winnipeg's Laurie Boschman rattled a Capitals player.

Murray hollered at me, demanding I do something about it. I tried to inform him that although Kypreos' hit was clean and I had told the Winnipeg side as much, the Jets' response was exactly what was to be expected. They hadn't crossed the line yet, either.

The actual conversation, however, didn't go as intended. The more Murray hollered, the more the spittle flew out of his mouth and right into my face. Expletives deleted, this is how it ended up going:

"Stop spitting on me when you talk!" I yelled.

That made Bryan even angrier. "You can't disrespect me! I'm going to report this to [supervisor] John D'Amico!"

I felt another stream of saliva. That did it. I bagged Bryan with a bench minor. I did not, however, eject him. I never ejected a single coach in my entire refereeing career.

The next day, the Capitals fired Bryan. They replaced him with his younger brother, Terry.

A year or two later, Bryan was coaching the Detroit Red Wings. I ran into him before I worked a game in Calgary. We were both in a relaxed mood and simply began to talk. We talked and talked about everything but hockey. We found we had a lot in common.

I got a different slant on Bryan Murray that day. What a soft-spoken, intelligent gentleman he was! In the years that followed, I found Bryan to be a caring person and a man of his word. I liked him. Incidentally, Terry is the same way, but usually more low-key behind the bench. Their styles were different but both were very good hockey coaches and good men away from the ice.

Knowing the person that Bryan was, when he was diagnosed with an aggressive form of cancer, I knew he'd battle it to his final breath and, for as long as possible, keep performing his responsibilities as Ottawa Senators general manager and executive vice president with every ounce of strength he could muster. That's exactly what he did until the end.

Over the years, I also grew close with Roger Neilson. Roger became one of my favorite people in hockey. Talk about men of honor, integrity, bravery and intelligence. Roger was all those things as well as a tremendous coach. He had a brilliant hockey mind and for all his absent-minded professor ways off the ice, was one of the most reliable and caring men the game has ever known.

When Roger was battling cancer and coaching in Ottawa near the end of his life, he and I were in touch frequently. I once got in trouble with the NHL for visiting Roger in Ottawa. I got written up for it, in fact. Some nonsense about the League not wanting to risk the perception of favoritism.

I couldn't have cared less. Roger and I had a bond. When I'd see him, I'd ask how his veins were holding up from all the injections. We both knew the feeling of turning into a human pin cushion. He'd smile knowingly and roll up his sleeve to show me.

In 2000, Roger was invited to the opening ceremony at the NHL All-Star Game in Toronto. He wasn't up to it, so he asked me to go in his place. I was honored to accept. As a thank you, the Senators gave my then two-year-old son, McCauley, a Sens sweater with the number "22 1/2" on it. I had McCauley wear it and we took photos.

I was reprimanded by my League bosses. I was told it was unbecoming for the family member of an NHL official to publicly wear the sweater of an NHL team. As far as I knew and heard, no one else minded under the circumstances.

At any rate, there were times Roger would get mad at me for a call on the ice. A devoutly religious man and a former teacher, swear words were not in his vocabulary (can't say that about many hockey people, including me). Even so, he would make it very, very clear to everyone in the building when he disagreed with an official's call. Waved a white towel once. Threw a stick on the ice another time.

In my case, Roger would simply look me in the eyes and then let it go. He never held a grudge, either. As coaches, Bryan Murray and

Roger Neilson and Pat Burns were all very different in their styles. As human beings, they shared a common bond that had nothing to do with whatever illness befell them. Cancer attacks your body, it does not define your humanity or crush your spirit.

Though I tried my hardest to get the calls right, like all officials, I made occasional errors in judgment. It was my intent to not make too many of them. In hindsight, it's hard not to see the humor in some of them.

I once disallowed a goal by then-Buffalo Sabres left wing Brad May shortly before the All-Star break in a game against the Islanders. I was friendly with Sabres trainer Jim "Pizza" Pizzutelli, a former Army medic in Vietnam, and Sabres equipment manager Robert "Rip" Simonick. I had always thought May was a good guy and I still do. I skated to the bench to explain my ruling. They challenged me to make a bet on the video review outcome.

"C'mon, just for fun," they urged.

"All right. We'll make it for charity. How about we make it twenty-five bucks to the winner's charity?"

They agreed. Brad was the head of the local Juvenile Diabetes Research Foundation, a cause he believes in strongly because his sister has the condition. May ended up being right. It was a goal. Rip came to collect the check after the game. I made the check out for two hundred and fifty dollars to the JDRF in care of Brad May, who was very appreciative of the donation.

The story ended up getting out. Matt Barnaby, probably not thinking anything at all about the consequences, told the Buffalo reporters after the All-Star Break, thinking it was a funny story.

It didn't take long for me to receive a call from the league : I was going to have to be fired for betting on a play on the ice. I explained I wasn't paying any money to May but, instead, to his charity.

"I used to be a player rep and I've been active in the NHL Officials Association. I know how to fight for my rights. You're a lawyer, right?"

"Yes, you know that," he said.

"Well, it seems to me you've got a dilemma here," I said. "It takes two sides to make a bet, right? So let me ask you this: If you fire me, how are you going to explain to the NHLPA that you are firing Brad May, too? How's the publicity going to look when the media finds out this is all over a charitable donation and was not a bet at all? Oh, and if you tell me you're punishing only me, how's it going to look in court if you've fired one person for a rule violation and let the other one slide for the very same thing?"

I ended up getting off with a fine and had to review our league policies with a couple league representatives, who had to brief me on sports ethics. They had the meeting with me in Phoenix before I reffed a Coyotes game that night and discussed, among other things, a blanket prohibition on betting.

Later, at the arena, as I was drinking my coffee outside the dressing room door, a Coyotes security guard asked me if I wanted in on the 50/50 raffle. I had done 50/50 raffles at several arenas as a player and referee and won a few of them too. I went into the referees' room and got two dollars each from each of the linesmen and also from the NHL reps who had gone over the ethics rules with me. They didn't know what it was for; I thought the less I told them the better. So when they asked, I brushed it off by saying it was for a post-game six-pack.

I took ten bucks from my own wallet and got our raffle tickets. I gave the tickets to the security guard outside the referee room for safekeeping. I received a bear-hug from the security guard after the game ended. We had won the raffle and each of us collected three hundred dollars. I gave everyone their winnings in the dressing room.

"What's this for, Paul?" one of the NHL security representatives asked.

"Trust me," I said. "Don't ask, don't tell!"

When McCauley died and after Scotty Morrison left his position as NHL vice president in 1992, I knew my avenue to the future was closed. Hall of Fame referee John Ashley told me that things had changed within the decision-making hierarchy.

"I won't be around to protect you anymore," Ashley told me. "Watch your back."

His advice was sound. For all the friends I had made in high and low places, the place that mattered for me most professionally, at that juncture, was a veritable vipers' den.

One of the incidents that affected me most resonates in my memory as if it happened just yesterday. The day after we buried my dad, I worked a game in Montreal. I brought with me a briefcase the

NHL had given my grandfather with the NHL crest on it. He gave it to my dad, who left it to me with a note in it telling me I should use it to carry my rulebook to games. If you can carry your heart in your hand, that was what this briefcase was to me; I felt like I was bringing a part of my dad with me during this trying time.

In the hotel lobby before the game, I stood with the briefcase and my equipment bag, about to head outside to flag down a taxi to the game. A high-ranking league official saw me there with the briefcase. He took me aside and told me to go bring the briefcase back up to my room. He told me I always had to make it known to everyone I was part of the NHL. He said it harshly and with a pointed comment that I felt was unnecessary. He never even passed along condolences about my dad's passing. I walked away and took a cab on my own. I brought the briefcase.

A couple of years earlier, I had been at a charity golf tournament. My golf shirt had the NHL logo on it. That same league official walked up and asked me if I had NHL stamped onto my privates. It wasn't asked in a good-natured way.

This same boss once asked me my plans for the All-Star break. I told him I was reffing a game in Washington and then flying to Tampa to referee a Lightning game the day before the All-Star break.

"I'm just going to stay in Tampa during the break," I told him. Next thing I know, I received a phone call telling me my schedule had been changed. I had to ref out west. I was re-routed to Vancouver to work a game there instead of Tampa before the break. Of course, Vancouver is the furthest point in the League from Florida. Make up your own mind on what happened and why.

People have told me I should forgive and forget. I try. I can forgive but I can't forget.

Something else that never would have happened under McCauley or Morrison's watch: I was called the night before I got remarried in 1991 and told I had to cut short my honeymoon in order to be back for a meeting in Buffalo in the middle of June. I had planned a trip to France to see the beaches of Normandy and take advantage of our new life together. It was supposed to be a trip we'd always have together.

I complied, came back, and was told I'd be sharing a hotel room with referee Paul Devorski. My wife wasn't even allowed to stay with me. I had to book her at the hotel next door at The Red Roof Inn. Some honeymoon.

"It's funny, because (longtime referee Terry) Gregson isn't here," I said. "Why is he not here but I have to be here?" Gregson had been on vacation in Thailand on an elephant safari.

A senior manager replied, "Because he's Terry Gregson and you're not."

Gregson, you see, was our union president and I was just a rank-and-file schmuck.

René Fasel, a dentist by trade and a former Swiss referee, is now the president of the International Ice Hockey Federation. René told me on more than one occasion that the NHL did not submit my name as one of the American-born referees to work the 1991 Canada Cup. "They said you had slumped terribly and couldn't recommend you," Fasel told me.

Fasel and the International Ice Hockey Federation bypassed the NHL list and I worked the tournament. I ended up reffing the championship game. At the game in Hamilton, another official (who was sitting in the toilet), overhead one of my bosses telling me to enjoy the moment because I would never work another international game if he could help it. Good stuff twenty minutes before a game. Really made me feel special.

The new powers-that-be were open about their dislike for me. Shortly after McCauley died, new management and I were at the home of Chicago Blackhawks president Bill Wirtz, who was also was the Chairman of the NHL Board of Governors. One of the new administration's very first actions was to fire me. They also rescinded the dismissals of two officials whom McCauley had fired for unprofessional off-ice conduct that affected their ability to work a game that spring in Philly.

My sin: I recently had run a clinic for graduated college students who went undrafted by the NHL. They were hoping to sign minor league pro contracts and some of them had told me they didn't know how to fight. They asked me what to do. They asked me what training camp would be like from a new player's point of view. I showed them how to protect themselves. I told them how to train, how to treat the trainers, the veteran players, the exhibition games. How to not drink the bars dry. I shared with them all the points I had to learn as a young player when I reported to training camps. A reporter and photographer were at the rink and the story and photo of me teaching them to fight went across the wires.

Senior management fired me for "conduct unbecoming" of an NHL official. The irony of pairing that decision with keeping others whom the previous administration let go for showing up unable to safely work was not lost on me.

Bill Wirtz saved me this time. Soon after my unceremonious dismissal from my job, Mr. Wirtz saw me at the pool and asked to chat with him in his study. We were at his house for an NHL meeting with officials, coaches, and general managers. Mr. Wirtz brought me into the study and started telling me stories about my grandfather. He loved my granddad for once letting him be a Black Hawks stick boy when my grandfather coached the Hawks, the year they won the Stanley Cup.

"He also used to bring me into the referee room and tell me great stories," Wirtz added. "I was so happy when I heard you were reffing in the NHL now and that you're here at my home. Welcome aboard."

"Well, I appreciate it, Mr. Wirtz, but I just got fired," I informed him, adding the reason why I had ostensibly just been canned.

"Just a second," Wirtz said, leaving the room. He returned with John Ziegler, Jr., who was then the president of the NHL. "Tell him the story you just told me," Wirtz said.

I repeated the story and, when asked, told them I made five hundred for the day at this hockey clinic for aspiring rookies.

"Five hundred dollars and they are going to fire you?" Wirtz said, surprised. "Go back out to the party and enjoy yourself. We'll be in touch."

Dinnertime came and everyone was seated. Mr. Wirtz gave a speech. He mentioned me.

"The NHL is about family," he said. "And I want you to recognize a young man here today whose family goes back to the NHL from the very first day of the league. This man's grandfather was a coach, a referee, and he won a Stanley Cup. And when I was a boy, his grandfather made me feel welcomed. And I want you to know that as long as I own the Blackhawks and I'm the chairman of the board, Paul Stewart will always have a job in the NHL."

I was taken behind the rhododendrons and rehired as unceremoniously as I had been fired just an hour earlier.

I guess the "Never Say Die" spirit isn't unique to me, though, because officiating management was undeterred by this failed attempt. Since they now knew it would be tough to actually fire me, a new tactic was adopted: grind me down psychologically and physiologically in the apparent hope that I'd quit.

Jim Gregory, in a closed session in Toronto that included only a few NHL officials and just the contracted refs and linesmen, pounded on the table, telling us we had to give the new administration a fair chance. This was our first day of training camp in 1989, just a few months after McCauley had died. Some people eventually came around; I wasn't one of them.

There were too many wounds inflicted. In Quebec, one night after I got hit with a Grant Ledyard slap shot and broke two ribs in my back, I got chastised for asking off my next assignment in Winnipeg. I couldn't breathe or bend over to untie my skates.

The response, "That's very convenient so you could fly home to be with your new wife."

That was 100 percent untrue. Anyone who knew the slightest thing about me knew how much physical pain I could withstand, and still work. Words can sting and bruise far more than any punch I ever took. I have no patience for those who are cruel for the sake of being cruel.

Management used to complain about how difficult their job was, how hard they worked to get the schedules correct, and how much work went into the careful wording of rules. "Arduous," they'd say. "The work is so arduous." Maybe for them, but I can tell you this: since my retirement, I've been doing exactly that job with five different leagues, twice the number of games to assign and four times the staff. It has been many things over the years—challenging, difficult, frustrating—but it has never been "arduous." It is a job that isn't work for me because I love doing it.

Management once told me how much paperwork the league did and how detail-oriented the administration was. Good with paper, bad with people apparently.

"All the details except ones that matter, like how to deal fairly with people," I responded.

The regime that followed McCauley's was oblivious to people management as well as the art and "science" of coaching officials. Trust, communication and teaching are all vital skills, and they just weren't there. That is probably the biggest shame of all of it. Hockey is about building trust and teamwork, fraternity and family. When that's lacking, one misses out on the best the game has to offer and can also destroy it for other people. It is real folly for people who are in positions of authority and control to allow those under them to run their fiefdom with no oversight, no restrictions and no reviews. That's is the *anti-Clemenza* effect—when management stops being about business and starts being personal. It is the epitome of ineffective management and everyone loses out as a result.

## CHAPTER 18: The C-Word

I made my mark in this world as a fighter. I was a fighter, and I am a fighter. I fought some of the toughest opponents in the NHL—both on-ice and off—and I held my own. I battled and beat the odds in making it out of the hospital when I was born, when I made it at Groton, at Penn, in the NHL, and then back to the NHL a second time. But that series of unending fights did little to prepare me for my next opponent, the most formidable by a mile.

In 1997, Lori and I got married on the bridge in The Boston Public Gardens, across from the Ritz Hotel, over the Swan Boat pond and just in front of the statue of George Washington. My dear friends, Twink and Theresa Walsh, two "cousins" from Orne Moor and Strathenwrey, Ireland were our witnesses. I had called Mayor Menino to get permission and a city permit for the ceremony in the park. A justice of the peace did the honors. We then had a champagne toast at the Ritz before boarding a limo to go to the famous chef and friend Todd English's restaurant, Olives in Charlestown, within feet of where Paul Revere waited for the signal to begin his ride. Todd cooked us a great dinner for four. The next day, Lori boarded a flight to London for work as a flight attendant. I drove to exit 16W to work a Devils game at The Meadowlands.

Within a year of marrying Lori, I became a first-time dad to a beautiful baby boy on February 22, 1998. I was just a month away from turning forty-five. I stood holding this eight-pound pumpkin, McCauley John Stewart, named for my friend and mentor. This child had red hair just like his gorgeous and proud mother, Lori. We were on top of the world.

And then I found out I had cancer.

I went from experiencing that euphoria for twelve hours to then, later, sitting in a hospital office being told I might not live to see

McCauley's first Christmas or to see him try on his first pair of hockey skates. It was worse than anything else I have dealt with during my entire life. It felt a trillion times worse than sitting depressed down on Cape Cod with a pistol sitting in my lap as I contemplated my end following my first divorce. It felt a trillion times worse than sitting on that freezing bus as a North American Hockey League enforcer with sixty-four stitches popping out of my brutally swelled face. It felt a trillion times worse than when I hid in the Zamboni pit after being cut from my college hockey team as a senior. It felt a trillion times worse than all those things combined.

But I'm a fighter, on and off the ice, and I knew I had to continue to fight. I couldn't give up. After all, wasn't I the one who'd fought Terry O'Reilly, Stan Jonathan, and Al Secord in the same NHL game just four years after hiding from teammates in that Zamboni pit at the University of Pennsylvania? Wasn't I the one who'd silenced the Hartford crowd by sticking with renowned World Hockey Association tough guy Jack Carlson of the then-New England Whalers punch-for-punch twice in the same game? Wasn't I the one who'd made it back to the NHL as a referee after selling Fords and working as the evening Laundromat manager after my NHL playing career ended? I was indeed.

If I could do all that, then why the hell couldn't I beat cancer, return to the NHL Official's Training camp and my officiating assignments, and also be there for McCauley's first skate when he was able to stand on his blades? There was no reason not to do all that except for the bleak odds presented by my doctors. If it meant a fight for my life and for everything that was precious to me, it was going to be a fight.

I'm a Stewart—a proud Stewart. I'm the grandson of a Stanley Cup-champion head coach and the son of a less well-known, but just as inspiring, proud and dedicated high school coach. Both had shown me, by their actions, never to quit.

I was blindsided by the diagnosis, but I shouldn't have been. The signs I had cancer had been there. But, foolishly, I'd ignored them for too long. In the midst of refereeing NHL games, I occasionally prayed silently for a stoppage in play or for the period to end quickly because I was experiencing such fatigue and brutal diarrhea that I sometimes couldn't hold it inside of me.

As awful as this might sound, I had occasional small accidents in my pants while reffing NHL games. I thought it might have been stress, or the extensive travel throughout the U.S and Canada, or from worry because my wife was pregnant with our first child, or even maybe the flu. Weeks turned into months. The symptoms grew more severe. My stomach constantly felt upset. I couldn't eat at a restaurant without using the restroom. My favorite meals began to have no taste to them.

My father always told me to wear suits to games, but I no longer felt in the mood or had the energy to dress up. I began to bleed from the rectum, but I thought this was the result of a hemorrhoid or fissure.

The signs were there and I ignored them. Despite watching other friends die of cancer, such as Barry Ashbee, Ray Schultz, and Christos Kaldis, the eight-year-old boy from my Cape Cod neighborhood, I somehow felt like it wouldn't happen to me. It wasn't even on my radar.

Isn't it crazy that I noticed Kaldis' fatigue and abnormal behavior as the summer of 1979 continued, and, without knowing he had leukemia, I'd asked his sister if he was feeling okay, yet I never read into my own warning signs enough to ask a doctor if *I* was okay? I was just like Vince Lombardi, Charles Schulz, Babe Zaharias, Audrey Hepburn, Elizabeth Montgomery and so many famous and not-so famous men and women. I just didn't realize that I was really sick. Or maybe it was pure denial on my part.

I began staring in the toilet every time before flushing. It looked like a can of Campbell's Tomato Soup had been dumped in there. During the rare time my excrement was solid, it looked like strips of red licorice had been sewn into it.

One February morning, during the Olympic break, I still was in bed, but Lori was awake watching *The Today Show*. Hosts Matt Lauer and Katie Couric were discussing how Couric had lost her husband of nine years, John "Jay" Paul Monahan, to colon cancer at forty-two-years old.

"Paul! Paul, watch this!" Lori said, as she elbowed me. "All these symptoms, all these are the ones you have!"

Lori immediately made me get out of bed to call my friend, Dr. Gary Kearney. I scheduled an appointment to see him the following

Monday. To get the ball rolling, he ordered some blood and lab work to be done before I met with him. After the blood work was complete, I headed to Springfield to be the toastmaster at the Springfield AHL Hall of Fame Dinner on February 21. Lori gave birth to McCauley the next day.

Even with the possibility of cancer looming in the background, I was on cloud nine the morning of February 23, even though I had received little sleep because McCauley skated into our lives at 11:22 p.m. I was euphoric when I first saw Gary—I'm on a first-name basis with Dr. Kearney because we're good friends—and I shared with him pictures of McCauley.

Our levity was not to last. The mood changed quickly as Gary's facts began to unravel my joy. He reviewed the blood test results with me. I was very anemic with the constant bleeding. My urine flow also was slow which caused Gary to wonder about my prostate. He decided to order a biopsy on my prostate, which wasn't too pleasant. We sat and talked there that day and Gary told me directly that all signs pointed toward cancer. He said it was perhaps prostate cancer, but we would know more when the biopsy results returned in a few days. But I was told it also could very likely be colon cancer.

"Is this a bad joke, Doc?" I asked. "We just had a baby. He's twelve hours old."

Gary was truthful and straightforward with me. "Paul, if we don't get at this right away, you likely won't see that boy's first Christmas," I remember him telling me. "Between your prostate and your colon, the excessive bleeding and your test numbers, it doesn't look good."

I left Gary's office for a few minutes to gain some composure. I was returning to work in Toronto in a few days and knew I had to try to downplay the blood work results with Lori. I also had to pick up my mother-in-law, Grandma Pat, from the airport (she had flown in from Minnesota), get ready to bring McCauley home, and try to enjoy the moment of being a new dad while also realizing I was about to be a cancer patient.

I called my sister and one of my brothers. I kept it light, then went back to Gary and said, "Okay, Doc, if we are in a brawl, let's get busy!" We sat and formed a plan that would be the first step in a war I never wanted to fight.

The plan was simple. I couldn't have a colonoscopy until the biopsy holes healed from the prostate exam. That would take me nearly to the end of March. The NHL finished its regular season in early April. One round of the playoffs was usually what I could expect. If lucky, maybe I'd make the Conference Semifinals. As I previously mentioned, people don't realize that every year I went to training camp knowing full well that management never would let me get to referee a Stanley Cup Final no matter how well I did or how hard I worked.

I asked Gary if a week or three more would matter. He shook his head, knowing a lot more than he was letting on to me. I left his office with this big secret, our plan and a new determination that I had to carry on as best I could. I had to start making plans to deal with this new reality.

I went to see Al Thomas at his funeral home to plan my funeral. I went to St. Joseph's cemetery to buy the plot next to my grandfather. I went to see my lawyer to draft my will. I went to see my accountant to get my finances in order. I went to see my financial planner to straighten out my pension and 401K. I got ready in case I was going to die. Yet I carried on with the rest of the season even as my symptoms continued.

Only three days after my diagnosis, on February 26, I worked a Rangers/Maple Leafs game in Toronto. The NHL had restarted after the 1998 Winter Olympics ended, the day McCauley was born. Like always, I never paid too much attention to who was playing beforehand. I was more focused on the city where I was scheduled to work and which linesmen would be working with me. Still, I knew it was the Leafs versus the Rangers playing when I, literally, almost bumped into New York Rangers star Wayne Gretzky that afternoon before the game while walking down the street near the CN Tower.

"Stew, hey good to see you," he said. "I read that you had a son and named him after John McCauley. That's terrific."

I was in a bit of a daze and responded with, "Hey Gretz, what brings you to Toronto?"

"Stew, you all right?" he asked. "We play the Leafs tonight. You okay?"

"Oh, I'm still tired from all the baby goings-on. It's been a long week with little sleep."

"Stew, after the game tonight, go over to my restaurant," Gretzky said. "John Bitove, my parents, my family, and some friends will be there. You will know a lot of them. Go on over."

"Gee, Gretz, that's nice of you, but drinking with the Rangers after the game might not look so cool to the Leafs, their fans or the league," I told him.

"We're flying out of Toronto right after the game, so no players will be there," he replied. "Will you go?"

"Yes, thanks. It will be good to see Phyllis and Walter again."

Gretzky, as usual, had a strong game, recording three assists in a 5-2 victory for New York over Toronto. To Gretzky's restaurant I went after the game. The maitre d' at the door escorted me into the back room for the private party. Tables and chairs were set up with an empty spot between Wayne's parents, Walter and Phyllis. The crowd was good-sized.

Hanging was a banner inscribed, "Congratulations, McCauley!" Near my seat also was a stick Wayne had used that night against the Maple Leafs autographed with these words, "To McCauley, health and happiness, Your Friend, Wayne Gretzky #99."

We then enjoyed a toast with a big magnum of champagne. Have you figured out yet why I love my life in hockey? As much crap as I swallowed during my refereeing career from certain bosses, occasions like that one in Toronto made everything worth it.

Little did Wayne know how much that meant to me with all that had happened the past ninety-six hours. Little did Wayne and his parents know they brought so much enjoyment into a week mixed with euphoria but also hidden sadness and anger. I cried when I saw the signed hockey stick and banner, but nobody at the time knew the real reason I cried.

Nobody there knew I cried was because I had been forced to wear Kotex in my underwear because I was leaking and that I had felt so embarrassed over the stains on my referee pants. Nobody there knew that whenever I used the bathroom a residual of blood typically remained in the toilet after I flushed and how I once told a linesman I had a hemorrhoid when he saw it and asked what the hell was wrong with me. Nobody knew it was because I had eaten at a Chinese restaurant with some linesmen not long before and used the bathroom at least three times during the meal and then couldn't walk the two or three blocks back to the hotel because I had such excruciating pain. Nobody knew I once blamed a broken whistle for a stoppage of the game so I could get myself cleaned up and changed.

Nobody knew it was because I not only dreaded death since I'd have to leave my newborn son and wife, but also because I loved hockey and didn't know if I was about to say goodbye to the game forever.

My season finally ended, and I was glad to return home, but unhappy about having the colonoscopy. I was never scared to fight anyone during my playing career, but I was scared of having this test and learning the results. I expected the worst. There was one bit of good news for me: the biopsy showed that my prostate was enlarged but not malignant.

Now I was off to New England Baptist Hospital for the colonoscopy in early May. It was a relatively simple procedure. I received a small anesthesia shot and off to sleep I went. When I woke, the gastroenterologist, Dr. Sue Kelly, looked a little troubled. She seemed to be avoiding eye contact with me. I touched Sue's back and asked her how the procedure went. She told me the results wouldn't be back for a few days. Meanwhile, I looked at the nurse in the room and she avoided looking into my face.

"Sue, please, you're telling me that after everything I've been through and everything I've read over the past couple of months that you're not going to tell me straight what is wrong?" I said. "I can read it in your face. You've been doing this for twenty years."

"Paul, what do you want me to say?" Dr. Kelly asked. "Your wife and son are outside. How do you want to handle this?"

"It's not good, is it?"

"No, it's not good," she replied.

The procedure had revealed a large tumor in my colon. I asked Dr. Kelly to give me a minute or two to think. I decided to act like nothing was wrong in front of Lori. I told Dr. Kelly that we'd tell Lori the results weren't going to be back for a couple days. I just needed a few days to get Lori ready for the news about to rock our lives.

Lori and I were in the process of moving out of our condominium in Dorchester at the old Baker Chocolate Factory. The plan was to live in my house in Hyannis Port on Cape Cod for the summer while our new house in Walpole was being built. We drove to Walpole to watch the builders lay the foundation. Everything was moving forward as scheduled, as if I had my whole life ahead of me. At the same time, I wondered whether I'd ever live in the new house.

A few days after the colonoscopy, Lori and I were moving furniture out of the condo when the phone rang. It was Dr. Kelly. Lori was holding a chair and she heard me ask when I needed to come to the hospital. I hung up the phone and just stared at Lori. She almost fainted. She dropped the dining room walnut chair and it broke. I did fix it, gluing it together. Some things can be more easily fixed than others. I looked at McCauley and wondered if I'd be alive to see him turn one. I told Lori I had a tumor and surgery was scheduled in two days. The next morning, I visited the hospital, bringing along my sister, Pat, a nurse. I thought she'd be a helpful person to take to the meetings because she dealt with ill patients constantly and is well-informed. I wanted someone unemotional who understood what the doctor was telling me. Education and knowledge is the key to victory. I didn't want to be lied to or bullshitted.

Little did I know, upon arriving at Baptist, that my surgeon, Dr. Stephen Camer, had worked with my sister for fifteen years. He immediately gave her a hug. Camer is an ace, the Madison Bumgarner of New England Baptist. He had operated on Rose Kennedy (gastrostomy procedure) and is a student of military history and an ex-Vietnam War Navy surgeon.

Being a history buff, Camer and I struck up an instant chemistry. He explained the surgery. The tumor was far enough up that he could avoid a colostomy. He asked about my family history with cancer. My lack of knowledge at the time was bitterly ironic, considering I now know that my maternal grandmother, her sister, her grandfather, and a cousin all had colon cancer. The Irish don't talk much about illness. They always pretend to be fine until the wake.

Pat and I then sat down with Dr. Jacob Lokich, the oncologist. He didn't mince words. He was blunt and I liked that about him. Lokich discussed how I would need lots of chemotherapy and possibly radiation. He said he'd know more after the surgery when the margins were in and he'd had a chance to review what the lymph nodes showed. The true test of patience is waiting for biopsy results.

I checked into the hospital under an assumed name (Dr. Kelly's daughter's name) to prevent the NHL or the public from learning about my cancer. I didn't want anyone's pity. I hardly wanted a stream of people at the wake before I actually died. But I also felt uncertainty about how NHL officials would react.

I didn't want the NHL to know until I knew whether I would survive or die. I had such a lousy relationship with my immediate manager and a few of his minions after John McCauley had died that I really didn't care to let them know that I might be leaving them, especially not in the manner they might have imagined. They had never done anything to help me when I wasn't sick, so I didn't need their phony baloney or pseudo-sympathy when I was.

I let very few friends know I was in the hospital. I hardly told any non-family members I had cancer. Paul Harrington is one friend I did tell. I played golf with Paul and had known he'd beaten cancer, but had lost one of his kidneys during the fight. I asked him to visit New England Baptist to talk with me about my diagnosis. He came, bearing a hat from the Masters Tournament as a gift for me.

I called another friend, John "Whip" Filoon, who had beaten prostate cancer. He visited with me and we talked about winning the fight. Whip had been a Harvard hockey player, a Marine, and a longtime friend from Hyannis Port. I needed Marine toughness, and, in case it didn't work out, I wanted to say goodbye to my friend.

The only other non-family members I told (other than my lawyer, my financial planner, and my accountant) were Junie O'Brien, my coach at Groton, and my great friend and teammate, Johnny Harwood. Harwood, my ex-Penn teammate, and I talked and laughed as best we could about it. He has been my friend since 1972 and I'd jump on a grenade to save him if it came to it. "That he was sick never worried me," Harwood said. "Absent the hand of God saying it's your time, I really believed in my heart, knowing him, and the way he fights and the way he works, that cancer wasn't going to beat him… I always had faith in him that he would win the fight because he won about ninety-eight percent of his fights."

I didn't feel the same confidence as Harwood did. As I mentioned before, I couldn't sleep at the hospital the night before undergoing surgery to remove the tumor from my colon, so I stripped off my clothes, went to the bathroom, turned on the shower knob, rested my head against the wall and prayed not only to survive, but I also prayed for my wife and newborn son.

I did not experience a single second of tranquility and peace in the hospital bed and shower. I wanted to fight someone but who? I wanted to blame someone but who? Keeping these emotions inside me made the anguish worse. I never shared those thoughts with anyone, not even Lori, and keeping them bottled inside made them that much more acute.

Not until right before I fell asleep, well past midnight and closer to 3A.M., did I experience an inner peace. That's when I heard from the God I knew as a child. The God I had known while attending Catholic grammar school. The God who had made Christmas mysterious and special. I thought about the tradition of attending Good Friday mass as a kid and watching the reenactment of the Stations of the Cross. All that made me forget the travesty of religion as we know it now, with many priests and brothers in the Archdiocese of Boston who were accused of pedophilia. It all made feel at peace with God.

Nobody but God was there with me.

For some reason, I remembered something I had learned from one of my former grammar school nuns, Sister Robard at St. Thomas' School in Jamaica Plain. It was a passage from the Bible that discussed God taking care of the birds and the lilies in the field. Did he not love me more than he loved those birds and lilies? I found solace and peace. I knew I could face the surgery.

I never wanted to admit it—and I'm holding tears back as I write this—but I had felt scared and pretty furious about having that surgery. But I shut it all out and found an inner calmness before finally falling asleep in the wee hours of the morning. When I awoke three hours later, I found I had begun to regain my courage. The emotions and feelings I built up inside of me back as an enforcer during my hockey playing career were the same ones I had to rediscover before heading to the operating table.

I found a sense of false courage to say "Eff you, cancer, I'm going to beat you!" It was the same mindset I'd brought when I'd entered the Boston Garden on Thanksgiving 1979 to make my NHL debut when I'd fought a Dorchester Hat Trick's worth of Bruins tough guys. I made a pact with myself: If I survived the surgery, I'd work harder in life, try to become a better person, and do everything I could to help my son.

The successful operation was the first step in a long road, a journey that continues to this day. I'm still not done. I'm still fighting and working toward a life with purpose. I wasn't my time to die. I lived and I have felt, ever since beating cancer, that God kept me alive to serve a purpose. I've been searching for the reason—the purpose—that I'm still here. Some people might think that sounds self-important, but I honestly believe there's a reason I am still here in this world. I fought like hell for my family. I wanted to see McCauley grow up and find his own happiness, whether with hockey or some other endeavor. I wanted to be with Lori until we reached a ripe old age together.

I also refused to accept Dr. Lokich's prediction that I wouldn't return to the NHL for the start of the 1998-1999 season. It was the example set by my father, who, even while he was growing sicker, refused to use any of his stored up sick days. He not only felt an obligation to his students and athletes, but he also felt a love for coaching and teaching. He did what he did because it felt right to him. I felt that same obligation to return to hockey in time for NHL officials training camp because it was my obligation and hockey always was my first love. Sure, I had cancer, but I wanted to continue to be who I was: a hockey man, a referee, a part of the game in any way possible. Like my dad, I didn't want to stop doing what I loved and what I did best. I didn't let anything step in my way of doing my job.

My life is a miracle in many ways, and not just because I beat colon cancer. My return to the NHL after a summer of chemotherapy and physical agony was nothing short of a miracle.

Even on the day of the operation, I had to do battle with the NHL's insurance carrier. The insurance company told me it had to tell the NHL I was having surgery. I told the insurance representative thirty minutes before I went under the knife that if he did tell the NHL, I'd live long enough to sue his company for disclosing my private medical history contrary to patient confidentiality laws. I was pissed and maybe that was a good thing because I went into the operating room with some attitude, the same way I used to feel as a player. If I was going to die, I was determined to at least go out fighting like when I'd entered this world fighting for my life in the neonatal intensive care.

I spent ten days in the hospital after the surgery. During my final morning there, all four of my doctors (Drs. Kearney, Kelly, Camer, and Lokich)—all came together to visit me.

"How do I rate a visit from all four of you at the same time?" I asked, laughing a bit. "You all look so serious." They told me to sit, then they delivered a rather disturbing prognosis. Kelly began talking, telling me that Camer did an excellent job with the surgery. They thought they had removed all the cancer. She used the word "optimistic."

"However, we haven't been a hundred percent honest with you," one of them said. "We told you that we removed all of the cancer during the surgery. We think that's true, but we also need you to know that you're a lot sicker than we let on. We didn't want you to be here worrying all the time, but you're not quite out of the woods. You're going to need chemo and lots of it. Even with that, we can't promise you that you will make it. It might be a year, it might be a lot of years. We can't tell you for sure."

For possibly the first time in my life, I was at a loss for words. Those four doctors in that one hospital room at Boston's New England Baptist Hospital in May, 1998 rendered me speechless. The four informed me I would need to undergo chemotherapy. I had a second tumor near my liver, but not yet growing on it. The chemo was the "mopping up" to get any cells that may have escaped, sort of like Lysol in the bathroom going after the invisible germs.

When I told them that I was going back to work in September even if I puked at center ice, my doctors thought I was slightly nuts. They told me January of 1999 would be the earliest I'd return to officiating NHL games. They formed their opinion about my condition and then I formed my opinion of their opinion; I couldn't miss any time.

Dr. Lokich said, "You're very cavalier about this. You're a sick man. You have advanced cancer. It isn't just a toothache."

My response: "Doc, cavalier is a three-dollar word. I'm from Dorchester, a two-dollar word will do. Besides, you never met anybody like me." Not only was hockey the way I made a living, but it also kept me focused, excited, and passionate each day of my life.

Boston Red Sox television color commentator Jerry Remy has said he couldn't bring himself to watch Red Sox games when his battle with cancer prevented him from working broadcasts one season. I think I would have felt the same way about watching hockey.

The doctors told me at the time that I had a 50/50 chance to survive. They eventually told me my survival was a miracle. Well, if God works miracles, He must have sent me Johnny Olsen. He was the key to my recovery.

My description of Johnny Olsen is twofold. First, he is ripped like Mr. Universe. More muscles bulge from his body than I ever knew existed. Second, he's a loyal friend and lifesaver who stood by me when I needed a loyal friend and motivator the most. Olsen and I connected when I was living down on Cape Cod after I left the NHL as a player. He interviewed me for a class project about the violence in hockey. Olsen grew up in Massachusetts. His parents could not afford to sign him up for organized hockey, but that never derailed his passion for the sport. As a ten-year-old, he watched the 1969-1970 Boston Bruins, led by Bobby Orr, win the organization's first Stanley Cup in twenty-nine years. That event especially sparked his hockey enthusiasm.

I lived in Hyannis Port during the summer of 1998. While I underwent chemotherapy, my house in Walpole continued to be built. Olsen owned Galaxy Fitness Center, in Hyannis, a stone's throw from Hyannis Port. I called him one afternoon and told him my situation. Olsen heard the pain in my voice.

"I was shocked and glad I was sitting down when I was listening," Olsen said.

I felt depressed, so Olsen drove to my house to talk. He promised to get me ready for the start of the NHL season, although he later told me he didn't know if he could keep the promise when he made it.

"We're going to get you going again," he assured me. "We're going to beat this together."

I started chemotherapy in June. It didn't take long for my skin to turn grossly pale because my doctors advised I keep away from the sun unless I wore a straw Panama hat and layers to cover my legs and arms. Without that protection, my skin broke out in rashes after ten minutes in the sun, a side effect of the chemotherapy. I didn't, therefore, spend much time outside during the day.

I occasionally went to Hyannisport Club, where I have a membership, to putt a few balls during the evenings. I also sometimes strapped McCauley's car seat to the passenger seat of a golf cart. We drove around the course in the evening, feeding the ducks, just to get out of the house. The golf pro, Rick Johnson, kept my secret and was a true friend.

One day, I accidentally showed up at a charity golf tournament that several Boston Bruins players attended toward the end of the evening. I didn't even know that a crowd would be there, never mind NHLers I knew. By then, I had lost forty pounds because almost nothing tasted appealing to me. Beer tasted briny and flat with a sort of aluminum taste from the can.

I drove a golf cart past some celebrities, including those players. I only said a quick hello as I passed. A day or two later, my brother called to tell me that the word on the street was that I had AIDS. I hardly cared what people said about me. Maybe I felt too sick to care. Maybe I found it comical to think how foolish they'd all feel when they learned I might be dying from colon cancer. If they wanted to talk behind my back, then more power to them. I felt no need to debunk the AIDS rumor.

But I did feel the need to get back in shape. In addition to my pale skin and weak appearance, I walked unsteadily and had a catheter placed in my chest. It included a battery-packed injector with a bag of chemo inside of it. The device made a zipping sound every thirty seconds as the chemo visibly shot up the tube. I hid the bag of chemo in a big Velcro fanny pack around my waist. The chemo pack was sensitive. An alarm sounded when the tube squeezed or was impinged. Several times the alarm sounded during the night causing my infant son to awaken in his bassinet beside our bed. The noisy alarm and my frequent inability to find a comfortable sleeping position often made me opt to sleep on a chair out in our screened porch.

The last thing I wanted to do most mornings after restless nights was lift my body from my bed or the porch chair, let alone run and lift weights at the gym. Olsen drove to my house every day to pick me up because I often felt too weak to drive. He made me get out of bed whenever I lacked any motivation. It took every ounce of my strength to get out of bed in the morning, even with Olsen's help. I felt like crap almost every day when we began training. My head ached almost constantly. It felt like someone had belted both my back and neck with a sledgehammer, but I went to his gym, sometimes twice a day. When Lori was away working as a flight attendant, I brought McCauley along with me.

Olsen put me through grueling cardio workouts. His wanted to increase my endurance so I could skate for sixty minutes a game. He jotted down detailed notes about every aspect of every workout. He wrote when I felt tired after an exercise. He logged workout durations, types of exercises, and number of repetitions for each exercise. He marked down how much weight I lifted and the number of push-ups and sit-ups I did each day. I followed a nutritional program he designed (foods high in protein, low in starch with necessary carbohydrates). Olsen literally did everything for me, including finding someone to cut my lawn.

I remember visiting the new Walpole house in July. I couldn't walk up the temporary staircase. I instead had to sit on the trunk of the car, I felt that sick. I still had a long way to go with Olsen. The NHL still didn't know in July what was wrong with me even as my medical bills grew into the hundreds of thousands of dollars. My doctors had told me I still needed chemo for another three or four months and they began to project I wouldn't return at all for the 1998-1999 season.

Several infections developed on my stomach and chest throughout the summer. They were beet red and tender to the touch. Thankfully, my neighbor, Katie Duggan, worked as an oncology nurse. She visited daily to dress the wounds. Her husband, Kevin, who once worked with my brother, visited each evening along with their son, Sean, and daughter, Kerry. A ritual happy hour became part of me reclaiming my life.

"It's cocktail hour," he'd say, telling me that his wife—and my nurse—had given the okay for me to have one drink. We spent two weeks experimenting with different liquors, trying to find one that actually tasted good. Finally, we discovered the right one: vodka mixed with grapefruit juice, the real pinkish grapefruit juice.

I eventually became Olsen's prized pupil in his spin class. Olsen recently reminded me that I continued to ride the stationary bike for a half hour after everyone else finished the forty-five-minute class.

"And the ones I taught were the hardest classes you can take—you wanted to get off that bike," Olsen said.

I began to adapt to the chemo. My strength grew with each workout. I forced myself to eat, too. As time passed, it became easier to get out of bed in the morning. I also spent more time at Hyannisport Club. By the end of July, I felt strong enough to golf.

On the course one day, a friend asked, "Why are you wearing that fanny pack?"

I brushed off his question with a little chuckle.

"You know that fanny pack isn't helping your golf game, right?" he remarked.

I lifted my shirt, showing him the catheter running into my chest. "Have another cigarette," I told him. "You'll be doing chemo someday, too."

This friend obviously looked quite shocked and embarrassed. He apologized immediately. Maybe I shouldn't have done what I did, but I didn't feel too rosy that summer.

# CHAPTER 19: The Comeback

It was getting to the point in late July when I had to tell the NHL about my cancer because I didn't know if my return would be possible. Calling the league took a prodding from longtime *Boston Globe* sports columnist, Will McDonough, my dad's ex-star athlete at Boston English.

I had called McDonough to tell him I'd decided to cancel the annual Bill Stewart Classic Golf Tournament, which honored my father's memory by raising money for inner-city student athletes. I lacked the strength to plan, organize, and execute the tournament. McDonough loved my dad and even had delivered his eulogy. He wasn't too pleased to hear I had decided to forgo the golf event that summer.

"Willy, I'm sick," I told him.

McDonough was a legend for his sports scoops and finding out private information about athletes. Like the excellent reporter everyone knew him to be, McDonough took fewer than ten minutes to get me to admit I had colon cancer. He was a friend and always direct. He got right to his point.

"Paulie boy, you have to tell the NHL," he said. McDonough wanted to write the story about my illness, too.

"Let me call the NHL first," I told him.

I called my supervisor. I remember feeling almost apologetic that I was sick because he always had made me feel like I was on thin ice. I never felt comfortable with him. The chemistry between us wasn't there. I thought he might use it against me to finally get rid of me as a ref. He might have said I wasn't physically well enough to do the job any longer. I told him everything. There was a long silence on the phone, but he did show compassion and told me he'd be in touch.

NHL commissioner Gary Bettman called within five minutes

after I hung up the phone. Bettman showed exceptional kindness and tremendous humanity. He insisted I take as much time away from work as needed to get healthy.

"What's the prognosis?" Bettman asked.

"We're not sure," I replied.

"I want you to know that no matter what happens, we'll take care of your family," Bettman said. "And if you don't come back to work, we'll pay you."

"I appreciate it, but my goal is to come back to work," I replied.

Bettman took a load of pressure off my shoulders because I knew what I had in the bank wouldn't be enough to take care of Lori and McCauley if I died. I didn't want to leave them destitute. They would never have been able to afford the house.

People aren't always kind when talking about Gary Bettman. He is who he is. But don't say anything bad about him in front of me because he was a friend when I needed a friend. He helped me. He promised to take care of my family and that meant the world to me.

I told Bettman that McDonough wanted to run the story. He was fine with it. Out of respect for my great friend, David Langford, the former *Globe and Mail* and Sun Media national sports editor, I also shared my story with him. McDonough, Langford, and I agreed both stories would run on the same day. Both did and both were terrific articles.

Thanks to Olsen's tremendous support, I made it back for the first day of NHL officials training camp in Toronto on September 10, 1998. I was in better shape than at previous camps. Olsen, his wife at the time, Lori, and I went out to dinner before I left for Toronto. During our casual dinner, I stood up and made a brief toast.

"I wouldn't be where I am without Johnny O," I said. Olsen and I cried together there at the table. We had defied all odds during a span of only twelve weeks. A year later, Olsen hosted a twelve-week fitness challenge for his gym members based on the idea of what he and I achieved during our three months training together. Olsen presented the competition's winner with a jet ski. He gave away mountain bikes to the runners-up. Each contestant wrote an essay on how the twelve-week training session changed his or her life. I sat in as one of the competition's judges. "The atmosphere and the energy level in the gym was ridiculous," Olsen said. "It was through the roof."

True. And what Johnny Olsen and I did together during summer 1998, well, that was pretty ridiculous, too. Thanks, Johnny.

I was now almost ready to go back on the ice and reclaim my life. The catheter wasn't removed from my chest until just before training camp. In the meantime, I attended a charity softball game where I ran into Bruins star defenseman Ray Bourque after the two articles ran. He walked up to me, hugged me, wished me the best, and patted me on the chest. He hit the catheter and I nearly fell to my knee.

My initial reaction: "Oooooooohhhhhh!" The catheter looked like a hockey puck under my skin. It was rather large.

"Oh, my God! What is that?" Bourque asked.

I told him he had hit my catheter.

"I'm so sorry!" Bourque said.

"Don't worry about it," I replied. "You didn't know."

John McDermott, the Scottish-Canadian tenor who sang the national anthem at my 1,000th NHL game as a referee, performed at the Cape Cod Melody Tent soon after. He phoned me, knowing I lived locally, and invited me to the show as his guest. We had seats down front.

"I want to take a second to introduce a friend of mine who lives here on Cape Cod," he said, about midway through the show. "We all know him from refereeing in the NHL and he's been sick lately, but he's a tough guy and he's going to come out of it. Here's my friend, Paul Stewart." McDermott hugged me and catheter pressed into my chest. I had the same reaction when Bourque did it: Ooooohhhhhhh! It hurt so much because it had a big needle inside.

My next visit to Dr. Lokich, I told him, "I don't think I can go back to reffing with this thing in my chest."

"Well, we're going to have to reevaluate your situation," he replied.

To make a long story short, the catheter was removed and I made it to the first day of NHL officials training camp. I changed chemotherapies from 5-Fluorouracil Leucovorin to a then-pioneering oral chemo called Xeloda (Capecitabine). I was told that it was a trial chemo. Beyond that, I never took any other type of medication. I told the doctors at the hospital to remove the intravenous painkillers. I never took one steroid. My return to the NHL was purely through my own strength and determination, unlike Lance Armstrong's return to his cycling career after battling testicular cancer.

Each Xeloda pill cost $75. I took five pills a day: three in the morning and two at night. Do the math. It cost a ton of money. In the meantime, my headaches persisted. The physical therapist recommended chair massages, but my insurance didn't cover it. I called Bill Daly, the NHL deputy commissioner.

"Sure, whatever you want," Daly said.

Bettman said, "Any bills, send them to me. We'll pay for everything." Bettman is a smart man. I recognized his superior intelligence the very first time I met him. He also exhibited some inner toughness. Anyone that successful must have some inner toughness. Bettman is at about the same height as was my father, so I was used to men who exhibited a certain swagger because of being short. Short people with power often are described as having a Napoleonic complex. I never sensed that with Bettman, but short people in charge must be in complete command and control. I understood that with Gary. I told Daly and Bettman once, "We've got Cornell, Dartmouth, and Penn all here. The Ivy League pretty well runs this league now."

I received tremendous support from my co-workers and my company. My relationship with certain people in the NHL hasn't always been peachy, but I don't dislike Bettman and I don't dislike Daly.

Before returning to the NHL, I worked four American Hockey League games starting October 24, 1998 in Springfield, Massachusetts. Those four games prepared me for my NHL return November 13, 1998, a Friday the 13th contest between the New Jersey Devils and Pittsburgh Penguins. The league wanted my comeback game in the New York Metro area, and New Jersey turned out to be the best place.

The press conference and everything went fantastically. New Jersey President/General Manager Lou Lamoriello even gave my family a suite, and I was awestruck when then-Pittsburgh superstar Jaromir Jagr skated out and hugged me at center ice.

I invited a young man who had lost a leg as one of my guests. He had been pursuing refereeing, but during the summer of 1998, he stopped to help someone change a tire on the Merritt Parkway in Connecticut and a car struck him. He lost his leg in the accident. I wanted him and my family there. Several league executives, including Bettman, attended.

I wasn't out of the woods yet. I couldn't work too many games in one week. I had to take off two or three days after working a game. My second NHL game back was in Nashville where the team gave a Predators sweater to my son, McCauley. I received a standing ovation at every arena I worked. My comeback tour rivaled Derek Jeter's recent farewell tour except the obvious difference: I'm a bit more handsome than the former New York Yankees' captain.

The NHL introduced its charitable foundation, Hockey Fights Cancer, in 1998. It became a widespread cause advertised quickly on the television and throughout NHL arenas. I became actively involved in it.

I didn't work my first game back in my hometown of Boston until January. When I finally did ref in Boston, Nate Greenberg, Boston's senior assistant to the president, and team President and General Manager Harry Sinden provided me one hundred tickets. I invited everyone who'd aided my return, including Johnny Olsen, the Duggan Family, my neighbors from Cape Cod, and the doctors, nurses, and techs who worked at Baptist.

Dr. Lokich, my oncologist, attended the game and sat beside my mother who said the doctor seemed in awe of the environment. Lokich is the doctor who told me I was very cavalier. That summer, in a moment of passion, I told him, "You know your problem? You should have spent more time at the gym and a little less at the library. Time in the gym would have taught you about guys like me." After he cured me, I told him, "Well, I take it back, I am really glad you spent a lot of time in the library."

My mother told me how Lokich raved about my hard work that summer and on the ice that night.

"This isn't work for him," my mother replied.

I became teary-eyed during the first stoppage of play in Boston when the Hockey Fights Cancer video appeared on the Jumbotron. The crowd roared, gave me a standing ovation, and I couldn't hold in the tears any longer. I don't know where the show of emotion came from. Mom never showed any emotion about the diagnosis, but then, neither of my parents acted too emotional or showed much affection throughout their lives. Mom had seemed confident I'd beat the cancer when I phoned her to tell her about my diagnosis. I don't know and will never know if she ever felt nervous. She has since passed away and is again sitting somewhere with my dad.

Dr. Lokich told my mom I was the toughest man he had ever met. I always remembered that because, the next year, I delivered a speech at a National Cancer Survivors Day event and Dr. Lokich introduced me. Soon after, I gave another speech at the Hockey Hall of Fame at an event several oncologists attended. I was asked to walk from the back of the room to the front with a spotlight on me. While sitting in the back before being introduced, two oncologists sat directly to my left discussing my case, unaware I was Paul Stewart.

One of the doctors said to the other, "Boy, his cancer was advanced. That he's here is a miracle."

Right after they got done talking, I was introduced. I stood up, looked to my left at the two doctors, and I joked, "We'll see how big of a miracle it is now!"

Linesman Brian Murphy said my survival extends beyond colon cancer. "He's a survivor in life, too," Murphy added. "I don't think Paul would ever say he had the greatest skill set [as a player] or anything like that, but he had the work ethic that I think he got from his father. And that's how he deals with his kids. He brings his kids everywhere because his father brought his kids everywhere."

I realized God preserved me for a reason and I've been trying to figure out the reason ever since. Maybe I've already fulfilled my purpose for living and don't even know it. Maybe I've accomplished it simply by preaching to everyone I know and meet to undergo routine colonoscopies.

"Have you had your routine colonoscopy?" I've even been known to ask friends at weddings. I feel angered when people ignore the signs, don't listen, and resist undergoing colonoscopies. Tim Taylor, the former Yale coach and Team USA coach at the 1994 Olympics, whose family owned *The Boston Globe* from 1873-1999, died from colon cancer at seventy-one-years old in April 2013. Are you telling me Taylor couldn't afford medical insurance and a colonoscopy? That's ridiculous.

Despite my strained relationship with senior management, I counseled my direct boss's wife about what to expect after being diagnosed with breast cancer. I advised her on the realities of being sick, how to combat it, the mental challenges, and how to prepare for chemotherapy. I told her about all she needed to know. He thanked me. He didn't have to. To me, it was simply the right thing to do.

Same thing with NHL coach Pat Burns, although we never spoke directly. I spoke with his wife, Line Burns, solely, after Pat's colon cancer diagnosis.

Oddly enough, Burns and I had a run-in during my final year of active refereeing. It was when he was the head coach of New Jersey and the Devils were playing in New Jersey versus the Florida Panthers, who were coached by Mike Keenan and assisted by George Kingston.

Keenan's mother was dying of pancreatic cancer. Keenan asked before the game if I could give him some Hockey Fights Cancer pins. The Panthers' dressing room was right near the referees' dressing room and Kingston came down the hallway with me after the period to retrieve the pins. In the meantime, Burns saw me talking with Kingston and came flying down the hallway and started yapping at me.

"Who do you think you are?" Burns asked. "You can't talk with one coach and not the other." He charged at me aggressively. I turned and looked at him, dumbfounded because Kingston and I weren't talking about hockey. I do understand that Burns perceived it differently.

"What's your problem?" I asked.

"You've been running around this league for twenty years doing anything you want!" Burns yelled. "You can't just walk down the hall and talk to him and not talk to me."

"I'll talk to you, Pat," I said. "He wants Hockey Fights Cancer pins. Do you want one?"

"What does that have to do with this game?" Burns asked.

"Nothing. That's why I didn't think it was that big of a deal. But, for some reason, you want to make a big deal out of it. Who are you kidding? You're trying to embarrass me. I frankly don't give a shit what you think. Matter of fact, I hate to tell you this, but I've got two weeks left and I'm out of here. So, if you want to pick a fight, then start today because I've got nothing to lose."

I also told him, "I hope you never get cancer and have to find out what it's all about."

Linesman Pat Dapuzzo stepped between us and blocked Burns. I turned and said, "Let him go. If he wants a piece of me, come on. Help yourself. You'll find out I'm just as tough as you. You think you're a tough guy, an ex-cop. I used to be a cop, too. Try me."

A priest had been standing there, and as Burns and I exchanged profanities. I turned to him and said, "Sorry, Father."

I gave Kingston the Hockey Fights Cancer pins and the dispute ended. Not too long after, Robbie Ftorek called me and asked if I heard about Pat Burns.

"He has colon cancer," Ftorek said.

I felt terrible.

"He'd really like to talk to you," Ftorek told me. "Could you call him?"

Pat never picked up the phone. He talked with me through his wife only. She asked me questions on his behalf. Maybe he felt embarrassed. Maybe he wasn't physically up to it at that point. I understood.

I emailed back and forth frequently, but never talked directly with Pat even once. I hope it was not because of what happened in the hallway. As I told his wife, "There's no harm, there's no foul. Friction is part of the game. It doesn't bother me."

I was concerned only with helping him through it. Let bygones be bygones. In a way, Pat and I did talk. His wife talked with me for approximately three or four years. I received emails and phone calls from her. I returned her messages to tell them what they wanted to know. I'm Irish; I forget everything but the grudge.

Another dispute I had with Burns came during 1997-1998 when he coached the Boston Bruins. I had yet to call a penalty on either team. I skated by the bench and Burns yelled, "You're a brilliant referee. You screw us to prove you're fair." Curious statement.

I blew the whistle, skated over to Burns, leaned over the bench, and asked, "What do you mean by that? I 'screw you to prove I'm fair?' That doesn't even make sense."

"Go f—yourself," he told me.

"You know what? A lot of guys tell me that," I said. "What are you going to do to back it up? You're shitting on me because your players suck. You're trying to get them motivated by using me. You know what? F—them and f—you, too. I'm not putting up with your happy horseshit, and you know what? Everyone thinks I'm going to give you a penalty—and I'm not."

I backed off and added, "Tell your wife she's got brilliant taste. I love your tie." The whole arena had grown silent. I had no reason to stop the game, though Burns and I had been screaming back forth at each other. I skated away. P.J. Axelsson, a rookie for Boston at the time, made some comment.

"When I want to talk to peanut gallery, then I'll talk to you," I told him.

Ray Bourque, one of the most respectful players of all-time, skated to me when the period ended and commented on how he had never seen Burns so hot.

"Yeah, so?" I asked.

"Well, you're not going to stick it to us now, are you?"

"No, that was between Pat and me," I replied. "You didn't say it. Your teammates didn't say it. Let me put it this way. When I leave this rink tonight and get on the plane tomorrow, I'm going to read the newspapers. If I see any comments from you guys on the TV when I get home, or if I read in the papers tomorrow what was said on the bench, you're going to hate it. Because tomorrow night, I fly to Buffalo. You guys are playing in Buffalo. You won't get a power play all night long and you'll be killing penalties. I promise you. Control the room. Control your teammates. I don't want to hear a word. It's between Burns and me. That's it. As for me, it's done."

A reporter asked Burns during the postgame press conference about the beef between him and me. Burns replied with something like, "Paul Stewart is one of our best referees. I don't think he had his best game tonight."

I was fine with his answer. It wasn't a fact. It was an opinion. He didn't blow it up. He didn't mention what was said. He just made an observation from his own side of the coin. I boarded the plane the next day and read nothing about it in the newspapers. Bourque skated by me in Buffalo before the game.

"You're the best," I told him.

"Well, are we going to get any power plays?" he asked.

"We shall see."

I then skated by Burns and commented, "Line chose another nice tie..."

He smirked. That was that. I refereed the game. That was good enough for me. I didn't have to be buddy-buddy with any coach or player during my NHL refereeing career. I felt so glad to see Pat Burns selected for the NHL Hall of Fame as a Builder in 2014. I just wished it hadn't come posthumously. He deserved it, having won the Jacks Adams Award three times and having led the 2002-2003 New Jersey Devils to the Stanley Cup title.

Pat went into remission after beating colon and liver cancer in 2004 and 2005, but the cancer returned four years later. The colon cancer had spread to his lungs. Burns celebrated the groundbreaking of Pat Burns Arena at Stanstead College in Quebec during March 2010.

"I probably won't see the project to the end, but let's hope I'm looking down on it and see a young Wayne Gretzky or Mario Lemieux,'' he said during his speech that day.

"I know my life is nearing its end and I accept that. As for my career, I always said to my kids, 'You don't cry because it's over; you're happy because it happened.' That's the main thing. I'm happy it happened.''

Burns died November 19, 2010. Pat Burns Arena opened the following September. A memorial game in Burns' honor took place in Quebec. Who did the organizers select to referee it? Yours truly.

I'm glad Pat found acceptance and tranquility before his death, but I have difficulty understanding why he left us too soon while I still remain here. The hardest thing for me at times simply is wondering why I was saved.

Sadly, cancer has touched the lives of many of my friends and colleagues. At NHL officials training camp in Barrie, Ontario in the fall of 1998 while I still was on chemotherapy, I met cancer patient Daniel Kruz, who was only about twelve years old. His sister had given him three bone marrow transplants and none of them had taken. He came to our training camp on his last legs. He was a friend of then-NHL referee, Lance Roberts. He sat beside me in the dressing room. He was a goalie and we dressed him up and gave him a uniform. He came out to our training camp and skated with us. A bunch of different people, including then-recently retired Mike Gartner, now a Hall of Famer, came by to be with Kruze and skate with him.

I met the boy's mother, father, and sister. We found out he was returning for more treatment at The Hospital for Sick Kids in Toronto.

"Well, I'm going to come by and see you," I told him. I was

walking up the street to The Hospital for Sick Kids in Toronto and ran into Walter Gretzky. Come to find out, Walter used to go in there quite often to visit with the ailing children, which tells you a lot about Walter's character.

"What are you doing?" Walter asked me.

"I'm going to see this sick boy who loves hockey," I told him. "He's up against it. Really tough."

"I'll come with you," Walter said. Walter put on the gown and mask, scrubbed up, then he went and talked with the boy and asked him, "If you could have any wish, what would it be?"

"I'd like to meet Patrick Roy," Kruze replied. The little boy was in the bed and you could see him failing. He was about to have another bone marrow transplant and his sister was there. It was painful for her, too, because they were taking the marrow right out of her hip. She's a hero, too.

Walter didn't tell the boy, but he took care of it. He told me he'd get several NHLers, including Toronto goalie Felix Potvin, Wayne Gretzky, Patrick Roy, and others to stop by the hospital to see Kruze. I thought it was great when he told me his plan. I was flabbergasted when he got everyone he asked to come visit this boy.

Daniel Kruze rallied and survived, and he's still alive to this day. I always think of him and his brave little sister. What toughness. The doctors credited Walter and all those players going to see him for reigniting his will to live. I still get emotional about it because that's the part of hockey that keeps me coming and makes me glad I was a part of it. So many players and others in the league—past and present—have that common decency and a concern for other human beings and it makes me feel gratitude toward the game.

I'll ask you again: Have you yet to figure out why I love my life in hockey? Despite the ups and downs with bosses, despite my own struggles as a player (getting cut in college and wading through the minors and the tough bus rides, etc.) I feel truly blessed because I have hockey, something beyond just family, that I truly love and can't live without.

During an appearance at the NHL All Star game in Toronto, representing the NHL Hockey Fights Cancer campaign and Roger Neilson who was also battling the disease, I spoke over a microphone to those in attendance at the Air Canada Arena. I held my son

McCauley's hand. He wore a hockey sweater with his name on the back and his number 22 1/2. His red hair glowed like his mom's. He stared up at me as I told the fans, "I'd like for you to say hello to my boy, McCauley John, the reason I fought so hard to come back to my life in the National Hockey League."

I love my own family the most. But like Kruze and his many other friends that he made due to Walter Gretzky, including many members of the hockey family, hockey was what ignited my will to live. I love being part of a hockey family that has afforded me the opportunity to skate on the same ice with legends such as Hall of Famer Gordie Howe and to go fishing with Hall of Famer Doug Harvey.

While undergoing chemo, I often thought about Harvey, who, like me, was sometimes a bit misunderstood as a man. I still often think about him. He was a brilliant hockey player—I was a two-goal guy—but his story sometimes makes me think about my own life, both the highs and lows. Many of Harvey's teammates disliked him despite his ability. He earned the James Norris Memorial Trophy seven times, but he did things to anger friends and teammates. He had some issues that led to his poor relationships. He battled bipolar disorder and alcoholism. Harvey died at age sixty-five in 1989 practically alone, almost indigent, and his body ravaged from the effects of cirrhosis of the liver.

I met Harvey in 1976 during my days as a player at New York Rangers' rookie camp in Décarie, Montréal. John Ferguson called me to the boards and introduced me to him.

"I'm going to give you the best teacher in world to teach you how to play defense in the National Hockey League," Ferguson said. "This is Doug Harvey. Montreal Canadiens, Number 2." Everyone in Montreal pronounced his last name 'arvey, never pronouncing the "H." He had a buzz cut and I recognized him from his playing days. I had watched him on television. He wore a plaid black-and-red hunting jacket and a pair of green work pants before changing into a sweatsuit. He then came onto the ice and showed me some techniques. Ferguson took the cigar out of his mouth and said, "Anywhere Doug Harvey goes, you go. If he wants to go somewhere, you drive him."

"Do you like fishing, kid?" Harvey asked me.

"I love fishing," I said. "Anything you want to do, I'm ready."

After practice, we jumped into his big old green car. I drove and we stopped to buy two six-packs of beer, then drove about forty-five minutes outside of Montreal into the middle of the woods.

"Pull up next to that fence," he instructed me. He went to the back of the car, popped the trunk and pulled out a Popeil Pocket Fisherman.

"Where's the lake, where's the stream, where's the river?" I wondered. Harvey walked to the front of the car, jumped on the hood and casted the Popeil Pocket Fisherman with a lure on it over the fence.

"What are you doing?" I asked.

"It's a trout farm," he said. "I catch fish here all the time."

The fish were active but he really didn't have much bait with him. I just stood, watched, and listened to his stories about the good old days. I was in a bit of shock and kept waiting for the gendarmes to show. I didn't drink any beer because I was playing that night at the Maurice Richard Arena against a Quebec Major Junior team.

We left when he finished all the beer. I drove him back to the motel we were staying at close to Concordia University. After the game, I ended up driving him and another gentleman back to the hotel from a Chinese restaurant. They both were gassed out of their minds. I put Harvey in his bed and then woke him up the next morning, poured him a cup of coffee, and drove him to the rink. I liked Harvey. He might have had his issues, but he treated me wonderfully and made me laugh. I feel bad thinking he died practically alone and in such tough shape. Nobody deserves that.

On the other hand, I was near death but wasn't alone. Kruze and I were lucky that others who loved us truly rallied around us. I had a beautiful wife, a handsome newborn son, a mother, two brothers, one sister, and several loyal friends. Still, I felt somewhat alone at times because I held so many emotions inside of me. Some strong advice I'll give you all: Don't ever hide what you're feeling. Let your loved ones know what's happening and how you truly feel when you feel it.

I reflect on that very experience with Harvey and so many other crazy moments with other hockey greats and feel extremely lucky. I rubbed shoulders with so many Hall of Famers, some of the greatest players ever to live, and they treated me like I should have been treated. They treated me like a guy who could play the game, and they knew I was tough. It was about respect.

My harshest critic within league management wasn't wrong when I was asked if I always felt the need to let everyone know I was part of the NHL. I was proud to be there. It was an honor to do what I loved for so many years. It was an honor to have made the NHL as a player and referee and been a part of such a terrific game. Not many get there and many try. I got there three times: as a player, a referee, and a cancer survivor who wasn't supposed to make it back.

My family gave me the strength I needed to fight cancer. But, ultimately, hockey gave me the drive to do it.

# CHAPTER 20: A Universal Language

I stepped off a bus in Russia during the fall of 2013 and noticed an elderly woman sitting on an old cardboard box near a fruit stand. Father Winter dusted the street with the beginning snows of a Russian winter. This old babushka was holding a tin cup and wore a Russian Orthodox icon of Jesus. I took a second look at the woman and said, "Screw it!" I took out all the Russian money I had in my pocket (it wasn't much), maybe 2,000 rubles, and put it into this woman's tin cup. She clearly needed it more than I did, though I was hardly flush at that point. I was barely even comfortable.

There I was, working as the officiating and league discipline consultant for the Kontinental Hockey League (KHL) in Russia, but still struggling to earn enough money to support to my family back home in Walpole. I started walking toward the train station, about a hundred yards away from the bus stop and fruit stand. I hadn't walked ten feet when my cell phone rang. SKA Saint Petersburg general manager Alexei Kasatonov was on the other line and told me the KHL wanted to renegotiate a new contract with me, meaning a salary increase.

I had recently called Kasatonov's son, asking him to talk with his dad about helping me renegotiate. I needed more money to support my two sons with their schooling back home. Kasy was close to the chairman of the league and, of course, everything always goes from there upward to the president. Things were tight. I had even considered selling the house we built in '98, downsizing to lessen the financial challenges.

I'm still plugging away, trying to make a buck just like most everyone in this world. I have been, for the most part, since I retired from the NHL. The NHL pension for players and referees is pitiful, especially for those of us who worked in the seventies through the nineties. We get our pension money in Canadian dollars with the exchange rate favoring everyone but us. Then we have to pay a foreign exchange tax plus the extra accountant fee to file the necessary paperwork. The NHL management and the owners should feel ashamed for the pitiful way we get our pension and the meager amount. It is a major league with all the big boys making millions and guys like me with twenty-plus years on the ice getting twenty grand—and in Canadian dollars, at that.

Going to Russia for work gave me a chance to catch up. I wanted Kasatonov's help pleading my case to Alexander Medvedev, KHL president and Deputy Chairman of the Board of Executive Directors for Gazprom Export LLC, the company that owns SKA Saint Petersburg. I also wanted Kasatonov to help me make my appeal to Saint Petersburg team president Gennady Timchenko, who served as the chairman of the KHL board of directors. Medvedev and Timchenko both work directly for President Putin. Everything in Russia is somehow controlled by The Kremlin and the man who lives there.

There are some certain things in Russia that are their lifeblood. They have those things in abundance. They include natural gas and oil, red and black caviar, vodka, and hockey. These aspects of Russia may well be important to the rest of the world, yet of all of those things (the hockey heroes of Russia and the way they play the game) is a source of pride and national identity for the Russian people. The reason I was asked to go to Russia was to try to improve Russian hockey officiating and to put some integrity into that aspect of the game that is oftentimes considered to be questionable.

Kasatonov did what he said he would do. He came through for me. Although… maybe God also intervened after I had helped the destitute woman just seconds before receiving Kasatonov's call. Who knows? Now, do you understand why I believe I wasn't meant to die of colon cancer? There are other things that I am meant to do.

The entire Atlantic Ocean and more stood between my apartment in Russia and my wife, Lori, and two sons, McCauley and Maxwell. Being so far away wasn't easy for me. I'd be home with Lori and the boys, working on their golf swings and hockey technique if I had enough money. But I don't. I traveled home every chance I got to be with them.

Life continues to present certain challenges, just like back as a kid when I moved to Jamaica Plain, or during my days at Groton and the University of Pennsylvania, or my grind through the minors, or the abrupt end to my NHL playing career, or my two failed marriages, or my cancer fight, or my struggles with certain bosses as an NHL official. I understand so many other people are struggling these days in a tough economy and changing world.

I've always come out on top and I'm confident that will not change as I continue to live. I've always liked the nickname "Stewcat." Not only is a cat always ready to pounce, but he gets nine lives. I've gotten so many chances to rise from the ashes. It's not that things came easily, it's more than I've scratched and clawed my way back.

My life sort of flows along like the lyrics from Bob Marley's song, "Three Little Birds." Unlike Bob, though, I do worry. A certain level of anxiety is inevitable for people with my personality. But I like to think everything has turned out all right so far because I'm a fighter in more ways than once. We all have that fight inside ourselves; we just need to find it.

I'm still fighting for my health. I suffered severe headaches a few years ago. I stood up as I got out of bed so dizzy after a nap to answer the portable telephone in the bathroom. On the way there, I fell over and took a header. The room was spinning. I thought I was experiencing a heart attack. After several MRIs, the doctors told me I had developed a pituitary adenoma, a non-cancerous tumor about the size of a golf ball in the pituitary gland in the middle of my brain. At that time, I opted not to undergo an operation because the tumor, they believed, was a noncancerous growth. I had some anxiety about another operation and exactly how it had to be done, thinking of the movie *Hannibal* and how he removed Agent Krendler's prefrontal lobe.

After I made the initial decision to forgo surgery, however, the size of the tumor increased and I needed that surgery. I suffered from more severe headaches and also short-term memory loss. I struggled to remember things. I began to struggle with my vision because the pituitary adenoma was pressing on my optic nerve. The surgery stopped the vision deterioration and, hopefully, will prevent the condition from worsening.

People heard my memory loss in my voice. I sometimes stopped sentences midway through and had to regain my thoughts. Still, my long-term memory remains strong. I reconnected with an old Groton friend on Facebook not too long ago, whom I hadn't seen since 1968. I reminded him of the exact location we were when we last met in-person. We both sat at a little cocktail party, him drinking a Miller beer and eating cheese and crackers.

"Don't put that beer down because I might drink it," I remembered telling him.

I remember the most amazing details such as from my days seeing Jackie Kennedy run the golf course every night during the summers as a kid when I caddied at Hyannisport Club and lived in *M*A*S*H*-style tents. She ran what we called the "inside-five"—holes one, two, sixteen, seventeen, and eighteen. She wore white slacks and a nice cotton shirt. Her hair was always pulled back in a bandana. She ran for a bit, then walked for a bit. Hole eighteen had a steep hill. She smoked a cigarette when she made it to the top.

I remember how Rose Kennedy wore a scarf around her head, pulled tight, and she wore big sunglasses. I remember one time I was near her when some tourists, having no idea who she was because of her scarf and sunglasses, asked her for directions to the Kennedy Compound. With her staccato voice, she gave them explicit directions to her home.

"If you go down the street, there's a fence on the right, it's behind the fence," she said. "But the best way to get a view of it is to take your first right and go along the beach road to the backside, otherwise the police will stop you ..."

Rose Kennedy golfed as well. She played what we called the "Wood Holes," or the one outside of the sight of the public. She occasionally came up to the club for lunch or to buy some golf balls. She drove a big white Chrysler Newport. She didn't spend too much time in the sun, but people in Hyannis Port knew her and she was engaging and friendly. She parked near our Caddy Camp, and after she finished playing, my brother who was the Camp Caddy Master, told me to go out and carry Mrs. Kennedy's bag. But she always refused.

"Oh, no, I'm fine, dear," she'd say. "Tell your brother no thank you." She knew my brother by name. When the ice cream truck was near the Caddy Camp, she'd stop and buy us all an ice cream—all fifty-six kids.

I remember almost every past event with such amazing clarity. I'm not infallible, but a vivid memory has always helped me. That's why I felt somewhat frightened when I lost my short-term memory and struggled to remember things I knew I should recall.

Since my NHL refereeing career ended, my life has been rocky at times, but wonderful in so many ways, too. The final year in the NHL was a whirlwind of emotions. During my first game back to the NHL in my return from colon cancer—November 12, 1998—I spoke over a microphone to the press at the Continental Airline Arena. Flash forward to November 15, 2003 in Boston, when I became the first American-born referee to work my 1,000th NHL game.

There I stood at another pre-game ceremony celebrating my career with Lori by my side and, not one son but two, McCauley and Maxwell. McCauley stood right beside me as he had in November 1998 and Lori held the very young Maxwell in her arms. Both sons wore referee sweaters.

How far I had come from my deathbed! How amazing it was my family had grown from three to four instead of decreasing from three to two. Interviewed on NESN, the Boston Bruins and Boston Red Sox television network, following my 1,000th game, I said, "When you love doing what you're doing and you have a lot of people who help and support you, and especially in the tough times when I was ill, I think that the proof is we've had a good kick at the 'Cat.'"

My 1,010th and final game as an NHL referee was just as emotional as my comeback game and number 1,000. Linesman Brian Murphy recalled, "Being in the room and seeing Paul in his last game and how much it meant to him and the accomplishments he made, to have survived and still have been there, it was a pretty emotional time. To see someone end their career... I think the heart and mind in him wanted to keep going, but he knew the body wasn't up to the level he needed it to perform at." He added, "To be there on his final days and see how emotional Paul was, he enjoyed officiating, he enjoyed working for the NHL, and thought about how much it really meant to him… But it wasn't about Paul. He was actually thinking about a lot of other people that day. People who helped him get there. He will never forget those people."

He's right.

During that final game, a lifetime of memories shot through me; from my days with my dad teaching me to skate, to Groton coach Junie O'Brien's lesson about never quitting, to John McCauley's compassion, to trainer Johnny Olsen's dedication, to sharing the same ice with legends such as my childhood idol, Gordie Howe, to family and great friends, such as Terry Johnson who came down from Toronto to help my wife move out of our condo and take care of McCauley when I underwent surgery to remove the tumors from my colon and my liver… I'll cherish them all.

Upon leaving the NHL, I worked as the director of the Boston Bruins Foundation for a few years. I even had three interviews for the Boston Bruins general manager position that eventually went to Peter Chiarelli. I put together a ninety-page report on how I planned to fix the team. I worked as a NESN television analyst during Bruins' pre- and post-game broadcasts for a brief time. Then-Boston GM Mike O'Connell telephoned me, upset about something I'd said on a post-game show. The Bruins had committed a blatant infraction resulting in a penalty shot for their opponent based off a recent rule change. I had explained the reasoning of Kerry Fraser, the referee who'd worked the game, for making the correct call. It should have resulted in a penalty shot.

But O'Connell wanted me to argue against the facts in favor of the Bruins. He wanted me to be in sports what is called "a homer," or believing your hometown team can do nothing wrong. He told me I'd never be on TV again. He's a small-minded person who had clout. I see him now, shake his hand, and then go wash my hands. "You could have been a Bruin," was all he kept saying.

If ass-kissing is what it takes to be a Bruin, I'll stay a Nordique, thank you. I'm no homer. I tell it like I see it. I tell it like it is. That's one of my main reasons for writing this book. I wanted to tell the truthful account of how things happen(ed) in the NHL and in my life. I will continue to tell it like it is because that's what's only fair. I do it on my blog at HockeyBuzz.com.

I wrote a blog post on the HockeyBuzz.com about NESN Bruins play-by-play announcer Jack Edwards; I called him out for being outrageously biased. This is the way things happen in the broadcast world nowadays with stations owned by teams. I don't like it. It's funny; I used to play golf with Fred Cusick, longtime Bruins announcer. As he said to me, the Bruins fans have been watching hockey for a long time and know the game. Tell it like it is because they can see the game anyway: don't make it up. I didn't, and so I got let go.

Anyway, these days, my goals are much grander, but also realistic now that I'm in my sixties. I underwent a hip replacement during summer 2013, not because I couldn't tolerate the pain, but because I wanted to keep doing things like cutting my own lawn and keeping up with my own landscaping at my Walpole house. I want my yard to look the way I want it to look.

A more important goal for me is to see my boys play and ref hockey, receive a strong education like I did, grow up into respectful men, and succeed at whatever they choose to do with their lives. I'll do anything to pay for their educations, just like when I was paying for my own tuition to the University of Pennsylvania and I walked up and down 30th Street Station in Philly wearing advertising sign boards on my chest to promote Friday Night Franklin Field games and other Penn events. Back in those days, I typically spent just five dollars on Sundays when the athletic training house was closed and I couldn't eat for free. Instead, I'd buy a quart of milk and a corned beef hoagie. I cut the corned beef hoagie in half, eating one side for breakfast and the other half for dinner. I'll reiterate again and again: no job was too big or too small. That should go for all of us as we work toward our dreams.

I currently serve as director of hockey officiating for the Eastern College Athletic Conference (ECAC) and I have a business back home called "Lest We Forget" where I maintain grave plots. It includes gravesite cleanups, trimming of shrubs, planting seasonal flowers, mulching, embedding flags and holiday decorations, and also stone cleanings. I do it all myself—sometimes in the dark and rain—and I send pictures to the families.

With the officiating work in Russia and with the ECAC refs, I have done and continue to do exactly what my mentor John McCauley did—teaching young officials and trying to make the game better for everyone.

A great boss is one who gains his workers' respect by teaching and helping them improve. John McCauley did that. It's what I strive to do with the people who work for me. After all, getting people to even *want* to officiate is hard enough. We need to get them to a place where they can succeed at it.

It's a never-ending job but, for me, it's never arduous. It's a labor of love because it's hockey and it's my passion. With so many changes over the course of my life, that is the one thing that has remained constant even to this day.

# CHAPTER 21: The Reason I'm Here

On the heels of the unthinkable Humboldt tragedy where a busload of young hockey players was injured and killed in a tragic accident, I shared on Facebook that I cry at the end of *Toy Story* when Andy gives away his toys and heads off to college. Thinking of the day when my own sons fly the coop and go out into the world makes me tearful. Parenting my sons has been at once the most gratifying and most humbling experience of my life. Teaching your kids how to fly is the fun part; letting them leave the nest is the terrifying part. Still, I know they are ready to take on the world in their own ways. I believe I have taught them how to compete in this world, both on and off the ice.

When I look back on my life and my career, I marvel at how things have come full circle. The ways in which I benefited from the teachings and role-modeling of my father and grandfather, I now see my own two sons continuing the cycle. Forced by a cancer diagnosis to face my own mortality, I have also been left to ponder my legacy. For what do I want to be remembered? What about my life has made an impact on others and given my life meaning?

First and foremost, being a father to McCauley and Maxwell has defined my life and my legacy. My boys, twenty and seventeen as I write this chapter, have accomplished so much and have given me so many reasons to be proud of them.

Just like my dad and grandfather were two of the most important people in my life, making me who I am today, I hope to be that to my sons as well.

Recently, both boys left home to go officiate local games. I couldn't help but get emotional, thinking about these two young men going forth in the world, each making his own mark to be sure, but also continuing in my footsteps along the path forged by their grandfather and great-grandfather. Hockey isn't just a game; it's a family business.

No matter what path they ultimately follow, their roots in this business run deep. It is a part of them as it was a part of me and that gives me tremendous satisfaction. They have the bloodlines.

While I can't overstate the meaning of my father's legacy in shaping my life, the importance of role models like John McCauley and Junie O'Brien who served as mentors shouldn't be understated either. After my NHL career ended, I found my way to the KHL. My official title was League Officiating and Discipline Consultant, and my official duties included teaching the Russians to officiate the modern pro game. Unofficially, I was doing much more. I was hoping to be somebody's John McCauley. I wanted to inspire and to teach young officials, and to help mold the officiating practices of a league where I could make an impact. I was trying to create a legacy in the spirit of those men and for the good of the game.

I have tried to make a similar impact in the ECAC. As the Director of Officiating, I've had a chance to work with very young officials, to help guide them through the ins and outs of officiating. Officiating is hard work and it is demanding, both physically and mentally. Good officiating is integral to the sport I love so dearly. Officials need support and guidance, and few people understand the demands of the job. I have tried to offer that support to those officials under my tutelage, whether instructing them on technical nuances of their job, or helping them navigate the emotional toll of time away from family and friends in pursuit of their calling. There are the ever-present challenges we all face in our lives. Gambling, drinking, drugs, injuries, and illness. Those items and trying to skate do not a happy mix make.

These are the things that define me and my life. It is fun to discuss penalty minutes and count missing teeth, but, at the end of the day, these are the things that matter the most and I can honestly say that I am proud of the marks I have made.

# CHAPTER 22: The Places You Will Go

I wrote this book to serve as a memoir. Many people have asked over the years when I planned to write a book about my experiences in hockey, having seen and done so much. I could fill a thousand pages with funny stories, sad stories, inspiring stories. But, in the interest of brevity, I will limit myself to just a few more favorite anecdotes. These are some of my fondest memories of my extraordinary life in hockey. If you are interested in hearing more, I guess you'll have to buy the sequel.

I mentioned previously that I was fortunate enough to be cast as an extra in the iconic hockey film *Slap Shot*. People always want to know what that was like and what it was like to work alongside Paul Newman. My extra role in *Slap Shot* was as a player. I earned five hundred dollars and received a Newman-autographed copy of the script which I still have. How I got picked to be in the film is a story unto itself. The filmmakers sent Paul Newman's brother, Art Newman, around to different NAHL cities with a Polaroid camera. At the time, I was missing a tooth, had a black eye and more than a few stitches. No big deal; I always seemed to have a black eye. I had a few different rough features that made me one of the guys they wanted as an extra.

Art Newman took my picture with his Polaroid. I asked him what he thought. "You are perfect, you are in," he said, and, thus, my fifteen minutes of fame was extended a few minutes more. The filming took place after the 1975-1976 season, my first in professional hockey, and happened in Johnstown. I had an absolute blast. I talked with Newman, actress Jennifer Warren who played Newman's ex-wife, actor Strother Martin who played the character Joe McGrath, actor Michael Ontkean who played the character Ned Braden, and actor Jerry Howser who played Killer Carlson and also starred in a great movie, *The Summer of '42*. Then there was the director, George Roy Hill.

"Where did you get all these fans for the filming?" I asked Hill once when there was a lull in the filming. He told me they were recruited from the welfare/unemployment offices around Johnstown and as far away as Pittsburgh.

"I can tell," I replied.

"Why is that?" Hill asked.

"There are more minorities at this game than I've ever seen at any hockey game in my life. I'd move them around a little bit if I were you."

He took my suggestion. It wasn't a bigoted viewpoint on my part. It is the truth about how hockey demographics were back then. I never saw seven black men sitting in the front row of a hockey game during the 1970s in any minor league town.

Hill asked me a couple more questions. We talked hockey. He didn't know much about the sport, but he learned quickly. He asked me if hockey players planned the violence that happened.

"I don't plan it," I replied. "I only plan how to handle it. It's like having four or five different pieces of equipment. I just pick out the one I need. It just depends on who I have to fight. If I fight a shorter guy, I fight him a different way from a larger guy. If I'm fighting a stick guy, I go about it in a different way. It's more theoretical and tactical-planning, and then, when the heavyweights get at it, it's just balls to the wall."

Lots of people are curious about what it was like to work with Paul Newman. What I recall is that Paul Newman ate fresh grapefruit on the set of the movie each day and was very health-conscious. He also enjoyed drinking beer with the guys. On the movie set, Newman owned and wore an insulated bandoleer holding his beer cans. He unsnapped it and handed out cans to everyone around him after filming ended each day, a time when the members of the crew kicked back, relaxed, and watched their "evening rushes." This turned out to be a thrilling opportunity to hang out with Newman, who sat with all of us hockey players during the evenings, drank beer, told fascinating stories, and asked us questions. We were in awe. Some of us asked him several questions and others just listened.

"Why don't you like it when the tourists take pictures of you after you're filming?" I asked him.

"It hurts my eyes and causes me to lose my focus," he replied.

Newman told me he didn't often sign autographs, but he signed for me and I appreciated it greatly. He attended a game I played in for Binghamton in Johnstown. I started a war that night.

"Is that the way you are every night?" Newman asked me.

"Just about," I told him.

Newman wasn't too tall just, like my dad, but neither man ever appeared short because of their great presence. After meeting Newman, we all had so much respect for him because of that presence. Another thing I noticed was that he was always smiling. He seemed genuine. That impressed me the most about him. He showed an earnest sincerity in us and our lives as hockey players and everyday people. I told him I liked his movies because they were a few hours of being able to retreat from the real world.

I also especially liked Jerry Houser. Houser skated pretty well and he was funny. He was just one of the guys like Newman.

People don't realize it, but just about six weeks earlier, I had fought all those players on the set, such as David Hanson and Jeff and Steve Carlson. Then, suddenly, we were buddies, eating at picnic tables underneath the stands and playing shinny hockey at one end of the rink.

I was an extra player on the ice when Newman's character heckles Long Island goalie Tommy Hanrahan, portrayed by actor Christopher Murney, telling Hanrahan his wife Suzanne is a dyke who "sucks pussy." Hanrahan finally throws off his goalie mask when Newman calls Suzanne a lesbian. I'm sure you remember, the Hanrahan character chased Newman off the ice, jumping into the penalty bench to attack Newman's character, Reggie 'Reg' Dunlop.

Murney is just 5'3" and the boards in Johnstown were not average height, but much higher. A ramp had to be placed by the penalty box board for Murney to run up because he was too short to jump over the wall. When watching the film, viewers obviously don't see him running up the ramp, but I look back on that and chuckle. Murney was cast in the movie because of his facial expressions. I remember Newman telling me all about his great facial expressions, having known him from other movie sets.

During that fight scene, where everyone was grabbing, grasping, and holding on, all the players in that scene are the ones who never fought. They were players on my team such as Steve Stirling, a Boston University alum, and Ken Davidson, a Dartmouth alum, who played with me on the Dusters but weren't fighters. So I always look back on that and chuckle as well.

Thinking of the few short days of filming *Slap Shot* and all the famous people I got to meet, I am still in awe. I pinch myself. Man, oh, man, I drank beer with Paul Newman. I was a part of an iconic and legendary film. It's almost comical to say I sat there at the movie theater shocked by the vulgar language in *Slap Shot* when I saw the movie for the first time in its entirety, especially since the "F" word and swearing is such a crutch for us in hockey. Its authenticity was a little startling.

Growing up a Catholic boy and never hearing my father or grandfather swear other than the odd "damn," I was shocked at the language in the film. I was not shocked because I hadn't heard that same language during my first year in the North American Hockey League all the time—but because I hadn't heard it spoken beyond the locker room or the ice. I certainly hadn't heard it in mixed company.

We lived such different lives outside the dressing room and off the ice. The shenanigans in the dressing room happened, but we didn't necessarily share it with the public. *Slap Shot* did. But the language was part of our culture. That curtness was part of our hockey daily life. An "eff you" was—and still is—more of a morning greeting than a curse or an accost on the listener.

They say that art imitates life. There was a certain way of life in the NAHL. *Slap Shot* wasn't a make-believe movie; it was a true depiction. I did the same with this memoir. I wanted to reveal a true depiction of my life on and off the ice. When we took long NAHL bus rides to places such as Lewiston, Erie, St. George de Beauce, and Utica, the beer bottles rolled from side to side after three and four days on the trip. The clinking of the beer bottles shifting constantly, constantly, constantly was heard after a while as a lullaby and not an annoyance. If it wasn't the beer bottles, it was the vodka and whiskey bottles. The point is that, for some, the drinking was the part of the game that became the lives of many NAHL players. Some even seemed to look forward more to the post-game drinking than the playing or their paycheck. One teammate drank a quarter or more of his beers, opened his Jack Daniels, and poured the whiskey into his can. He drank boilermakers the whole way. By the time we arrived at our destination, he'd be shit-faced and a little hostile.

Here's another story that might make some readers uncomfortable. I won't tell which team did this because there were some still-married men on the bus. I don't want their wives to think about it out now years later, but one of the teams picked up a prostitute in a city after a game. Some of the guys had their fun as she made her living on the bus during the eleven-hour ride. Once the team reached the destination, she was paid and given enough for her plane ticket back to the city where she had joined the ride. Nowadays, they have TV and WIFI on the buses. There's hardly any conversation. The players play video games or text on their cell phones. Times have changed—maybe (or maybe not) for the better.

The casually vulgar language, the womanizing, the card playing, the cigarette smoke, and the violence was a reality during that time. It is what helped me learn the game and helped me become a tougher guy as I fought my way to the majors. The violence in the NAHL—fighting the Carlsons (Jack and Steve), Dave Hanson, and the Blake "Badman" Ball of the league made me tougher. *Slap Shot* was not quite a documentary, but it also wasn't so far off from our reality.

I was so happy to be invited to the set and have that experience as part of my history and life. I mention that because some people have formed certain perceptions of me I deem false. People think I craved being on-camera. Some think I had to make it my business to appear in *Slap Shot* as an extra because they think I was a showboat who wanted all the attention both as a player and later as a referee.

But I wasn't. I was just happy to be included. Same thing goes for the NHL. I was happy to be a part of it all. It wasn't all about me. I wasn't trying to be the constant attention-getter, but I did want to make a name for myself. I wanted not to live a life where I was the last guy picked.

At the same time, I admit to being starved for approval and a sense of belonging as a young player. I wanted people to like me. I wanted my teammates to like me. However, I think if I knew then what I know now, popularity and acceptance would not have been such a goal in my life. I wouldn't have elevated the approval of my peers and rivals to such a high priority.

It was my life in hockey that made me feel important. It gave me an identity I could hold onto, and that makes me most proud when I reflect back on it today. The fraternity of hockey was what has defined my life, both the game and the friendships and relationships I've built. Of course, not all brotherhoods lead to close bonds—Cain and Abel were brothers, too, after all.

Actor Strother Martin, who appeared in *Slap Shot* and also played the captain in the 1967 film *Cool Hand Luke*—the one in which Paul Newman starred as Luke—delivered one of the most famous lines in that movie, "What we've got here is failure to communicate." Maybe I feel misunderstood to some degree because of a failure to communicate. There have been many times that I've failed to communicate my expectations, my feelings, my needs to the people who most needed to hear them. Others have failed to communicate with me in a way that I felt was productive or appropriate at the time. That is now done. I feel I have communicated my message through this autobiography.

I wanted this memoir to right that situation; I wanted to provide the readers with a true depiction of not only my life, but the culture of hockey when I played and refereed. I also wanted to convey that you don't have to be a minority to feel excluded or discriminated against. It is part of the human experience, and one that everyone endures—even people who seem to have it all. It is almost the most difficult aspect of my life to comprehend. To think and believe that there are actually people who are that jealous, that insecure, that diabolically petty that they go out of their way to destroy others and for what? That is the part of this whole mix that befuddles me beyond belief. Frankly, I can't think of a moment in my life when I have envied anyone, except maybe Sonny Bono and John Derek.

I set goals for myself and I achieved them. When most people say that the road to success is paved with blood, sweat, and tears, they are speaking metaphorically. I am not. But all of those moments prepared me to fight some of the most renowned NHL enforcers, such as Terry O'Reilly, Stan Jonathon, and Al Secord in my NHL debut.

I wasn't afraid of O'Reilly. I wanted to fight him. He was massively tough and strong but was slightly unstable on his skates when he fought. He almost always tried to wrestle his opponents down and pop them a few times. I planned to get underneath him and come up on him. I planned to hit him with upper-cuts and that's what

I did. Let me put it this way: fighting O'Reilly gave me a reputation and I always appreciated that he fought me. It wasn't a bad thing; it was a good thing. Every player wants to establish a certain reputation. That's how a player without the most talent, whatever that talent is, makes a name for himself and stays in the league.

I was at a card show once where Terry was signing. He didn't know I'd be there, and I brought the photo of the two of us just about to fight in my NHL debut. I placed it in front of him and simply asked, "Can you sign that?" He looked up and never said anything like, "How you doing, Paul?" Instead, he circled the gloves and wrote, "You started it. Best wishes, Terry O'Reilly." It's exactly the reason I love the guy, why I respect him and why I wish that we had been teammates. He was tough, smart, and he got it.

I watched a ton of movies as a player and referee and still do, especially during my downtime when I was in Russia. I like to study the characters and how actors/actress portray a variety of regular, everyday people, then transform back into their own regular, everyday selves off the set. I think that's fascinating.

I also use several movie references as analogies to my own life because I sometimes have difficulty expressing what I want to say about my life and the obstacles I overcame. I have said I feel there is a reason I survived cancer, a purpose for which I lived. I also have said that I hope that doesn't come off as self-important; I just believe it to be true. In the same way, I don't mean to sound self-important when I say my life has been like a fascinating, must-see movie, having taken many twists-and-turns like Forrest Gump's adventure, and a story of courage and determination comparable to Rudy Ruettiger's story.

Except my story is better than Rudy's in my opinion, because I was there longer and accomplished more. I made the NHL as a player and referee and I returned to the NHL after beating colon cancer. Rudy got a break because everyone loves Notre Dame and all that it means to football and our Irish lives in America. Along the way, I had fun and gained the attention that I'd been starved for from teammates after being an outsider before turning pro. I wanted a team that appreciated what I could do.

I earned the acceptance and respect of my colleagues throughout the industry. I have so many stories to prove it, like when I was sick with cancer and ex-teammate and current ESPN-hockey analyst Barry Melrose and his wife Cindy, who had been a cheerleader with the Cincinnati Stingers when Melrose and I played there together, sent me a beautiful teddy bear for my son McCauley.

I remember clearly and with awe when Hall of Famer Rod Gilbert took me, along with Danny Newman and Nicky Fotiu, to dinner at Il Vagabondo on East 62nd Street in New York City. We walked in there and everybody knew Gilbert. He took us around and introduced us. Fotiu, Newman, and I were much larger than Gilbert, but it was clear who was the king and who were the serfs. I remember every second of the dinner and how delicious the veal parmigiana, the chianti, antipasto salad, and Amaretto Disaronno tasted. Several celebrities, including boxer Jake LaMotta, approached the table to shake our hands. We played bocce after dinner and every second of that night will always stay embedded in my mind.

When I retired as a referee, Gilbert sent me a handwritten letter congratulating me on my career. He used to visit with me when I refereed games in New York.

I gained the respect of so many and that made me feel so good.

My seat in the Cincinnati Stingers dressing room was between Rick Dudley, now the assistant GM of the Montreal Canadiens, and Jamie Hislop. Once, I mistakenly grabbed Dudley's equipment bag and put on his jock. I learned that Dud's hands are much bigger than Donald Trump's.

Dudley was always nice to me. He always had time for me. He didn't prod me to fight, but he'd say, "You can take that guy. You're the toughest guy I've ever seen." Dudley gave me loads of confidence with his words. I had watched him score thirty-one goals for Buffalo during the 1974-75 NHL season. I just appreciated sitting next to him. On the other side, meanwhile, Hislop was one of my best friends and one of the men who I respect the most for his courage, athleticism, and dedication.

Hugh Harris was another who made time for me when I played for Cincinnati. I was part of a play that ripped up Harris' knee. Harris retired immediately thereafter, took his money, and bought a pizza place in Indianapolis, so I always tell him I deserve a free slice. Harris was a veteran player and he made time for me.

So did Dennis Abgrall, who picked me up from the airport when I arrived in Cincinnati and took me out to The Lighthouse bar my first night there. I remember how accepting and accommodating those teammates were and how well they treated me. I was fortunate to hang with the cream of the crop.

If anyone wants to know how much I loved those guys, just ask. Billy Gilligan and I roomed together in an apartment in Cincy. We still see each other as friends and hockey teammates. I know his brother, Mike, who coached at UVM. I know his beautiful sister, Carol, who was office manager for Dr. Diane English, the orthopedic surgeon for Boston College hockey and football. Dr. English is a gorgeous, tall redhead. I didn't mind getting hurt or a needle from Dr. English. Carol always made it so that, with all my injuries, I could get to see Dr. English when I needed to be there, tout suite. I am a lucky guy to say they are my lifetime friends.

Pat "Whitey" Stapleton is easily one of the greatest teammates and friends I could have ever had. How small is the hockey world? We were teammates in Cincy, then I played against his Indy Racer team when he first signed Gretz. His son, Mike, played OHL and in the NHL for Edmonton. I reffed his games. Whitey and his wife, Jackie, visited me when the 1972 Summit Series and the 1987 Canada Cup team had their reunion in Russia. Whitey's dad, Frank, used to stay at my house on Cape Cod. Sadly, I knew all the Stapleton children and grieved when I heard of their tragic losses of two daughters from cancer. I feel their pain and pray for them often. They are my friends and the classiest people you could know.

Imagine, Whitey, a former Bruin and a Black Hawk, a stalwart D man for the 1972 Team Canada and I got to play as his D partner when we played Red Army in 1977.

"Get me the puck, kid, and then stand behind me. Don't get fancy. Leave the puck handling to me." Ha, Ha. I chuckle now when I think of that game and playing with Whitey against Kharlamov, Tretiak, Mikhaelov, and all those Russian legends. It was a long way from Groton School, a long way from sitting in the stands at Penn and a really long way from those bus rides in Binghamton. Then, years later to be treated so well by the Russian Hockey Federation, President Medvedev, Chairman Timchenko, Commissioner Dmitry Efimov. To be treated so respectfully by all the Soviet legends of hockey—I am in awe. I'm a lucky guy. I got the life I'd dreamed about as the rink rat at the old Boston Arena.

Some disparage that I only played twenty-one NHL games. It's okay; one would have been enough. I am happy because I earned the respect I'd sought. It may have been because of my toughness, persistence, and the assistance of some great people, but I got there. I reached my Mecca. The respect I received isn't something given. I learned that. It is something earned. I paid the price and would do it all again if I could.

Fighting is not an easy way to make a living. I fought some of the game's best enforcers. I was prepared for each one, win, lose or draw. My gold medal came when Stan Jonathan whispered in my ear during the final game at the Boston Garden that I was the toughest player he ever fought. Trust me, he was pretty tough himself and, without him, I was just a wannabe.

There are others who make me shake my head and stand in awe. Hall of Famer Phil Esposito always greeted me warmly. I appreciated that and that he thinks of me as a friend. Again, I never backed down even dealing with Hall of Famers. I respected them. That I did my job made people, including Phil Esposito, respect me.

One great illustration was the night that, as GM of Tampa, Esposito challenged me when I officiated a game in Tampa. At the time, he served as the Lightnings' GM besides being the founder of the franchise. Tampa player Enrico Ciccone shot a puck at one of the linesman. I gave him a misconduct penalty. Espo met me after the game in the dugout walkway and started to complain loudly. I had a puck in my hand. I threw that puck at Espo as hard as I could, although it went well over his head. I never intended to hit him, but he dropped to the floor like Sargent York in the trenches.

"What the hell are you doing?" he yelled.

"How do you like it?" I asked. "How do you think my linesman liked it? You have a cinder block playing for you and he has no respect for the officials. Maybe the linesman's not going to call it, but I'm calling it. And you're lucky I don't go down to that dressing room and kick his ass. You can do what you want. You can call Toronto and complain about me, or you can handle it man-to-man like we're doing right here."

"No, that's the end of it. I get it," Espo replied.

I had respect for Esposito and I think he shared a mutual respect. He was one of the strongest guys I ever played against. He could hold me off with one hand, no problem, and I was a strong guy. I was 210 pounds and lifting weights constantly. I could move skaters with ease, but I couldn't move him.

He is an icon and I was just happy to be one player doing what I loved among these icons. Who could ever forget his performance in 1972 versus the Soviets? Who could ever forget that speech he made in Vancouver chastising all of Canada for being so fickle in not supporting that team?

I like to think I made my own reputation and spot in history among these legends, and that's pretty damn good for a freckled-faced kid from Dorchester who had no skill to be in the NHL in the first place, let alone multiple times. No coach of mine had to look too far down the bench to find who could straighten things out on the ice. I was that guy. Why was I that guy? I don't know. Maybe simply because I was tough and willing. Toughness was what I had to have to get in the door and stay there.

A former adversary, Steve Short from the Flyers, once knocked me down in a fight. I then proceeded to fight him about ten times after I got knocked down. One night after a game, he approached me in a bar and asked why I kept fighting him.

"Because you knocked me down a while back and it's not going to be right until I knock you down," I replied. The next game, we fought and I knocked him to the ice.

"How do you feel now? Do you feel better? Can we now just go play?" he asked.

I feel fortunate. I have lived a Zelig-like life—an ordinary man who has found himself among extraordinary people and improbable situations—and I hope you enjoyed reading about it. Life can be great without being easy.

Remember when I felt so depressed after my first marriage ended that I'd contemplated suicide? I met my second wife in 1989 at a Super Bowl Party. We married in 1991. By 1992 it was all done. One night I flew home from an NHL refereeing assignment—a Stanley Cup playoff game in LA—and walked into my house to find all the furniture gone except for one couch and a dining room table. There was an eighteen-page "Dear John" letter leaning against the kitchen wall. That day, after flying all night, I came into the apartment and looked at the emptiness of the apartment and saw this letter. I looked at the letter, reached into the cabinet for a bowl, saw none left in there. She had taken all the spoons so I couldn't eat the ice cream in the freezer.

"The hell with this," I said to myself. I went to Eire Pub in Dorchester and spent the next three days going back and forth from there to another local Dorchester bar and a nearby diner. My friend Bill Garrahan called, looking for me. I told him what had happened.

"I'll be right over," he said. Garrahan drove there, grabbed me, told me to fetch my golf clubs, and we then went and played in a tournament. In 1993, the divorce was finalized. I never looked back after that. And I never did read that letter.

I met my third wife, Lori, and finally found the optimism of having a wife and family. Lori absolutely saved my life. I'd be dead now if she hadn't been watching the television that morning listening to Katie Couric talk about her late-husband's colon cancer symptoms. Lori made me get out of bed and call Gary Kearney. From there, Mary Hickey took charge of my treatments and all at New England Baptist saved my life.

See how everything eventually works itself out in the end? Maybe it's God's will or maybe it's from my own doing. People say everything happens for a reason. Maybe that's so. Maybe that's bull. But everything seems to turn out fine. When fighting all those other tough NAHL enforcers, I often wondered if I would have real guts if I faced a life-and-death situation. I got my answer in 1998.

I was a good referee because I was never afraid. When diagnosed with cancer and told I could die, I never fixated on the fear. I fixated on what I could do to make it right. I never learned the word *quit*. I knew I could do something. I've always known there's something to be done. That's what makes me who I am: a tough guy, a survivor, a worker. To me it wasn't just the fight, it was what I was willing to invest.

For some reason, as I take to this keyboard to wind down this book the haunting Frank Sinatra tune, "My Way" keeps popping into my head. As much as I like the song (having heard Frank actually sing it during his comeback at the old Philadelphia Spectrum), somehow I keep putting off my conclusion for as long as I can.

Behind these aging eyes, there is still the passion and persistence that took me through all the years of victories and defeats. It does take some extra effort these days. I can actually tell you a day or two ahead when it's going to rain or snow. The knees, the wrists, the back—like that song that my body knows so well—"Hips Don't Lie."

The memories I have of the life I chose to live bring a bit of a smile to my heart. I think of the wonderful people who took the time to care about me, liking me even when I got in my own way, even during those dark times when I was less than fond of myself.

I was blessed with great teammates like Groton's Billy Larkin, Larney Fowler, Steve Borgerson, David Key, Morin Bishop, Bobby Peabody, and Springer Miller. Teammates and friends from my UPenn days including Johnny Harwood, Peter Roche, Peter McNamee, Tim McQuiston, Brian Jacks, and Paul Akey. My Binghamton team that initiated me with Billy and Jiggs Gratton, Ken "Ivy" Davidson, Gary Jacquith, Peter Millar, Cap Raeder, Rick Pagnutti, Larry Mavety, "Gypsy" Joe Hardy, Ken "Dutch" Holland, Rod Bloomfield, Dr. Joel Schnure, and the best owner ever, Jim Matthews. My WHA- and NHL-mates including Robbie Ftorek, Jamie Hislop, Mark Messier, Mike Gartner, Rick Dudley, Tim Sheehy, Paul Henderson, Bryan "Bugsy" Watson, Butch Deadmarsh, Richard LeDuc, Billy Gilligan, Pat "Whitey" Stapleton, Barry Melrose, Nick Fotiu, Phil Esposito, John Van BoxMeer, Jim Schoenfeldt, and the great Rod Gilbert.

I've played with many more—some unforgettable, some very forgettable and a few I'd like one more shift against, like Rick Jodzio and Bobby Schmautz.

I had the good fortune of having coaches from the start who were patient and selfless including Eddie Dalton, Eddie Kirrane, Jon Choate, Frank "Junie" O'Brien, Dave Rogerson, Larry Davenport, Bob Crocker, Peter Yetten, Jacques Demers, and Johnny Cunniff. Officiating mentors who never quit on me nor tried to beat me down psychologically, including Ian "Scotty" Morrison, John McCauley, Frank Udvari, Lou Maschio, John Ashley, Wally Harris, Sam Sisco, Dutch Van Deelan, Jim Gregory, Ray Gregory, Gordie Anziano, Jack Butterfield, and Ray Miron.

My "Brothers in Stripes" are too numerous to mention. I loved these guys. A few of the many: Pat Dapuzzo, Brian Murphy, Mark Pare, Gerard Gauthier, Dan Schachte, Kevin Collins, Randy Mitton, Swede Knox, Ryan Bozak, Ron Asselstine, Dave Newell, Andy Van

Hellemond, the late Romeo LeBlanc (whom I greatly miss to this day) and so many more—too many to name them all.

There are many others whose absence from my life has been a blessing; a few who distinguished themselves with their antipathy towards me and whose names barely warrant mention, except that they, too, unfortunately, are a part of my story. If small was big, you'd all be huge.

I know that I am good at teaching officiating. After all, the Russians hired me for the KHL and MHL for three years to help better their officiating. I only came home because of a brain tumor. Who knew how much time I would have if the seven-hour operation didn't go well? Besides, I had already missed three years of watching my kids grow up; in the wake of another health scare I did not want to risk missing any more time. But I left of my own accord, and by the necessity of my circumstances. I was doing great work there and was proud to have the chance to actively improve the game of hockey.

The ECAC Commissioner, Steve Hagwell, and I have worked together for thirteen years. ECAC Men's and Women's officials are recognized as being in shape, mobile, accountable, and consistent. Don't take my word for it: ask the NCAA, as they use our people often, even to officiate the final game in The Frozen Four. The ISL New England Prep School Hockey League has hired me for ten years as the Co-Commissioner. The New England Pro-Am Chowder Cups has had me as Referee-in-Chief for the past ten years.

One has to wonder what it was that turned me away from the NHL, my home for so many years. I think it's like the book, *Pride and Prejudice*, except it was neither my pride nor my prejudice that stood in my way. One thing is clear in my heart: I did a great job in the NHL and earned the respect of legends in the sport. Whatever the issues might have been, the quality of my work was not among them. To me, that is everything.

There was a desire in me for so many years to write a book relaying some of the moments that made up my life, that some of my moments could be of interest to others who have never experienced the cauldron of sound I stepped into for so many nights. I am also compelled, even at this point in my life, by the lessons lives by my grandfather and father. I enjoy telling the stories of my life, some almost unbelievable in their irony and their outcome. Like my grandfather and my dad, who also had lifetimes of interesting stories, I so much wanted to be like them.

I've used tons of metaphors and comparisons to themes in my life from movies and songs and literature. So many great poets, authors and songwriters mention roads. "Life is a Highway," the song by Tom Cochrane, "The Road Not Taken" by Robert Frost, "The Long and Winding Road" by the Beatles. The list is probably longer than this book. But life is indeed a journey, and I believe mine has been a remarkable one. Best of all, I still have a long way ahead of me.

The ride may be bumpy, but I have to ask one last time: Ya wanna go?

# EPILOGUE: A Call From The Hall

In July 2018, I received a call from USA Hockey. I was informed that I had been selected to the U.S. Hockey Hall of Fame's induction class of 2018. It takes a lot to render me speechless, but I was truly at a loss for words. I am very grateful to the selection committee for including me among so many of the sports luminaries.

My congratulations go out to my fellow inductees: David Poile, Red Berenson, Natalie Darwitz, and to the family descendants of the late Leland "Hago" Harrington.

There's a joke in hockey circles that goes back to the days my U.S. Hockey Hall of Famer grandfather, Bill Stewart, Sr., was coaching and refereeing in the NHL. It went like this: Want to spread hockey gossip in a hurry? The three fastest ways: telegram, telephone, tell-a-ref. After being told of my Hall of Fame selection, I was sworn to secrecy until the official Class of 2018 honorees announcement from USA Hockey. Although I shared the good news with my family, I have kept it otherwise quiet until the news went public.

Being inducted in the U.S. Hockey Hall of Fame is something that I never dreamed would happen. I'm just a rough-around-the-edges kid from Dorchester and Jamaica Plain who would do anything to be at the rink. When I look at the company into which I am being included—the best officials, the great players, coaches, and builders of the game in our country—it is humbling. So many thoughts have raced through my head upon learning of my induction.

I have thought a lot about my late grandfather and dad. I think about my kids, McCauley and Maxwell, who are a bigger part of the reason I am still alive to see this day than I could ever explain to them. I think about how my wife, Lori, heeded Katie Couric's warning message on a *The Today Show* broadcast and alerted me to the fact that I had all the symptoms for colon cancer. It was caught in the nick of time and I was saved to continue to live on in my life and to return to hockey.

I think about my teachers and coaches. I think often about my officiating mentors and those whom I hope I have been able to pass along what I learned through the years. I think about my officiating teammates, especially the many amazing linesmen with whom I've worked, and about many of my teammates and opponents from my playing days. I think, too, of the scores of talented people with whom I was lucky enough to share the ice first as a player and then as a referee. I think about the police, the rink crews, the team equipment and athletic trainers.

I think of all the wonderful people from all walks of life I've gotten to know over the years, both at and away from the rinks. Thank you all for friendship and kindness.

Lastly, I think about all of the learning experiences and example-setters over the course of my life. Many were positive. I even learned from those that were not-so-positive, but each and every one shaped me in some way or another. This famous expression is a quotation from John Donne's "Devotions" (1624): "No man is an Island, entire of itself, every man is a piece of the continent, a part of the main."

I have always viewed myself as an ordinary man who found myself in unusual circumstances. I was never a star player by any stretch of the imagination. I literally fought my way into playing in the World Hockey Association and National Hockey League because that was my ticket to living out my dream. Later, I made it back to the NHL in a striped jersey with orange bands. I refereed 1,010 games in the NHL before moving on to the supervisory and administrative side of officiating at the collegiate, local, and KHL levels. I believe that officiating is a noble profession.

Two decades ago, when I was told that I had an advanced stage of colon cancer, I bought a cemetery plot near that of my grandfather who'd been inducted into the U.S. Hockey Hall of Fame 1983. Thanks to my doctors and nurses, the love and support of my family, my many friends in and out of all those rinks and my own will to fight, I am still alive to share a whole different type of real estate with Grampy: a spot in the U.S. Hockey Hall of Fame.

Thank you all, from the bottom of my heart.

—PAUL STEWART

# CONTRIBUTORS

Christopher Smith reports about the Boston Red Sox and Major League Baseball for MassLive.com. He has worked in sports journalism for 10 years. The Syracuse graduate lives in Georgetown, Mass., with his wife Kristi Smith, a special education teacher.

Bill Meltzer is a writer for PhiladelphiaFlyers.com, the content manager for the Philadelphia Flyers Alumni Association and a longtime blogger for HockeyBuzz.com. He is the co-author of *Pelle Lindbergh: Behind the White Mask* and has assisted on several other books.

# Index

**C**

**D**

**E**



**F**

**I**



**J**

**K**



**L**

**M**

**N**

**O**



**P**

**Q**



**R**



**S**

**T**



**U**

Manufactured by Amazon.ca
Bolton, ON

18971605R00201